Constructing Gender

FEMINISM AND LITERARY STUDIES

Edited by Hilary Fraser and R.S. White

with a preface by Penny Boumelha

UNIVERSITY OF WESTERN AUSTRALIA PRESS

First published in 1994 by
University of Western Australia Press
Nedlands, Western Australia 6009

National Library of Australia
Cataloguing-in-Publication entry:

Constructing gender

941226

Bibliography
ISBN 1 875560 34 3

1. Feminism and literature.   2. Women and literature.   3.
English literature — History and criticism.   4. Women in
literature.   I. Fraser, Hilary, 1953–   .   II. White, R.S. (Robert
Sommerville), 1948–   .

809.93352042

Cover painting: *The Kiss in the Glass* by Jo Darbyshire

Consultant Editor: Amanda Curtin, Curtin Communications, Perth
Designed by Robyn Mundy, Mundy Design, Perth
Cover designed by Susan Ellvey, Designpoint, Perth
Typeset in 9½pt Garamond Light by Lasertype, Perth
Printed by Scott Four Colour Print, Perth

CONSTRUCTING GENDER

FEMINISM AND LITERARY STUDIES

ACKNOWLEDGEMENTS

The editors and publisher are grateful to the Trustees of the British Museum for permission to reproduce *Adder's Tongue*, by Edward Burne-Jones; to the National Gallery for permission to reproduce *Apollo and Daphne*, by Antonio Pollaiuolo; and to Judy Dater for permission to reproduce *Imogen and Twinka at Yosemite*. Every effort has been made to obtain permission to reproduce *Roots* and *Luther Burbank* by Frida Kahlo; if for any reason a request has not been received, the copyright holder should contact the publisher.

CONTENTS

PENNY BOUMELHA   **'Go litel bok':** A Prefatory
Benediction   *vii*

HILARY FRASER AND
R.S. WHITE   INTRODUCTION   *xiii*

LUCY DOUGAN   **Women's Bodies and
Metamorphosis:** Thoughts in
Daphne's Shade   *1*

ANDREW LYNCH   **'Be war, ye wemen':** Problems
of Genre and the Gendered Audience
in Chaucer and Henryson   *19*

PHILIPPA BECKERLING   **Perceval's Sister:** Aspects of the
Virgin in the *Quest of the Holy Grail*
and Malory's *Sankgreal*   *39*

ANN CHANCE   **Black Widow:** Death and the Woman
in Early Modern English Texts   *55*

R.S. WHITE   **Jephtha's Daughter:** Men's
Constructions of Women in *Hamlet*   *73*

CHRISTINE COUCHE   **Tears and Tushes**: Images of
Gender and Power in *Venus and
Adonis* and *The Rape of Lucrece*   *90*

D.W. COLLIN   **Space, Time and Pastoral** in
Elizabeth Gaskell's *Cranford*
and *Cousin Phillis*   *109*

HILARY FRASER   **'Love's citadel unmann'd':**
Victorian Women's Love Poetry   *132*

CONTENTS (continued)

TIM DOLIN
Fifteen Scenes Towards **A Melodramatics of Hardy**   *157*

CARMEL MACDONALD-GRAHAME
Angled Vision: D.H. Lawrence's Narrative Gaze   *179*

IAN SAUNDERS
'The most difficult love': Expectation and Gender in Barnard Eldershaw's *Tomorrow and Tomorrow and Tomorrow*   *199*

JANE SOUTHWELL
Mapping 'the labyrinth within us': The Search for New Ontological Territory in Angela Carter's *The Passion of New Eve*   *223*

AMANDA NETTELBECK
The Ambivalence of Women's Experience in Elizabeth Jolley's *My Father's Moon* and *Cabin Fever*   *242*

SUSAN MIDALIA
Art for Woman's Sake: Kate Grenville's *Lilian's Story* as Female *Bildungsroman*   *253*

ALEX SEGAL
Gender, Ethics and Literary Theory   *269*

VERONICA BRADY
Towards a New Geography: Body of Women, Body of the World   *287*

NOTES ON CONTRIBUTORS   *303*

'GO LITEL BOK': A PREFATORY BENEDICTION

PENNY BOUMELHA

IT may well be the only remaining truth universally acknowledged within the discipline of English that things are not what they used to be. Whether this is seen as a crisis or a revolution, as occasion for regret or cause for celebration, it is at least undeniable that it is a discipline that has changed a great deal in recent years. English departments (or their equivalents in the various institutional nomenclatures) around the world have relinquished the moral high ground on which they once took their stand: their claim to provide a necessary civilizing influence, to be part of the educational baggage of every humane man (and I do mean 'man'). Practitioners of literary studies, by and large, no longer see the purpose of their subject as that of demonstrating eternal truths and affirming aesthetic values once postulated as universal, but rather as that of attending to the ways in which societies construct meanings and aesthetic value. The object of study is not, so to speak, an *objet trouvé* but a *construction* that bears upon it the marks of its society; cultural meanings and evaluations have come to be seen as, of necessity, *social* meanings and practices, and therefore to be related on a daily and intimate basis to the societies in which we live and work, as writers or readers.

The forces for such change have come from a number of directions, including the recognition that it is no longer possible, in a society increasingly oriented towards film and television, the video and the computer, to regard the primacy of cultural place of the book as axiomatic. (Hence the rise of cultural studies, in which literature takes its place as only one among a number of forms of textuality.) But there is certainly a widespread perception that feminism — to bestow upon it, for the moment, a singularity that risks disguising a plurality of debates and contestations — has made a substantial contribution to transforming the practices of literary criticism. Feminist critics over the last fifteen years or so have engaged in a variety of tasks and addressed themselves to a broad range of issues, among them insisting on reading and writing as gendered activities, drawing attention to the historical construction of a predominantly male canon, rediscovering neglected women writers, remarking and analysing stereotypes of femininity, engaging in debate about pornography and its relation to representation in general, theorizing the specific relation of female subjectivity to language, and critiquing and challenging the systemic and institutional constraints and pressures that reproduce differential access to cultural and educational practices. And in addition to posing these questions of their own, the various feminist theories and criticisms have also served, as John Frow points out, as a forceful and effective 'critique exemplary to other groups excluded from representation in the canon',[1] and so have aided in the establishment and growth of other new areas within the discipline, such as, for example, gay and lesbian studies.

It is one of the starting points of feminist criticism in all its forms that cultural meanings are always and undeniably social meanings; that, whether we speak of the 'high' culture of literature or of the less prestigious cultural products such as advertisements or pop songs, cultural signification is inextricably intertwined with questions of history, questions of power, systems of difference, by which identity, whether of individuals or groups or societies, tends to be constructed. Feminist critics have argued that the whole matter of gender is prominent among those systems of difference. It is sometimes suggested that gender differences and constructions are 'mere conventions'. I do not agree; this way of looking at things seems to reduce one of the categories by which we are most clearly, if contradictorily, produced to the status of table manners or handshakes. If masculinity and femininity have no necessary grounding in objective reality, then we are not entitled to deduce from that that they are merely illusory, because their effects are undeniably real. Gender, I would suggest, can best be named a social fact with which it is always and everywhere necessary to deal. It is impossible simply to stand outside the systems of gender difference (certainly not impossible to *change* them, but that is another question); none of us can say, 'That doesn't affect me'. Nor does literature stand outside them.

After all, those things that a literary critic, even of the more traditional kind, might most expect to encounter in a text — say, themes, images, ideas of character, generic conventions — do not halt politely at the frontiers of the book, but shape and are shaped by the discourses and institutions of our society. It has sometimes been assumed that, for the oppositional or politically committed critic, reading is equivalent to a process of unmasking or denunciation: we seek out the guilty traces of racism or sexism or imperialism or whatever it may be in order to pillory the book or the author. This is not so, though in my opinion writers should take as much responsibility for the views they hold as must the rest of us. But what would be the point of taking up the practice and teaching of literary study in order to show that the texts on which we spend our time are without either value or pleasure? Better, surely, simply to turn our attention to something else. What is at stake is not the question of the ideological acceptability or otherwise of a particular work — in the currently fashionable hostile caricature, its 'political correctness' — but the critical demonstration and analysis of the ways in which it is a site of social meaning, its imbrication in the societies in which its writer, readers, teachers or students are placed. I do not mean by this that a literary text is best approached as if it were a straightforward historical document (to postulate such a thing for the moment), from which it might be possible simply to read off facts about the time and place of its writing. Rather, I mean that the forms taken by literary texts and histories of their reading stand in meaningful relationship to the social structures and individual options of their readers and writers, and to the ideological and discursive conditions of possibility of those structures and options. The methodologies for establishing that relationship and subjecting it to examination are various, but it is one of the strengths of the current feminist criticisms that they can address and inform so many of them.

For example, it is perfectly clear that being, or becoming, an author is a process in which gender differences and conventions operate at many levels; to look only at the period on which my own research primarily focuses, the second half of the nineteenth century, such matters as male pseudonyms, the issues of professionalism and access to publication, and the different opportunities for education are all traversed by (though not only by) gender. And so it is for readers, for students, for academics, for publishers, for literary critics: questions of authority, of interests and expectations, of reading histories, of the relative roles of the humanities and sciences, of canons of what is deemed to be worth attention, and, yes, of *pleasure*, cannot be separated from the practices and ideologies of gender difference. Whether we read, write, cannot read or write, study, or teach, literature (in this exemplary of culture more broadly conceived) is embroiled continuously and intimately with our lives and the societies in which we live. I have often thought that it is this undeniable centrality of gender in our experience, together with an unwavering conviction that literature actually *matters*, that helps to account for the fresh intellectual excitement that feminist criticism has generated for many within the study of English.

Certainly, such pleasure of intellectual engagement can be seen at work in the essays that follow. They do not display the entire range of current feminist theories and concerns, of course, but they do exemplify much of what is exciting and productive about them. They range across historical, generic, thematic and theoretical starting points and address works from the fourteenth to the twentieth century. What is most evident about them, taken as a group, is that they show how gender helps to form all aspects of the literary experience and system: actual and implied authors, actual and implied audiences, narrative and poetic structures, the conditions of possibility for generic and other experimentation, theorizations of literature and representation, and the circulation of meanings and reception through perform-ance and criticism. It is this extraordinary breadth of address that best answers a charge sometimes still brought against feminist criticism: that it is a kind of superfluity arising from a narrow special interest group, to be dealt with in the time left when all the *real* material has been covered. The range and variety of this collection help to show that there is no element of reading or writing which is not permeated by issues of gender.

But if these essays are notably and productively varied, they are also fascinatingly interrelated by the way in which a question fundamental to the impulse of feminist criticism in all its forms, the question of authority, is both critically considered and played out across the collection. Carmel Macdonald-Grahame's study of Lawrence's narrative technique draws upon theories of the authority of the gaze; Andrew Lynch, Susan Midalia, R.S. White and Hilary Fraser all begin from the authoring voice; Tim Dolin, Susan Midalia and Hilary Fraser invoke and examine the authority of genre; Dorothy Collin examines the abrogation of masculine authority in the female society of *Cranford* and Gaskell's use of the autocratic or authoritarian father; Ian Saunders and Christine Couche consider authority as a theme; Ian Saunders documents the authority of the publisher; Tim Dolin exemplifies the impact of feminist writing in transforming criticism into a less impersonally authoritative, more conspicuously authored mode. More institu-tional forms of authority flit across the arrangement of the essays, the professorial Introduction, the academic weight of the University Press, and, not least, this legitimizing Preface by a supposed 'authority' in the field.

Because it is time for me to position myself in relation to

a volume emanating from the Department of English at The University of Western Australia. I was a member of that department from 1985 to 1990. I was not the first to teach there in the area of feminist criticism; that is, I believe, an honour due to the pioneering Dorothy Collin. But I *was* the first member of staff to be appointed as a specialist in such work, and I retain a real sense of both gratitude and gratification at the response of students and colleagues to the challenge of a new area. During my time at The University of Western Australia, I lectured from an explicitly feminist standpoint at every level from first to fourth year, in units on medieval literature, Victorian literature, contemporary literature, Augustan literature, narrative, literary theory, modernism, and semiotics, as well as establishing my own Honours subject called 'Feminist Perspectives on Fiction'. I enumerate these not to suggest that I worked harder than my colleagues but because it shows how receptive the department was to feminist work and to the critiques it brought to bear on the existing programme taught there. Having encountered and greatly benefited from such a generous response, I am not at all surprised to see that feminist criticism of such variety and sophistication now flourishes there; I am only delighted.

Penny Boumelha
University of Adelaide

---

1   John Frow, *The Social Production of Knowledge and the Discipline of English*, Inaugural Lecture Delivered at the University of Queensland, 18 April 1990 (St Lucia: University of Queensland Press, 1990), p. 9.

INTRODUCTION

HILARY FRASER AND R.S. WHITE

THIS collection of essays by writers who are or have recently been working in the English Department at The University of Western Australia is designed to demonstrate the vigour and diversity of feminist criticism and gender studies in the 1990s.

Feminist criticism and gender studies are central to the study of literature today, informing research in all periods, genres and theories, and available, at least potentially, in all conceivable courses in universities and schools. Feminist criticism can be oppositional and challenging, but it is also recuperative and conservationist, bringing back to bookshelves and conscious-nesses neglected women writers of distinction and whole areas of lost or suppressed experiences in women's writings. At its most exuberant, gender-based criticism is reviving literary studies with a spirit of excited commitment, identifying and analysing the close relationship that exists between texts and social and political realities.

Although literature may seem genteelly removed from the fray of feminist politics, in fact it has always held a uniquely strong position within the women's movement. Foundational works of feminism such as Mary Wollstonecraft's *A Vindication of the Rights of Woman* (1792), John Stuart Mill's *The Subjection of Women* (1861), Virginia Woolf's *A Room of One's Own* (1929) and Simone de Beauvoir's *The Second Sex* (1949) are taught, if anywhere outside Women's Studies, in literature courses. Literary texts and other cultural artefacts give insights into the social practices and popular attitudes that contribute to the manufacture of gender identity at different places in different times, including our own. Moreover, literary critics have guided or led the feminist movement as a whole, to a degree exceptional in the social application of literary studies. Feminist writers from Germaine Greer and Kate Millett to Hélène Cixous and Julia Kristeva have mediated between cultural texts and the societies which write and read them, bringing their literary training and an acute critical sense to bear upon a considerably broader field of analysis. Women's Studies centres are often run by women who made their reputations as professional literary critics, and yet many of the key figures in gender studies are identified with something much broader than a phrase like 'professional literary critic', let alone the word 'academic', would lead us to expect. Gender does not just determine reading and writing positions; it is implicated in every aspect of our personal, social and political existence.

Each essay in this book was written independently of the others, and yet it is fascinating to see how much implicit dialogue and debate goes on between them. Moreover, the inter-connections are multi-layered, in ways that we hope to indicate in the rest of this Introduction.

Gender as construction

One virtual axiom assumed by all the writers is that while every-body is born either male or female in terms of biological differences, all definitions of femininity and masculinity are provisional, culture-specific models which are far from 'given' or 'universally true'. Simone de Beauvoir's celebrated paradox 'One is not born, but rather becomes, a woman' is a central text in that it suggests biological differentiation is a neutral fact of no special signification in itself, and that the more crucial forces that seem to create gendered identities are social and cultural in origin. Such constructions may be observable in literature, but they are not confined to books. Institutions — financial, political, legal, and social — have traditionally and firmly underwritten a whole set of tightly integrated attitudes and assumptions about what is 'natural' or 'innate' about feminine or masculine behaviour. The legal maxim to explain why statutes have in the past referred only to male agencies — 'the male embraces the female' (chortled over by generations of mainly male Law students) — is a small but potent example of how constructions based on inequality have prevailed in the public sphere. Only in the last decade have they been challenged.

In this book, every chapter at least tacitly, and often overtly, recognizes that gender construction can be observed and analysed in so-called literary works. If we are tempted to confine stereotypes to earlier ages, such as the virgin in medieval writing (Philippa Beckerling), the 'black' widow in Renaissance texts (Ann Chance), power relations in Shakespeare which depend upon male sexual penetration or female penetrability (Christine Couche), and in the nineteenth century, Elizabeth Gaskell's reticent and indomitable spinsters (Dorothy Collin), or the Pre-Raphaelite woman seeking to escape subjugation (Hilary Fraser), it is salutary also to read the essays on twentieth century writers. Carmel Macdonald-Grahame, through pertinently chosen quotations, demonstrates the underlying stereotypes of femininity and masculinity presumed in D.H. Lawrence's novels, invariably derogatory to women, and Veronica Brady locates in inscriptions of Australian history the marginalization or erasure through stereotype of women and Aboriginal peoples. Lucy Dougan muses on the curious and ambiguous potencies of the culturally widespread link between women and nature. On the positive side, Jane Southwell, Amanda Nettelbeck, Susan Midalia and Veronica Brady examine powerful attempts by women writers to subvert stereotypes and construct new representations of gender.

Gender and genre

Some of the essays explore a particular problem for women writers: that the literary genres available to them are typically gendered male. (The problem is just as acute for the homosexual writer of either sex finding available only genres which take for granted heterosexuality as the norm.) A writer seeking to destabilize conventional notions of gender is obliged to adapt or subvert existing genres, or to create some new literary form which challenges readers' assumptions. For example, in her essay, Susan Midalia points out that the *Bildungsroman*, the novel of education or identity formation, 'both requires and valorizes what is usually denied to women — autonomy, independence, self-determination'. The female *Bildungsroman* either is condemned to detail the obstacles to education or formation for a woman, or it must fashion alternative female destinies.

In other essays we are shown how female writers appropriate male genres. D.W. Collin, for instance, shows how Elizabeth Gaskell's allusions to the pastoral endow the heroine of *Cousin Phillis* with a regenerative and creative power which had not been available to the women of Cranford, an approach which can be supplemented with Lucy Dougan's caution against accepting at face value constructions of women and nature in various genres. By contrast, Tim Dolin looks at the work of a male writer, Thomas Hardy, in the light of melodrama, which has frequently been identified as a female genre. Hilary Fraser's essay is also concerned with questions of gender and genre. She recuperates a genre of poetry by women which has been neglected by traditional critics and feminists alike: Victorian women's love poetry. Love poetry has perhaps more than most been a masculine domain. Fraser looks at the diverse strategies adopted by women poets in the last century to write in the tradition sanctioned by Dante and Petrarch, which typecasts woman as the silent object of male desire.

Romantic love provides a focus for discussion of sexual ideology in a number of other essays in the volume, too. Alex

Segal, for instance, examines Paul de Man's presumed complicity with patriarchal ideology in his reading of Rousseau's *Julie ou la nouvelle Héloïse*. Segal argues that de Man endorses Julie's replacement of the putatively 'natural' relationship of love with the contractual agreement of marriage as an instance of the unmasking of ideology. Ian Saunders elucidates Barnard Eldershaw's articulation of a 'difficult love' that is other than the 'easy love' of either nature or institution. R.S. White argues that even in a Renaissance play such as *Hamlet*, which appears to conform to a male-dominated genre of political tragedy, the active silencing of women is highlighted, and that Ophelia in fact does her best to subvert and even change the rules of the generic game.

Gender and readers

So far we have implied that gender is constructed by writers, and it is time to emphasize that readers are equally instrumental in the process. In the relatively recent development of reader response theory, which takes as its starting point the claim that readers create meaning in literary works, feminist readings which 'resist' a dominant reading are providing a paradigm for the whole approach:

> The woman reader, now a feminist, embarks on a critical analysis of the reading process, and she realizes that the text has power to structure her experience ...The reader can submit to the power of the text, or she can take control of the reading experience...She *should* choose the second alternative.[1]

Reading with a conscious policy of resisting the universalizing tendency of imaginative literature, the reader scrutinizes a text for signs of hidden bias due to what one of our writers terms 'angled vision', which depends, in a phrase taken from film criticism, on 'the male gaze'. Carmel Macdonald-Grahame turns a spotlight on D.H. Lawrence's loaded language in describing what are claimed to be archetypal masculine and feminine feelings, and the results are uncomfortably revealing of an inbuilt prejudice against women.

Other writers in this book employ resistant readings, such as Ann Chance in her interpretations of some Renaissance male texts which equate death and the woman, and Christine Couche, who digs beneath the surfaces of Shakespeare's poems to locate and identify underlying attitudes to sexuality, perhaps held only unconsciously by the author but no less potent for that. R.S. White suggests that critics, audiences and readers of a play like *Hamlet* are inevitably constructing and reconstructing the play themselves, and that the result can be a plurality of readings which may be in direct opposition over the depiction of gender issues. Andrew Lynch, in examining the imputed 'gendered audience' in poems by Chaucer and Henryson, concludes that 'Though a "women's meaning" may be uttered, it is not necessarily the only one heard'. Tim Dolin turns on himself a critical gaze in meditating what act of construction is occurring when a male reader attempts a feminist understanding of male novels such as those by Hardy. In this piece of ficto-criticism, Dolin positions himself as father, as does Ian Saunders in his essay. Saunders examines an Australian text by two women, *Tomorrow and Tomorrow and Tomorrow*, partly from the point of view that readers' expectations are activated by a novel which appears to challenge orthodoxies of gender identity. These writers explicitly address questions of the extent to which readers accept or resist assumptions about gender in literary works, but all our writers imply that readers and writers alike are part of a continuum in the process of constructing representations of gender.

Gender and history

Context is all-important, for writers and readers alike. No matter how we may attempt to escape the confines of our personal, historical locations, we shall always, despite ourselves perhaps, reveal the preoccupations, anxieties and confidences of our debates and disputes with the times we live in. This is why a book called *Constructing Gender* can appear in 1994 and could not in 1894 or 1394. This is also why the most immediately noticeable structuring of this book lies in chronology, in historical sequence. We presume no grand narratives of progress, or repetition, or periodicity, or cyclicity, but it does seem, to the editors of this book at least, that modes and strategies of gender construction are crucially effected within historical conditions, opportunities, and constraints. The kinds of questions addressed by writers and readers in the fourteenth century are different from those raised in the sixteenth, nineteenth or twentieth centuries, just as criticism informed by debates about gender will be different from those conducted before women could vote. Appeals to universalizing and essentialism no longer stand up against the argument that dominant assumptions about gender are culture-specific, and the essays here confirm this conclusion.

In analysing gender construction in medieval and Renaissance literature, one approach is to examine specific texts against a literary convention such as the cult of the Virgin. Another is to interpret literary works against social realities like those faced by widows. The conclusions may be particularly adapted to the context of early modern poetry and drama, but the methodologies employed can fruitfully be extended into other times and other genres such as the novel and poetry in nineteenth-century England (or, for that matter, Russia, America or Australia). Overarching myths — for example, the metonymy of women and trees traced by Lucy Dougan — might be most prominently exemplified in a specific time such as an England dominated by Darwin's thought, but again the general approach is applicable to such myths generated in different times. The study of gender in literary works can contribute to what is often called 'herstory', a tracing of women's experience through time and political change, calculated to rectify, and potentially to dislodge, assumptions of progress and historicity imposed by patriarchal assumptions and structures. In various ways, sometimes overt and sometimes covert, all of our essays are part of this enterprise. In a more conceptually innovative way, gender specific history might reach towards what Jane Southwell, borrowing a phrase from Angela Carter, calls 'mapping the "labyrinth within us"', a viewing of history as a personal rather than national construct. Both Tim Dolin and Susan Midalia revise notions of history and narrative to include 'personal' time and autobiographical chronology as factors overlying and crucially determining the ordering of ideas about gender in the context of passing time. Writers make gender, and so do readers, and they do so with reference to very personal experiences and evolving belief structures which are by turn fluctuating, changeable, spasmodic and constant. A new kind of literary history may be forecast in this set of essays, one which complements and intersects with radical developments in women's history.

Gender and geography

Contexts in which gender construction operates will include place and region. There are, for example, obvious parallels between gender oppression and oppression based on race or class in particular regions, and postcolonial theory in recent years is enabling us to analyse these links. In her essay in this volume, 'Towards a New Geography: Body of Women, Body of the World', Veronica Brady looks at some of the ways in which colonial settlers set about the ideological reconstruction of their appropriated territories, bearing with them the class distinctions, the racial hierarchies and the gender ideologies of the old country into the quite different social and racial context of the 'new'. Drawing an analogy between settlement and rape, Brady explores the link between the situation of women under patriarchy and that of colonized Aboriginal Australians, and goes on to contrast with her earlier colonial texts some recent Australian literature by women which foregrounds the country and its Aboriginal inhabitants as a way of suggesting affinity rather than alienation and difference.

Since this volume emanates from Australia, it is appropriate that it contains several essays on recent literature by

Australian women: Ian Saunders' piece on Barnard Eldershaw's *Tomorrow and Tomorrow and Tomorrow*, a novel written by two women, Marjorie Barnard and Flora Eldershaw, in the early 1940s and republished by Virago Press in 1983; Amanda Nettelbeck's on Elizabeth Jolley's novels *Cabin Fever* (1990) and *My Father's Moon* (1989); and Susan Midalia's on Kate Grenville's *Lilian's Story* (1991). All three essays offer readings of these novels which reveal their disruption of patriarchal norms. Jolley's and Grenville's fictional heroines are subversive women, and so are their authors subversive of patriarchal language and literary forms. Nettelbeck draws on Kristeva's theory of the semiotic and her articulation of the position of 'the in-between, the ambiguous', that position which 'does not respect limits, places or rules', to argue that the spacelessness which disables women in Jolley's novels may also be empowering. Jolley's heroines may be 'crippled' but they are also creative, and in a similar way Grenville's misfit heroine Lilian achieves fulfilment as an artist. Midalia argues that artistic vocation functions as a potentially emancipatory plot in *Lilian's Story*, as it does in a number of other recent Australian works about female artists, and thus offers an alternative *Bildungsroman* structure, one that is available to women as well as to men.

Gender and teaching

All the writers in this book have been involved in teaching institutions, and our final comments in this Introduction concern the pedagogical implications of the study of gender construction as shaped mainly by feminist criticism. It should be clear by now that we consider this emphasis to be necessary, healthy and irreversible in the world of criticism and teaching at all levels. It is an emphasis, moreover, which is now demanded by students, female and male alike. When feminism was first recognized in the late 1970s as a valid approach to the study of literature, special courses on women's writing and feminist readings began to be offered in English departments around the world. But while this was a crucial stage in the proper assimilation of feminist theory into the discipline, the practice of hiving off gender studies from mainstream, literary criticism had the effect of consigning such an approach to the margins, categorizing it as a passing academic fashion which did not significantly impinge on the dominant, institutional practice. Denominated feminist and gender-based courses still, of course, crucially act to foreground gender issues and to critique and subvert the politics and values of traditional literary criticism. But more recently, as consciousness of gender issues has heightened, there has been a more general demand for such issues to be addressed in all areas of literary study, and at all levels. This activity involves not simply including on courses texts written by women, but incorporating approaches which are alert to issues of gender. In this sense, even works which largely exclude women can fruitfully be analysed and taught with reference to constructions of masculinity and the absence of the feminine.

This book, as a whole, stands as evidence that feminist and gender-based approaches are important, relevant and interesting in fields stretching from Chaucer and Malory to literature written today. Together, these essays explore the significance of gender issues in very different literary texts written in different times and places and informed by a range of reading practices. They demonstrate the complex and subtle interconnection of gender politics and cultural politics in literary history and theory. It is to be hoped that, as well as constituting a significant contribution to feminist scholarship, the essays will introduce students to some of the interpretative richness opened up by gender criticism in all areas of literary study. After all, to adapt de Beauvoir's pungent formulation, feminist critics and readers, like women, are not born but made.

---

1   Patrocinio P. Schweickart, 'Reading Ourselves: Toward a Feminist Theory of Reading', in Elizabeth A. Flynn and Patrocinio P. Schweickart, eds, *Gender and Reading: Essays on Readers, Texts, and Contexts* (Baltimore and London: Johns Hopkins University Press, 1986), p. 49.

WOMEN'S BODIES AND METAMORPHOSIS: THOUGHTS IN DAPHNE'S SHADE

LUCY DOUGAN

I N thinking and writing another version of Daphne's
body, I found myself in a position analogous to hers;
that is, one of being in between two states, of
becomingness and hopefully of possibility. I knew that I believed
in the importance of recognizing the social construction of the
body, but at the same time, I also had — call it nostalgia — a
hankering for a more rooted sense of embodiment.[1]

If artefacts made by women are perceived as having a
direct and uncomplex relationship to their lives, then body
theory in actually challenging any simple state of real body/real
life brings a complexity and rich texture, or rather textuality, to
lived experience itself. I want to suggest that there is a different
relationship between women's lives and works and men's lives
and works and that this, in part, stems from different experiences
of embodiment.

In Western culture there has long been an imaginative
connection between women's bodies and trees. In the beginning,
the Bible tells us, there was a woman in a garden and a snake
in a tree. In a small, circular watercolour by the late nineteenth-

century artist Edward Burne-Jones entitled *Adder's Tongue* (1882–98, Figure 1), a snake-coloured devil-woman metamorphoses from the trunk of a tree, presenting herself to an apprehensive Adam and a more thoughtful Eve. As in many medieval and Renaissance representations of the drama before the Fall, some feature of the snake echoes Eve's, to indicate their infamous collusion.[2] In Burne-Jones's work the snake-woman could be Eve's twin. I open with this image not only because it is about beginnings but also because it is immensely suggestive. It indicates that the cultural confluence of the representational sites of women and trees is very old. But more importantly, it suggests that there is something subversive about this

Figure 1. *Edward Burne-Jones.* Adder's Tongue*: 1882–98, watercolour, The British Museum, London.*

relationship; that women and nature, in some respect, talk to each other, reflect or answer each other, in a way that men and nature do not.

The perception of a closeness or likeness between women and nature as categories is an insistent theme in Western literature and art, and scholars holding different feminist positions are invariably involved in the contentious issues that this material raises.[3] Critiques of this perception of women and nature contend that it is dangerously reductive and that it serves only to further discrimination and conservative gender politics.[4] However, I wish to argue in the following that this culturally inscribed relationship carries (like Eve's exchange with the snake) the potential for a subversion of patriarchal epistemologies and ontologies.

The *locus classicus* of tree women is Daphne, and in reading her representations one is compelled to negotiate certain tensions: movement/arrestment, narrative/stasis, culture/nature, body/tree, and lover/celibate.[5] A particularly fruitful way of reading Daphne is provided by Mikhail Bakhtin's study of the grotesque medieval body in *Rabelais and His World*. With her protuberances, the transgression of her old body and her merging with the world, it could be argued that Daphne works as a mythic literalization of Bakhtin's grotesque body.[6] In describing the character of the grotesque body, Bakhtin relies on organic analogies, on 'the shoots and branches...all that prolongs the body and links it to other bodies or the world outside'. The grotesque body, that is, 'is a body in the act of becoming'.[7]

Two elements concern me most here. Firstly, Daphne in her becomingness, her indeterminacy, offers a position beyond the enclosing binaries of the essentialist/anti-essentialist debate, because she privileges process over closure.[8] Secondly, she raises some very important questions about women's bodies enacting resistance, and about the complex issue of women's bodies as spectacles of power.[9]

The readings below, then, attempt to explore a space in some written and visual texts by women that I have called Daphne's shade, to reanimate nature's nunnery, that cultural locus of retreat, with a radical tension. The word radical means, aptly, to return to the root. I propose to show, through a re-reading of the Apollo/Daphne myth and narratives of metamorphosis in texts by women writers and artists, that there lies a space of respite from the defining rays of Apollo's gaze, cast by Daphne's shade. In using the term shade, I also wish to draw attention to the echo of Daphne, or a woman transforming into a tree, filtering down through later texts. In all but one of my examples, the Daphne myth is not used as a specific source, therefore I am not so much interested in direct after-texts of the myth but the ways in which the myth resonates in other texts. Neither are the works under consideration all necessarily explicit representations of a woman's body metamorphosing, although the ways in which this might be represented are of concern; instead they may suggest metamorphosis in the form of cycles or process.

The history of the myth of Apollo and Daphne, its sources and its religious, political, allegorical and symbolic uses, forms a massive area of inquiry.[10] The core of the myth describes how an amorous Apollo pursues a virgin Daphne, a nymph who wishes to live forever in the band of the virgin huntress Artemis, and so calls upon the mercy of her father (or in some versions upon the earth) to work a transformation that will eradicate her beauty. Sometimes the earth swallows Daphne's fleeing body and a tree emerges from this ground, and in other texts there is an explicit description of a metamorphosis, as in Book 1 of Ovid's *Metamorphoses*:

> a deep langour took hold on her limbs, her soft breast
> was enclosed in thin bark, her hair grew into leaves,
> her arms into branches, and her feet that were lately
> so swift were held fast by sluggish roots, while her
> face became the treetop.[11]

In her study of after-texts of Ovid's Daphne and Apollo, Mary E. Barnard comments on the metamorphic nature of myths themselves:

> A myth, by its very nature, is fluid. It undergoes con-
> stant changes when variants are introduced as the tale

migrates from region to region, as it passes in the oral tradition from generation to generation...And the adaptability continues as Daphne, along with Apollo, enters the world of literature; both the god and the nymph serve the wishes and whims of writers, who construct new stages on which the mythical figures play new roles.[12]

Just as writers and artists in different historical and cultural contexts have manipulated the material of myth, so do readers.[13] In looking at the myth of Daphne and Apollo from a feminist reading position, it seems at first glance to be a fairly predictable fable about male creativity. Brenda Walker writes:

in a metaphorical sense women poets are canopied by the laurel tree. The laurel is the traditional emblem of achievement in poetry and this achievement has, in the past, conventionally been the prerogative of men. The very term 'laureate' is gendered masculine. This identification is strengthened by the connection between the laurel and Apollo, the god of poetry.[14]

Walker's image of the canopied woman recalls representations of woman-as-muse, where her position as bestower of the wreath (maker of leaves as Daphne) always encodes her as passive figure of inspiration rather than active artist.

But there is a sense in which this position as tree-woman need not necessarily be construed as a silent foil to male creativity. In her suggestive essay 'On Becoming a Tree', the feminist classicist Mary Lefkowitz, in discussing women, education and celibacy, claims that:

Daphne...by refusing Apollo's advances, managed to survive at least as a representation of herself, a laurel tree, fixed in one place, with her own name (*daphne* means laurel).[15]

Being free to become a representation of oneself may not at first appear to be a position of power, but if we consider the representation of women's bodies in the history of art, the radicalism of Daphne's narrative emerges.[16] Daphne's transformation into a tree follows the maintenance of her virginity. Just as in other famous metamorphosis myths from Ovid, the shape reinforces the psychological drama of the myth. In the more tragic narratives of Io and Callisto, who are both raped by Zeus, these mythical women assume animal forms, respectively the cow and the bear. Their extreme physical and emotional debasement is symbolized through their animal forms. Unlike these examples of therianthropism, the tree has far more positive symbolic connotations and is connected in numerous belief systems with the sacred.[17] The narrative of becoming a tree offers a new, imaginative allegory for women's bodies. Daphne is taking flight by staying still, by wearing motley, by becoming one of the many in a wood, by making her own *hortus conclusus* (enclosed garden) and by resisting male inscriptions of beauty on the body.

Lefkowitz's essay suggests that autonomy is only attainable through the choice of celibacy. Her work is a celebration of single-sex college life and a dire warning about the constraints that come with heterosexual marriage.[18] But her argument also raises questions. Does the attainment of autonomy for women depend on a denial of sexual life? Or a denial of heterosexual life? Does the maintenance of feminine identity require the metaphorical loss of the female body?

Whilst metamorphosis is often read as a challenge to assumptions about identity, and whilst it evokes the philosophical debate of where the self resides,[19] what preoccupies me most is Lefkowitz's point that, despite the loss of the human bodily self, some sort of new self-possession takes place.

But is self-possession gained by resistance? Human bodies, it has been argued, are potent sites for acts of resistance. Western histories, myths and stories are full of instances of their use as such. In *Monuments and Maidens*, Marina Warner gives many examples of women using their bodies as sites of resistance, both ancient and contemporary: from Lady Godiva to the women of Greenham Common.[20] Warner writes:

the Greenham drama belongs to the long tradition of expressing virtue in the female form...They have made fundamental sexual difference the premise of their vision, and they ground that difference in the body.[21]

The resistance that self-possession implies is a resistance to the possessiveness of the male gaze. That the male gaze has determined the shapes women's bodies are allowed to take is well documented.[22] In *Possession: A Romance*, a recent novel largely concerned with both mythical and scientific metamorphoses, A.S. Byatt's narrator has her heroine question: 'Who knows what Melusina was in her freedom with no eyes on her?'.[23] In the Melusina narrative, a myth most explicitly about bodily taboos and women, the hero is prohibited from witnessing Melusina bathing or giving birth. The myth's subversive power lies in its indication that without the censure of the male gaze, Apollo's eyes, women are free to appear as themselves, or at least to partake in the construction of their physical selves.

In Thomas Hardy's novel *The Woodlanders*, the heroine, Grace Melbury, experiences what the narrator calls 'a Daphnean instinct'[24] and runs from her husband, Edred Fitzpiers, to take to the woods. What I want to suggest here is that the myth's very intrusion into another narrative signals a subversive impulse that is not complicit with the conventional expectations of a heroine's narrative destiny. While Grace's 'Daphnean instinct' proves to be only a temporary escape from her patriarchal complicity, the naming and presence of the myth within Hardy's narrative haunt the reader with at least the idea of resistance and self-possession.

Jane Marcus has considered the Daphne myth, or the motif which she calls 'lady into tree', in feminist fantasy novels of the 1920s. Marcus locates the central meaning of the myth as 'really about an imagined transition from a matriarchal order to a patriarchal one'. Narratives in which the Daphne figure emerges, argues Marcus, are haunted by a nostalgia for 'preclassical feminine power', sisterhood, the maintenance of virginity, sacred wilderness and the lost body of the mother.[25] One of the feminist fantasy novels considered by Marcus is Sylvia Townsend Warner's little known novel *Lolly Willowes* (1926). A pivotal narrative event of the work occurs when Laura, the dependent spinster heroine of the book, trapped in London, imagines another woman's body into a tree and then, by extension, her own. Wandering in a shop 'half florist and half greengrocer', Laura envisions:

> A solitary old woman picking fruit in a darkening orchard, rubbing her rough finger-tips over the smooth-skinned plums, a lean and wiry old woman, standing with up stretched arms among her fruit trees as though she were a tree herself, growing out of the long grass, with arms stretched up like branches...
>
> As Laura stood waiting she felt a great longing. It weighed upon her like the load of ripened fruit upon a tree. She forgot the shop, the other customers, her own errand...She forgot the whole of her London life. She seemed to be standing alone in a darkening orchard, her feet in the grass, her arms stretched up to the pattern of leaves and fruit, her fingers seeking the rounded ovals of the fruit among the pointed ovals of the leaves...The back of her neck ached a little with the strain of holding up her arms. Her fingers searched up among the leaves.[26]

A mythic dimension in the text here is explicitly connected to a longing, Laura's, and it calls up the reverie of the tree-woman. This vision impels Laura into a Daphnean flight from her brother's rule as she is transformed from town spinster to country witch. The emphasis on physicality in the description above, on stretch and strain, on lengthening and growth, recalls to mind the iconography of Daphne, as in the mid-fifteenth century oil painting *Apollo and Daphne* by Antonio Pollaiuolo (Figure 2).

The heroine of *Lolly Willowes* experiences what the artist Frida Kahlo called 'the vegetable miracle of my body'.[27] In Kahlo's painting *Roots* (1943, Figure 3), the seemingly barren landscape is broken by the vigorous growth of stems and leaves that spread from the open trunk of the artist's body. Hayden

Figure 2. *Antonio Pollaiuolo.* Apollo and Daphne: *mid-fifteenth century, oil, The National Gallery, London.*

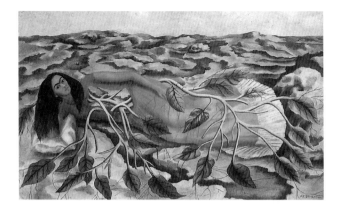

Figure 3. *Frida Kahlo.* Roots: *1943, oil on metal, private collection, Houston, Texas.*

Herrera has written of this image in the context of Kahlo's childlessness:

> Frida's childlessness lent urgency to her connections with all forms of life. She nurtured plants in her garden as if they were offspring, she painted flowers and fruit with such a passion that they look alive. Not being able to root her body in the world by bearing children, she dug her roots into the universe, embracing a philosophy that saw all aspects of life as intertwined.[28]

Roots records a metamorphic letting go of the boundaries of both the bodily and psychic self. Most of Kahlo's oeuvre can be read as a resistance: to an ailing body, to colonization by male Surrealism and, most importantly here, to the expression of motherly tenderness in only one form, biological motherhood.

In another image, *Luther Burbank* (1931, Figure 4), Kahlo portrays the famous horticulturalist as half tree himself. Herrera comments that 'Frida's inventiveness...came straight from Mexican popular culture, where the metamorphosis of humans into plants

Figure 4. *Frida Kahlo.* Luther Burbank: *1931, oil on masonite, Collection of Dolores Olmedo Foundation, Mexico City.*

or animals is common'.[29] Both these images about roots and bodily and psychical health implicate bodily change in social change. They are texts in which the body changes for change, and where the self, in feeding the self, feeds other selves — Burbanks's portrait through a literal feeding of the community and Kahlo's self-portrait through a spiritual feeding that suggests that there are other stories of interconnectedness for women's bodies besides biological birth. The visual trope of metamorphosis here partakes in the artist's rhetoric of regenerative cycles.

The cyclical changes of bodies require explanation and context. Cecil Helman writes that myth

> provides people with ways of perceiving themselves, and their own bodies, and how they function in both health and disease. It offers a repertoire of concepts, words and images which helps each of them to organise, and to make sense of — the shapes of their body — as well as its symptoms and cyclical changes...[and their] relation to other human bodies of the same society.[30]

As Germaine Greer notes in her book *The Change*: 'Women's lives are constructed of changes so vivid that they might well be called metamorphoses...often these changes...are signalled by contrasting body states'.[31] In a woman's case, then, the other bodies through which she makes sense of her own (the process Helman describes) may well not be other. It may be her own body in any one of the different phases of her body's history.

Elsewhere in *The Change*, Greer describes the possibility of the menopausal woman recovering within herself the relatively less gendered girl child:

> Women will have to devise their own rite of passage, a celebration of what could be regarded as the restoration of a woman to herself. The passionate, idealistic, energetic young individual who existed before menstruation can come on earth again if we let her.[32]

Even though Greer's conception romanticizes a traumatic event, it indicates its poetic potential for spiritual change and both physical and emotional freedom. Similarly, in a short, dramatic poem by the neoplatonist Kathleen Raine, an old woman rediscovers the young girl inside her:

> I felt, under my old breasts, this April day,
> Young breasts, like leaf and flower to come, under grey
>   apple-buds
> and heard a young girl within me say,
> 'Let me be free of this winter bark, this toil-worn body,
> 'I who am young,
> 'My form as subtle as a dream'.

Here, the extended metaphor of the woman as tree is being used to represent a narrative of change, a delving under the present old woody self (both bodily and psychically) to renewal. The tree like the body is a continuum that ages in time, dies and is renewed:

> And I replied, 'You, who are I,
> 'Entered a sad house when you put on my clay.
> 'This shabby menial self, and life-long time,
> 'Bear with as you may
> 'Until your ripening joy
> 'Put off the dust and ashes that I am,
> 'Like winter scales cast from the living tree.'[33]

Whilst the poem is muted in tone and the older voice's sentiments are coloured by the neoplatonic belief that the body is something to be rid of, there will be a 'ripening' and a casting off of 'scales' suggesting rebirth. The extended image of the young girl-tree inside the old woman-tree, flowering beneath the 'winter bark', calls to mind a gestation, a being pregnant with the self.

Rosalind Coward argues rightly that a Western woman's health is always constructed by commercial culture as residing on the outside of the body.[34] Just as the eyes figure in Western culture as the windows of the soul, the surface of the body, particularly the skin, equals the window onto a woman's health. But narratives of metamorphosis, with their challenge to the boundary of that surface, radically call into question this limited notion of health.

In using the term health, I want to suggest not only its physical implications but more pressingly its political ones, and what concerns me here is a health of representation in images of women. In a photographic portrait of Imogen Cunningham and her favourite model Twinka by Judy Dater, Cunningham peers around the base of a majestic tree to discover its shy residing spirit (Figure 5). This image parodies depictions of male voyeurism in the history of Western art, as it playfully amends all those mythical violations of sacred places. It juxtaposes the city against pastorale: Cunningham's technological baggage of city life/city-seeing hangs around her neck in the form of a large camera, but here it is obsolete and new ways of seeing and old narratives come together. There is much of Raine's 'I felt, under my old breasts...Young breasts, like leaf and flower to come', but with a much lighter tone of heart. Between the old citified woman and the nymph stand the grand tree and an even grander number of myths and stories about imagining women's bodies into trees.

In my readings of the novel, poem and images above, I have attempted to reappropriate the Daphne myth in order to radicalize the representational possibilities for women's bodies. Finally, while I cannot claim to have found Virginia Woolf's tantalizing sentence for a woman's body,[35] I would like to proffer that the mutable and organic character of metamorphosis expresses for women as writers, artists, readers and viewers a poetics of the body — making it an aptly expressive parallel for the experience of being in a woman's body.

In three instances above — Warner's novel, Raine's poem and Dater's image — younger women and older women observe one another, and the space between them speaks a tale of change. These textual situations reveal the liminally charged position of points in the physiological narrative of women's lives. If the mythical Daphne is motherless and can only call upon her father for help, then certainly in Daphne's shade the

Figure 5. *Judy Dater.* Imogen and Twinka at Yosemite:
1974, photograph.

mother or a like figure is recalled.[36] Again, I would argue that as
a semantics metamorphosis itself may come to represent the
somatic narratives of women's lives. It is a text that accom-
modates and honours the mutability of women's bodies through
their different ages and changing shapes.

I would like to thank Tim Dolin and Lesley Dougan, who both read and discussed this essay in all its stages; and also Hilary Fraser, Gail Jones, and Sally Scott for their comments and suggestions. I would also like to give special thanks to Peter Bryant who is currently involved in researching metamorphosis myths. He has given generously of his wide knowledge of classical culture, and his enthusiasm for the subject provided me with the impetus to write about Daphne.

1   See Carol Bigwood, 'Renaturalizing the Body (With the Help of Merleau-Ponty)', *Hypatia*, vol. 6, no. 3 (Fall 1991), pp. 54–73. Bigwood argues that 'The body must be understood as culturally and historically contextualized on the one hand, and yet as part of our embodied givenness, on the other', p. 57.

2   Marina Warner, *Monuments and Maidens: The Allegory of the Female Form* (London: Weidenfeld and Nicolson, 1985), p. 296.

3   On feminist readings of women and nature, see for instance Warner, pp. 263–265. See also Marcia Pointon, *Naked Authority: The Body in Western Painting 1830–1908* (Cambridge: Cambridge University Press, 1990), pp. 17–34, and Vicki Kirby, 'Corporeal Habits: Addressing Essentialism Differently', *Hypatia*, vol. 6, no. 3 (Fall 1991), pp. 4–24. The latter critic questions, 'is it possible that our vigilant opposition to arguments that associate woman and nature has become so automatic and prescriptive that it risks intellectual complacency?', p. 7.

4   Warner, p. 325.

5   Proceeding from the idea of a mythic mode, Gillian Beer suggests that myth 'makes endurable the contemplation of irreconcilable contraries'. See Gillian Beer, *Darwin's Plots: Evolutionary Narrative in Darwin, George Eliot and Nineteenth-Century Fiction* (London: Routledge and Kegan Paul, 1983), p. 113.

6   Refer to Lynda Nead, 'Framing and Freeing: Utopias of the Female Body', *Radical Philosophy*, no. 60 (Spring 1992), pp. 12–15. In considering the Bakhtinian body, Nead notes that 'the *female* body is undoubtedly central to Bakhtin's definition of the grotesque body — the body in process, liberated from boundaries'. In closing, Nead argues that feminism itself must embrace a future of 'change and process' against one of fixity and finalities. Extending Nead's conclusion to Daphne, it would seem that her figure offers to feminism(s) an allegory of process between two states.

7   Mikhail Bakhtin, *Rabelais and His World*, trans. Helene Iswolsky (Bloomington: Indiana University Press, 1984), pp. 316–317. Elsewhere Bakhtin refers to '(sprouts, buds)', p. 318.

8   See Kirby, p. 10. See also Diana Fuss, *Essentially Speaking: Feminism, Nature and Difference* (New York: Routledge, 1989), p. 4. Both Kirby

and Diana Fuss note the complicity that exists between essentialist and anti-essentialist (or constructionist) positions. This study posits Daphne's simultaneous natural-cultural states as figuring a way of moving beyond the stalemate of the essentialist/anti-essentialist bind.

9   See Janet Wolff, *Feminine Sentences: Essays on Women and Culture* (Cambridge: Polity Press, 1990), pp. 120–122. Wolff summarizes varying positions held in relation to the issue of women's bodies as the 'site of feminist cultural politics' and argues convincingly 'that a feminist cultural politics of the body is a possibility...[and that there] is every reason...to propose the body as a privileged site of political intervention, precisely because it is the site of repression and possession' (p. 122).

10 See Mary E. Barnard, *The Myth of Apollo and Daphne from Ovid to Quevedo: Love, Agon and the Grotesque* (Durham: Duke University Press, 1987), pp. 4–17. See also P.M.C. Forbes Irving, *Metamorphosis in Greek Myths* (Oxford: Clarendon, 1990), p. 261.

11 Ovid, *Metamorphoses*, trans. Mary M. Innes (Harmondsworth: Penguin, 1976), pp. 43, 548–551.

12 Barnard, pp. 15–17.

13 In considering the interpretation of myths, Jane Marcus argues that the critic's gender bias can repress key elements of a myth, particularly those concerned with female power. See Jane Marcus, 'A Wilderness of One's Own: Feminist Fantasy Novels of the Twenties: Rebecca West and Sylvia Townsend Warner', in Susan Merrill Squier, *Women Writers and The City: Essays in Feminist Literary Criticism* (Knoxville: University of Tennessee Press, 1984), pp. 137–138. See also Nancy K. Miller, *Subject to Change: Reading Feminist Writing* (New York: Columbia University Press, 1988), pp. 90–94.

14 David Brooks and Brenda Walker, eds, *Poetry and Gender: Statements and Essays in Australian Women's Poetry and Poetics* (St Lucia: University of Queensland Press, 1989), p. 3.

15 The idea for a study of Daphne was conceived after reading Lefkowitz's work. See Mary R. Lefkowitz, *Heroines and Hysterics* (New York: St Martin's Press, 1981), p. 89.

16 For an overview of the inscription of male power in the representation of the female body in Western art history, refer to Rozsika Parker and Griselda Pollock, eds, *Old Mistresses: Women, Art and Ideology* (London: Routledge and Kegan Paul, 1981), pp. 114–116.

17 For a brief comparative mythology of the tree as symbol, see Roger Cook, *The Tree of Life: Image for the Cosmos*, The Art and Cosmos Series (New York: Avon Books, 1974), pp. 7–31.

18 Lefkowitz, p. 93.

19 See Harold Skulsky, *Metamorphosis: The Mind in Exile* (Cambridge, Mass.: Harvard University Press, 1981), pp. 1–3.

20   In her interpretation of the Greenham Common protest, Warner demonstrates how women can radicalize traditional signs of femininity, such as weaving, through their reappropriation. See Warner, p. 58.

21   Warner, p. 59.

22   For an analysis of how particularly contemporary commercial culture has promulgated an ideal body type for women, refer to Rosalind Coward, *Female Desire: Women's Sexuality Today* (London: Paladin, 1987), pp. 19–55. See Parker and Pollock, and Pointon, pp. 11–34, on gender issues and the male artist, and the implied male viewer.

23   A.S. Byatt, *Possession: A Romance* (London: Vintage, 1991), p. 373.

24   Thomas Hardy, *The Woodlanders*, ed. James Gibson (Harmondsworth: Penguin, 1981), p. 362.

25   See Marcus, pp. 136–137. In considering Daphne, Marcus reiterates Lefkowitz's point about sexual autonomy: 'Central to the concept of female wilderness is the rejection of heterosexuality. It is a flight into a pre-patriarchal magical world of trees and transformations, animals and plants, and proud inviolateness.'

26   Sylvia Townsend Warner, *Lolly Willowes, or the Loving Huntsman* (London: The Women's Press, 1978), pp. 83–84.

27   Marina Warner, 'In the Garden of Delights', in Helen Chadwick, *Enfleshings* (London: Secker and Warburg, 1989), p. 56.

28   Hayden Herrera, *Frida Kahlo: The Paintings* (London: Bloomsbury, 1991), p. 84.

29   ibid., p. 86.

30   Cecil Helman, *Body Myths* (London: Chatto and Windus, 1991), p. 6.

31   Germaine Greer, *The Change: Women, Ageing and the Menopause* (London: Hamish Hamilton, 1991), p. 55.

32   ibid., p. 61.

33   Kathleen Raine, 'I felt, under my old breasts, this April day', in Jeni Couzyn, ed., *The Bloodaxe Book of Contemporary Women Poets: Eleven British Writers* (Newcastle: Bloodaxe Books, 1985), p. 66.

34   Coward, pp. 19–25.

35   Virginia Woolf, *A Room of One's Own*, ed. Morag Shiach (Oxford: Oxford University Press, 1992), p. 99.

36   Marcus, p. 138.

'BE WAR, YE WEMEN': PROBLEMS OF GENRE AND THE GENDERED AUDIENCE IN CHAUCER AND HENRYSON

ANDREW LYNCH

I

In later medieval Europe, an extension of the role of literacy had gained for the thinking subject some of the authority formerly vested mainly in objects of thought themselves. The onset of literacy, Brian Stock suggests, meant a growing individualism in interpretation and a disturbing of

> the concept of a single, stable, external reality, because the inherited idea of the real was now denied by the fluctuating forms of consciousness by which the real was brought into being. Every person who read, listened, debated and thought could potentially arrive at somewhat different conclusions about what a text meant.[1]

Stock's comment looks forward to the idea of the individual reading subject as the ground for establishing meaning in utterance. But, as he also points out, written tradition did not simply replace oral tradition. Instead, 'there was a realignment of oral discourse within a real or implicit system of meaning involving texts, readings, interpretations and audiences'.[2] In later medieval England, even when the idea of writing for readership had become well established, many vernacular texts were still highly conscious of an 'audience' — both a communal hearing, and a group which hears — not only as an interpretative community but as a primary condition of utterance. The comment in Chaucer's *Tale of Melibee* 'Thar as thou ne mayst have noon audience, enforce thee nat to speke' is thoroughly commonplace in medieval rhetorical theory.[3] The reception of texts was understood to be 'aural' and 'communal', but 'various', with 'a diversity of listening styles'.[4]

While the convention of a diverse 'audience' persisted, even solitary reading could be affected by it to the extent that any interpretative position became more conscious of its place as one amidst a range of possible positions which the idea of a group of hearers, heterogeneous or homogeneous, could be employed to evoke. This applied whether or not such audiences actually existed. It may be true, as has been claimed, that addresses to a (supposedly) present audience in later medieval poetry might sometimes have been deployed as a trope of intimacy for readers, or to evoke the ways of a past world.[5] But in the case of Chaucer, at least, the trope of an audience is extremely persistent. 'It is written to be read, but read *as if* it were spoken. The poem is a literary imitation of oral performance.'[6] The Chaucerian reader is surrounded by the shadowy presence of others in the audience. The form of *The Canterbury Tales*, alternating stories supposedly told by different narrators in different genres with their imagined reception in a mixed company, seems designed to exploit to the full a consciousness of variance both in utterance and textual reception, reproducing something of what Walter Ong calls the 'agonism' of an oral culture. Even the bookish narrators of Chaucerian dream-vision and of *Troilus and Criseyde*, who can be seen as surrogates for the confused Chaucer reader,[7] refer equally to oral and written sources. In *Book of the Duchess*, for example, the narrator reads to himself Ovid's story of Ceyx and Alcyone, but adds that he had never previously 'herd speke' of the gods of sleep.[8] There is no consistent division made between representations of hearing and reading. Instead, as in *The Parliament of Fowls* and *The House of Fame*, part of the prototype reader's confusion is the perception that books are marked by personal and political interest, as embodied by quarrelling *voices*, more than by the sublime and permanently authoritative wisdom attributed to themselves or their writers.[9]

In tracing textual gendering of the audience, the invigoration of English vernacular writing in the fourteenth century is a major factor. Whereas Latin was the written language of clerks, and therefore overwhelmingly of men to men, many English vernacular works of the later medieval period were not restricted in their address to men but, certainly in theory, and potentially in practice, addressed to both women and men. This did not mean that writers found in English a language equally accessible to the experience and outlook of men and women, or that vernacular writing was in some way naturally androgynous or epicene. Women's interests, if one takes them to be legitimately different from men's, were rarely consulted by the male voices women heard, scarcely more than were the interests of the servants also within earshot. But anyone hearing in the vernacular, or reading a work with 'oral' characteristics, could easily be made conscious that the audience included women as well as men. Even if the solitary male reader silently imbibed the words on the page, he could still be influenced by conventions of utterance which invoked a gender-mixed reception.

It was clearly possible to acknowledge or imagine the presence of a female audience for vernacular literature. Many later medieval English texts were addressed to both women and men, whether earlier minstrel work like *Havelok*, pitched at 'gode men-/Wiues, maydnes, and alle men',[10] or manuals of piety like *The Abbey of the Holy Ghost*, directed to 'My dere brother and sister',[11] or histories like *Le Morte Darthur*, with its writer's final prayer to 'all jentylmen and jentyllwemen that redeth this book'.[12] There are many devotional pieces and sermons — like Repentance's sermon in *Piers Plowman*, which has a lesson for Pernele and Bette, as well as Tom and Watte.[13] From the thirteenth century onwards, there were numerous narrative and other translations into English from French, presumably making these texts available to more women. In particular, there were also many more vernacular love lyrics, mainly of the courtly variety, consisting of male-voice addresses to women, though intended for reception by mixed audiences.

In this study, I examine a few instances where Chaucer and Henryson signal a female component amongst their general audience, or suggest that their audience is partly or predominantly female. These texts link the (sometimes fleeting) idea that they are addressed to women with other indications of genre and interpretative closure. The audience of women amongst men, and addressed by men, is first entertained as an idea within the fictive and poetic structures of the text, permitting a kind of secondary narrative which makes of the supposed female audience a group seen to be experiencing social pressures which are likened to those felt by women within the primary story. These pressures are linguistically constructed in so far as they are made evident by forms of poetic address. Nevertheless, the linguistic forms carry within them some traces of the powerful and male-dominant institutions in whose interests the interpretative closure effected by genre has produced a 'women's meaning' for the text. To look at the representation of men addressing women is, at least, to understand something of the condition of women as constructed by established discursive regimes. Moreover, the regimes themselves are understood more fully when their construction of women receives specific attention. Such scrutiny, by highlighting the gender assumptions of the generic and interpretative stances outlined within the poem, can disturb the 'women's meaning' there and make room for a freer and more sceptical analysis.

There can be no simple equation of literary form and ideology. As Rita Felski puts it:

> If ideology is understood as the cultural legitimation of
> the interests of dominant groups, then it becomes

clear that the ideological status of texts can be ascertained only by examining their functions in relation to existing constellations of social and political power, and not by attributing an inherent value to particular linguistic forms.[14]

I wish to examine the possible meanings that a particular formal feature, the male address to women, might carry in some texts of Chaucer and Henryson. But to do that will mean paying attention to the broader generic and discursive conventions within which these meanings might be generated, in this case the poetic traditions of 'noble love' (*fin' amor/fin lovynge*), and warnings of death (*memento mori*). In turn, these conventions are connected with two major power centres of medieval life, the court and the church. It is their manner of determining the meaning of women, and its limitations, which is ultimately at issue.

II

Like many of Chaucer's works,[15] *The Legend of Good Women* itself focuses attention on the problems of interpreting Chaucer. In its *Prologue*, Cupid berates the poet-figure for translating *The Romance of the Rose* and writing *Troilus and Criseyde*, on the grounds that these works offend against Love's law and all good women. As reparation for *Troilus*, the god, guardian of the ideology of Love, prescribes an entire narrative series built on the names of famous women in Chaucer's ballade to his lady, 'Hide Absolon, thy gilte tresses cleere' (F, 249–269):

> These other ladies sittynge here arowe
> Ben in thy ballade, yf thou kanste hem knowe,
> And in thy bookes alle thou shalt hem fynde.
> Have hem now in thy legende al in mynde.
> [*Legend*, F, 554–557]

The series, like the revised ballade in the later (G) version of the *Prologue*, is to culminate in the praise of Alceste, as model of perfect noble lover and wife:

> For she taught al the craft of fyn lovynge,
> And namely of wyfhod the lyvynge,
> And al the boundes that she oghte kepe.
>
> [F, 544–546]

Out of the male love lyric are to be drawn 'legends' — lives of saints, that is, of the kind of women Cupid admires. The purpose of these lives is to provide exemplary studies of correct female behaviour. This prescriptive containment of women also involves an abridgement in literary form, a briefer summary method. The poet is instructed to tell only the gist ('grete') of each story (570–577).

There follows an unfinished set of brief histories proving the duplicity of all men, and equating female 'trouthe' and 'goodness' in love with naiveté and an inexhaustible appetite for suffering. These narratives are ostentatiously presented as *for* women in several senses: to vindicate the name of women,[16] to encourage them to be true lovers, and to warn them of the falseness of men. The female audience is closely kept in mind. Within the frame-narration of the *Prologue*, Cupid tells Chaucer to present the completed legends to Queen Anne at Eltham or at Sheen (F, 496–497). It is possible that the poem's intended first audience was predominantly courtly and female.[17] The individual legends also include some direct addresses to women; these provide evidence of what a male poet-figure, acting on behalf of a male God of Love, might think his female readers and hearers had to learn, but in a way that compromises its supposed function as authoritative, disinterested advice:

> O sely women, full of innocence,
> Full of pite, of trouthe and conscience,
> What maketh yow to men to truste so?
> Have ye swich routhe upon hyre feyned wo,

And han swich olde ensaumples yow beforn?
Se ye nat alle how they ben forsworn?
[1254–1259]

The exclamation is partly an apostrophe of female victims within the stories, such as Dido, Hypsipyle and Phyllis, and partly an address, citing the stories as already 'olde ensaumples', to contemporary womankind in general. The commentary assesses the potential for *all* females (and males) by reference to the exemplary stories. In consequence, the legends seem to provide no useful exempla for their female hearers, only a matrix which they will be powerless to escape: trusting women and deceitful men. In a later legend, the narrator makes this shift in address more plain by confirming the logic of its direction. He turns from bewailing the death of Phyllis, and admonishes all women, including specifically the female component of his own audience:

She for dispeyr fordide hyreself, allas.
Swych sorwe hath she, for she besette hire so.
Be war, ye wemen, of yore subtyl fo,
Syn yit this day men may ensaumple se
And trusteth, as in love, no man but me.
[2557–2561]

Through this comic strategy, men's advice to women is implicated in their continuing real-life perdition. For if the stories are truly exemplary, what can real women do but continue to provide awful examples, and how is any man's advice to be trusted, including the moral poet's? The genre of instruction — the moral exemplum — is collapsed into a form of seduction-speech, recalling the deceptive 'aparaunce' (1372) of Jason, and Theseus's false 'countenaunce' (2076).[18] The *Legend* is so far from revising *Troilus and Criseyde* here that these lines specifically recall an address to women in *Troilus*: 'Beth war of men, and herkneth what I saye' (V, 1772). In both cases, a comic version of the male poetic voice fails to establish that it is seeking the good of women. The desire to *advise* women, to be the *single* authority they are to credit, replicates the seducer's strategy and his urge towards possession. Women in the audience, supposedly outside the fictions which offer to instruct them, are nevertheless enticed (under the appearance of good counsel) into a further plot that seeks to entrap them through language as the story's heroines have been entrapped. The duplicity of men within the primary fictions (Pandarus, Diomede, Aeneas, Jason, Theseus, etc.) can also be attributed to the fictional commentators, and, more importantly, to the discursive and institutional frameworks within which they operate.

Such a combination of sermonizing and predatory self-interest is characteristic of the courtly complaint lyric, in which the lover accuses some unwilling woman of cruelty and coldness if she will not have him. The language of courtly lyric, in which Chaucer was an acknowledged master,[19] provides, along with that of Christian moral instruction, the standard form for vernacular male writers speaking to women in the Middle Ages. In Chaucer's *Franklin's Tale*, noble love diction saturates Aurelius's speech to Dorigen, the woman he desires. Aurelius is a practised lyric love-poet, a maker of 'many layes/Songes, compleintes, roundels, virelayes' (947–948). In the circumstances of the story, a rash promise spoken (clearly not meant) by Dorigen permits Aurelius to supplement his initial lyric plea — 'Have mercy, swete, or ye wol do me deye' (978) — with an appeal to her 'trouthe', the quality of faithfulness to one's word which ideally underwrites a person's moral and social standing in medieval aristocratic society:

> 'My righte lady,' quod this woful man,
> 'Whom I moost drede and love as I best kan,
> And lothest were of al this world displese,
> Nere it that I for yow have swich disese
> That I moste dyen heere at youre foot anon,
> Noght wolde I telle how me is wo bigon.
> But certes outher moste I deye or pleyne.
> Ye sle me giltelees for verray peyne.
> But of my deeth though that ye have no routhe,
> Avyseth yow er that ye breke youre trouthe.
> Repenteth yow, for thilke God above,
> Er ye me sleen by cause that I yow love.'
> [1311–1322]

Aurelius's full speech (1311–1338) performs the functions of a standard love complaint, interspersed as it is with moral coercion. But since we already know that Aurelius is motivated by sexual attraction, and is aware that any submission by Dorigen will be against her will, his stance as adviser is severely undercut. Within the context of a temporal, contingent narrative, the strong reminiscences of atemporal, performative lyric conventions make the love-speech seem hardly *addressed* to the woman at all, but almost wholly solipsistic. Even within Aurelius's discursive range, the old feudal, even religious, diction of the courtly lyric genre (a 'sovereyn lady deere' [1310], extending 'grace' [1325] to the dying male servitor) coexists very uneasily with the construction of Dorigen as fellow-party to a freely entered into contract (her 'trouthe'), and with her further status as recipient of disinterested counsel ('Madam, I speke it for the honour of yow/Moore than to save myn hertes lyf right now' [1331–1332]). In a polyvocalic narrative like *The Canterbury Tales*, as in later fourteenth-century English society, a woman can, of course, be a focus for these competing discourses. But the attempt to pass them all off within a version of *fin' amor* address overloads and breaks the genre, partly through the sheer visibility of courtly lyric conventions *as* conventions in this more complex narrative surrounding.[20] Aurelius is discredited, and with him the discursive definitions conventional male address offers women as disguises for their lack of power: sovereign, partner, pupil. There are other ways to express Dorigen's situation:

> He taketh his leve, and she astoned stood;
> In al hir face nas a drope of blood.
> She wende nevere han come in such a trappe.
>
> [1339–1341]

III

A notable and problematical address to women occurs in the last stanza of Henryson's *The Testament of Cresseid*. After a brief account of Cresseid's burial, the poem concludes:

Now, worthie wemen, in this ballet schort,
Maid for ȝour worship and instructioun,
Of cheritie, I monische and exhort,
Ming not ȝour lufe with fals deceptioun:
Beir in ȝour mynd this sore conclusioun
Of fair Cresseid — as I have said befoir;
Sen scho is deid, I speik of hir no moir.

[610–616][21]

The *Testament* is 616 lines long, not very 'short'. Nor is it a 'ballet' (ballade) in the normal Middle Scots sense of a 'short poem to be sung'. Even in Middle English, the term 'ballade' refers to a short song or poem in stanza form. It often denotes a love song or poem, sometimes a poem of satiric or moral comment. A 'ballade' never seems to mean a substantial narrative like the *Testament*.[22]

'In this context', concludes Denton Fox, '[ballet] is a deprecatory term'.[23] But even if we take these lines to be an address by Henryson *in propria persona*, as a poet really or apparently deprecatory about his work, along the lines of Chaucer's 'Go, litel bok' (*Troilus*, V, 1786),[24] the poet is still referring to the guise his 'tragedie' (4) would wear were it to be perceived for the moment as a 'ballade' composed for the edification of women. The change in addressee has coincided significantly with a change in genre. The *Testament* in this women's version is now understood as a lesser form, and one associated with lyric address rather than an extended story.

It is also just possible, though less plausible, that 'this ballet schort' refers only to the last of the *Testament*'s rhyme royal stanzas, thereby singling it out as a kind of coda added by a narrator, who briefly comments in his own voice on a history meant to be reported from another source, the book he has found (57–63). The single stanza is 'short', after all, and in a ballade metre (rhyme royal). The brevity of the narrator's signing-off is reminiscent of the brief post-dream sections in Chaucer's completed dream-visions, but the impulse to moralize the end imitates and narrows even further the conclusion of *Troilus and Criseyde*. Where Chaucer's poem addresses 'Yonge, fresshe folkes, he or she' (V, 1835) on the vanity of earthly love, Henryson's addresses only 'worthie wemen' on the necessity to be faithful earthly lovers.[25]

Whatever 'this ballet schort' refers to, and whether offered as by 'poet' or 'narrator', the question remains: what does it mean, and what does it mean to address it specifically to women? The moral is certainly selective, not only in emphasis, as Douglas Gray has noted,[26] but in suggestion of audience and of genre, as we have seen. It also gives interpretation an anti-feminist slant. The admonition 'Ming not ȝour lufe with fals deceptioun' chooses to read Cresseid's conduct as a planned deception of Troilus, ignoring the political circumstances outlined in Chaucer's poem — Criseyde is given to the Greeks against her will, to ransom Antenor, a Trojan prince (*Troilus*, IV, 176–217). And there seems a further strong hint that sexual infidelity to Troilus is the cause of Cresseid's wretched disease and death. If that is not the implied logic of these lines, it is hard to see how women who are tempted to deception in love could be presumed to benefit from bearing Cresseid's 'sore conclusioun' in mind.

Such an implication raises more problems. Although it was not uncommon in medieval times to view leprosy as a venereal disease, and a divine punishment for lust, one might question why 'worthie wemen' in the audience need the 'instructioun' any more than worthy men. If the disease is venereally contracted, then Cresseid has caught it from a man. And even if all women may be deceivers like her, as the stanza seems to imply,[27] the story teaches that all men are not, like Troilus, 'honest and chaist in conuersatioun' (555). Is there to be no warning for them?

Moreover, if the story of Cresseid's disease and death is held to bear some moral significance, as a punishment of the woman for her deception of a true lover, then one must ask by whom, and in whose interests, the punishment is supposedly administered. To take the usual 'principal efficient cause', in the late medieval view, is God punishing Cresseid for an offence which excludes the original liaison with Troilus, but consists of later unfaithfulness to him?[28] If so, the putative God of the final stanza's analysis would seem uncannily careful of both *fin' amor* values and the rights of male sexual partners. What seems to be taking place is an extension of Christian ideas of punishment for sin into the judgement of conduct in a courtly love affair. The hybrid of Christian and courtly terms ('cheritie' and 'lufe') hints at an authoritative external sanction for what might well appear a partial and inadequate reading.

The last stanza's version of Cresseid's punishment is tendentious partly because the issue is otherwise severely circumscribed within the narrative. There, Cresseid is merely said to be punished by the planetary deities for blasphemy against them, especially against Venus and Cupid, not for any infidelity to Troilus. Cresseid herself is the only witness of this punishment, and that only within a dream, in which the deities figure 'be apperance' (141–147). I do not accept that Henryson or anyone else can care about blasphemy to these figures of speech as individuals. They must be understood as something else.[29] As Jill Mann has written, ascription of punishment to the planetary gods indicates that Cresseid's disease is an ineluctable fact, consequent on her behaviour, but without any wider endorsement as a moral punishment, and truly understandable as a 'misfortune'.[30] There must therefore be considerable doubts over what, if anything, Cresseid's leprosy might mean to *others* in moral terms, as distinct from her need to come to terms with it as a fact in her imagined situation. If the position assumed in the last stanza, where man instructs women, encourages an interpretation which ignores those doubts, and suggests that the disease is an apt punishment for infidelity, then the value of the interpretation must come into question, including the gendering of its address, and its apparent misappropriation of religious diction.

The standard modern interpretation of the *Testament* is one in which Cresseid's moral vision is corrected by suffering until she is able to say 'Nane but myself as now I will accuse' (574). This is indeed the only utterance of Cresseid's which has drawn widespread critical endorsement.[31] In this way, understanding the poem has meant knowing better than Cresseid what is going on, finding a meaning for the woman that she must finally learn to see for herself. We could, for once, vary this process by noting that the full meaning of the story as stated through Cresseid is very different from that implied in the poem's ending, and asking if 'her' version must necessarily be all invalidated. Instead of reading her disease as a lesson on unfaithfulness, as the last stanza seems to, Cresseid separates the two issues, in two great set-piece speeches. The first of these (407–469), distinguished by a change in stanza form, laments her misfortune, and offers herself to young women of the court as an example of the instability of earthly wealth, beauty and reputation, a *memento mori.*

> '3our roising reid to rotting sall retour;
> Exempill mak of me in 3our memour
> Quhilk of sic thingis wofull witnes beiris.
> All welth in eird, away as wind it weiris;
> Be war thairfoir — approchis neir 3our hour —
> Fortune is fikkill quhen scho beginnis and steiris.'
>
> [464–469]

Cresseid is especially appropriate as a reminder of approaching death to courtly women because she is now aged, poor and ugly, like the figures excluded from the garden of the *Romance of the Rose.*[32] Cresseid is supposedly a pagan, ignorant of Christian revelation, but she speaks to a medieval Christian audience in a familiar language. Her leprosy merely replicates faster the processes of ageing in life and decay after death which are standard topoi in medieval death literature.[33] Although she addresses only women — first herself, then others — the *memento mori* theme has already been sounded for men by the male narrator's discovery of his own age, in the poem's opening section. (Henryson's *actual* 'ballet schort' on death, *The Thre Deid Pollis*, is addressed to both sexes: 'lusty gallandis gay' and 'ladeis quhyt, in claithis corruscant'.)[34]

The second lament (540–574), begun by three stanzas with the refrain '...fals Cresseid and trew knicht Troylus!', is concerned with Cresseid's unfaithfulness, regarded not as a misfortune but as her own fault: 'Nane but myself as now I will accuse'. She speaks first to herself and Troilus, then to 'lovers', especially male lovers, it seems, with the warning that other women are like her, 'unconstant' — 'Quha findis treuth, lat him his lady ruse' (573).

I have no wish to literalize Cresseid as a real entity capable of generating a woman's perspective on her condition. Clearly, 'her' voice occupies a discursive position marked by male interests. But it is still important to note that the view expressed through her is in conflict with the implication of the final stanza. Taking Cresseid's viewpoint, it is only because she considers the leprosy and the unfaithfulness separately that she can be seen to reach the moral awareness critics have so prized, separating the fact of her disease from a conviction of personal wrongdoing to Troilus as lover. When the two are confounded, as in the instruction to worthy women, the possibilities for moral vision attributed to Cresseid are annihilated. Furthermore, if Cresseid is right to accuse only herself, then the direction of the poem's moral towards *others*, an otherness quickly established by sexual discrimination, is a response which badly misses the point.

The view attributed to Troilus is different again, but far closer to Cresseid's. A debilitating lovesickness comes on him when he sees her begging, weakening his value as a defender of Troy (514–516). Though there is no recognition, his mind's eye is so preoccupied with the image of the lost lover that even this disfigured crone's blinking can bring Cresseid's love-glances to mind (498–504). So Troilus unwittingly gives alms to the leper, in memory of the same woman's beauty when she was his lover — 'For knichtlie pietie and memoriall/Of fair Cresseid' (519–520). On hearing soon after of her death, Troilus is forced to connect the two images of her so far received as separate; his feelings find expression in two utterances which replicate, in reverse order, the substance of Cresseid's two laments (407–469; 540–574). First, Troilus laments Cresseid's 'untruth' in a way that displays his own 'truth' (fidelity): 'I can no moir;/Scho was vntrew and wo is me thairfoir' (601–602). Second, he makes of her tomb a *memento mori* for women, with this inscription:

'Lo, fair ladyis! Cresseid of Troy the toun,
Sumtyme countit the flour of womanheid,
Vnder this stane, lait lipper, lyis deid.'
[607–609]

So both Cresseid and Troilus perceive as separate to the very end
her mortality and her conduct as a lover. This fact might be read
to their discredit in terms of medieval Christianity, for instance in
the terms adopted at the close of Chaucer's *Troilus and Criseyde*,
where the young are urged: 'Repeyreth hom fro worldly vanyte',
and instructed to love only God, who will never betray them
(*Troilus*, V, 1835–1855). For if the *memento mori* theme were
taken in its normal spirit, as a teaching to despise the world, then
love of a worldly object for its own sake would be reproved as
a 'pagan' folly (*Troilus*, V, 1849–1855). It would then become
untenable to alternate laments couched in *fin' amor* language
with meditations on death, as Henryson's Troilus and Cresseid
both do. One would rather expect, in Christian terms, that with
the sudden realization of earthly transience, such as Chaucer's
Troilus achieves after his death (*Troilus*, V, 1807–1834), would
come either an abandonment or religious appropriation of noble
love language. Instead, the advent of Cresseid's death leaves both
of Henryson's lovers in an impasse of tragic regret, and radically
undecided. Cresseid, after making a testament within the spirit of
contemptus mundi (contempt for the world) — though without
a Christian hope of salvation (Mann calls it 'Stoic')[35] — bursts out:

'O Diomeid, thou hes baith broche and belt
Quhilk Troylus gaue me in takning
Of his trew lufe' and with that word scho swelt.
[589–591]

Troilus, wrecked by unhappiness, simply 'can no moir' (601), a
phrase also employed by Chaucer's Love-stunned narrator in
The Parliament of Fowls (1–7), but then, according to some
(603), he writes a lesson in mortality on Cresseid's tomb. Each of
the discourses of love and death is resistant to the other. The
integrity of their utterance seems to depend upon that separation.

Neither can be abandoned *or* subordinated if the tragic situation is to be fully realized.

The major oddity of Henryson's clerkly last stanza is not, however, that death and deception in love are for the first time linked. *Troilus and Criseyde* had already done that, in the interests of Christianity. It is that they are implicitly hierarchized in a way which offers Cresseid's sorry end as a lesson in fidelity to *fin' amor* principles. The poem seems to conclude within the boundaries of the same love ideology which its evocation of the *memento mori* tradition has allowed only a partial hold on the story's meaning. In this context, the sudden association of the last stanza with a new genre and a new audience suggests some instability in the interpretative closure obtained, however grave and compassionate it may sound.

One possible view is that the poem, in the manner of Chaucer's *Clerk's Tale*, offers at the end a ballade counter-moral especially for women which satirically offers to replicate the attitudes of its supposed audience.[36] The poem *might* be read to suggest (and implicitly to deplore) that women are incapable of understanding any conclusion deeper or less carnal. But that reading is no more persuasive than its reversal, which would question the motivation of the instructing voice rather than of the audience. The conclusion so gravely protective of noble love doctrine would then appear as a male ploy, morally impoverishing of its female addressees. That is, the stanza would seem to function in the interests of male sexual dominance, to keep women afraid, 'faithful' and pitiable within the confines of *fin' amor*, whatever the cost to them of submission to its discourse.

In this last reading, the ballade moral to the blanker tragedy makes of it retrospectively a seduction of women, praising a male-dominant 'love', excluding any application for men. The meaning of Cresseid's story, in this analysis, is to warn women to do what their lovers want. That is, she is offered as an exemplum which endorses the preconditions of her own suffering. The plenitude and indeterminacy of the 'narratioun' in which she figures are traduced by a false closure, whose 'deceptioun' lies in the moralist's language itself.

Genre provides a contract of expectations between writer and reader/hearer, but individual texts may employ it in order to display their own variance.[37] In any case, as many critics have shown, genre in narrative is rarely single, without a sense of competitors.[38] When linked to generic traits, therefore, conventions of gender in poetry become less, rather than more, stable, and may themselves become objects of revision and critique. In Chaucer and Henryson, I believe, versions of lyric and moral address to the female audience, especially when inserted in volatile narrative contexts, can be seen to provide what Carolyn Dinshaw calls 'a double perspective — the awareness of what is left out by the literary act even as that act is performed'.[39] Through that double perspective, standard generic evaluations and definitions are acknowledged but not unchallenged, and some resistance is offered to the institutional pressures that normally underwrite the meaning of women in medieval poetry. Though a 'women's meaning' may be uttered, it is not necessarily the only one heard.

1   Brian Stock, 'Historical Worlds, Literary History', in Ralph Cohen, ed., *The Future of Literary Theory* (New York and London: Routledge, 1989), p. 52.

2   ibid., p. 47.

3   *The Riverside Chaucer*, ed. L.D. Benson (Oxford: Oxford University Press, 1988), VII, ll. 1045–1046, quoted in Paul Strohm, *Social Chaucer* (Cambridge, Mass.: Harvard University Press, 1989), pp. 47–48. All subsequent Chaucer line references are to *The Riverside Chaucer*.

4   V.A. Kolve, *Chaucer and the Imagery of Narrative: The First Five Canterbury Tales* (California: Stanford University Press, 1984), p. 15.

5   Thorlac Turville-Petre, *The Alliterative Revival* (Cambridge: D.S. Brewer, 1977), pp. 36–40. See also Derek Pearsall, 'The *Troilus* Frontispiece and Chaucer's Audience', *Yearbook of English Studies*, no. 7 (1977), pp. 68–74. Kolve, p. 8, gives more credence to the *Troilus* frontispiece (Corpus Christi College MS 61) than Pearsall does.

6   H. Marshall Leicester, 'The Art of Impersonation: A General Prologue
       to the *Canterbury Tales*', *PMLA*, no. 95 (1980), p. 220. See also
       pp. 223–224, n. 25: 'The poem presents not merely stories but stories
       told to an audience that is part of the fiction, and this circumstance
       allows Chaucer to register the effect of a range of conditions of
       performance'. A summary of views on textuality and performance in
       Chaucer is in Carolyn Dinshaw, *Chaucer and the Text* (New York and
       London: Garland, 1988), pp. 99–109. See also Walter Ong, *Orality
       and Literacy* (London and New York: Methuen, 1982), pp. 43–44, 103.

7   Dinshaw, p. 188: 'the role of the reader is inscribed in the text in the
       narrator's role as reader, and our response is thus already written'.
       (The reference is to *Troilus*.)

8   *Riverside Chaucer, Book of the Duchess*, ll. 231–237.

9   See Jill Mann, 'The Authority of the Audience in Chaucer', in P.
       Boitani and A. Torti, eds, *Poetics: Theory and Practice in Medieval
       English Literature* (Cambridge: D.S. Brewer, 1991), p. 5, n. 16. See
       also *The House of Fame*, ll. 1475–1480.

10   *Havelok*, ed. G.V. Smithers (Oxford: Clarendon, 1987), ll. 1–2.

11   N.F. Blake, ed., *Middle English Religious Prose*, York Medieval Texts
       (London: Edward Arnold, 1972), p. 89.

12   *The Works of Sir Thomas Malory*, ed. E. Vinaver, rev. P.J.C. Field, 3
       vols (Oxford: Clarendon, 1990), p. 1260. In Caxton's Preface of 1485,
       the *Morte* is directed 'unto all noble prynces, lordes and ladyes,
       gentylmen or gentylwymmen, that desyre to rede or here redde' of
       Arthur, ibid., p. cxlvi.

13   *Piers Plowman: The B-Version*, eds G. Kane and E.T. Donaldson
       (London: Athlone Press, University of London, 1975), V, ll. 24–33.

14   Rita Felski, *Beyond Feminist Aesthetics: Feminist Literature and Social
       Change* (Cambridge, Mass.: Harvard University Press, 1989), p. 63.

15   Judith Ferster, *Chaucer on Interpretation* (Cambridge: Cambridge
       University Press, 1985), pp. 11–12.

16   See Sheila Delany, *Medieval Literary Politics: Shapes of Ideology*
       (Manchester and New York: Manchester University Press, 1990), p.
       103: 'As a defence of women essentialism destroys itself. To argue
       that women are by nature good is to accept the conceptual founda-
       tion for the opposite view.'

17   See *Riverside Chaucer*, pp. 587–588, and *Legend*, F, ll. 496–497 and
       notes.

18   On the instability of Chaucerian exempla, see J.A. Burrow, *Ricardian
       Poetry* (London: Routledge and Kegan Paul, 1972), pp. 88–92, and
       Janet Cowen, 'Women as Exempla in Fifteenth-Century Verse of the
       Chaucerian Tradition', pp. 51–64, in Julia Boffey and Janet Cowen,
       eds, *Chaucer and Fifteenth-Century Poetry*, no. V (London: King's

College, Centre for Late Antique and Medieval Studies, 1991), see especially pp. 49–50.

19   See *Confessio Amantis*, VIII, ll. 2941–2949, in *The English Works of John Gower*, ed. G.C. Macaulay (Oxford: Early English Text Society, 1900–1901, Extra Series 81–82).

20   See W.A. Davenport, *Chaucer: Complaint and Narrative* (Woodbridge, Suffolk: D.S. Brewer, 1988), p. 8: 'The complaint as lyric perhaps seemed to Chaucer inadequate to deal with particular circumstance, more apt to the expression of mood or general aspect of state of mind'. I would argue that Chaucerian use of complaint lyric language, even when not in stanzaic form, can often be regarded similarly.

21   Line references are to Denton Fox, ed., *The Poems of Robert Henryson* (Oxford: Clarendon, 1981).

22   Fox, p. 383, n. 610. See also H. Kurath and S. Kuhn, eds, *Middle English Dictionary* (Ann Arbor: University of Michigan Press, 1952–), pp. 621–622, under *balad(e*.

23   Fox, p. 383, n. 610.

24   See *Riverside Chaucer*, p. 1056, n. 1786, for a list of antecedents, beginning with Ovid. Chaucer also calls his love story a 'tragedy', perhaps following Ovid's definition. For examples of Scots ballades of Henryson's period, see J. MacQueen, ed., *Ballattis of Luve* (Edinburgh: Edinburgh University Press, 1970).

25   Henrietta Twycross-Martin, 'Moral Patterns in *The Testament of Cresseid*', in Boffey and Cowen, pp. 49–50.

26   Douglas Gray, *Robert Henryson* (Leiden: E.J. Brill, 1979), p. 207: 'the narrator...speaks earnestly and directly to his audience, selecting, as in the moralitates of the fables, a single important strand from his story for emphasis'.

27   Delany, p. 159: 'To let the individual stand for the sex is a standard tactic of misogyny'. For 'worthy', see N. Davis, ed., *A Chaucer Glossary* (Oxford: Clarendon, 1979), where it is described as 'often ironical', especially in Chaucer's *General Prologue* to *The Canterbury Tales*. (The phrase 'worthy woman/women' may be ironic in two of these instances: l. 217, l. 459.)

28   C.S. Lewis understood Cresseid's offence in that way: 'The same pliancy which ennobled her as the mistress of Troilus, debases her as the mistress of Diomede...Her further descent from being Diomede's mistress to being a common prostitute, and finally a leprous beggar, as in Henryson, cannot be said to be improbable', *The Allegory of Love* (Oxford: Oxford University Press, 1936 and reprint), p. 189.

29   Jill Mann, 'The Planetary Gods in Chaucer and Henryson', in R. Morse and B. Windeatt, eds, *Chaucer Traditions, Studies in Honour of Derek Brewer* (Cambridge: Cambridge University Press, 1990),

argues, p. 95, that Henryson represents 'the physical forces of the cosmos in the personalised forms of gods'. She cites J. MacQueen, *Robert Henryson* (Oxford: Oxford University Press, 1967), p. 169, who sees the gods as 'the indifferent laws of the universe'.

30   Mann, 'The Planetary Gods', pp. 95–96.

31   For example, Mann, 'The Planetary Gods', p. 95; Gray, p. 205: 'She has come to some kind of self-knowledge', quoting line 574.

32   See Chaucer's translation, *Riverside Chaucer*, ll. 301–412, 449–474.

33   These processes are emphasized by the descriptions of Saturn (ll. 155–168), and of Cresseid's punishment (ll. 308–343), especially l. 318: 'Thy moisture and thy heit in cald and dry'. Fox, p. 351, notes that Saturn's old age replicates the condition of leprosy.

34   Fox, p. 182.

35   Mann, 'The Planetary Gods', p. 95.

36   *Riverside Chaucer, Clerk's Tale*, ll. 1163–1212.

37   See Jonathan Culler, *Structuralist Poetics* (London: Routledge and Kegan Paul, 1975), p. 147.

38   For extended studies of competing genres in Chaucer, see Strohm, and C. David Benson, *Chaucer's Drama of Style* (Chapel Hill and London: University of North Carolina Press, 1986).

39   Carolyn Dinshaw, *Chaucer's Sexual Poetics* (Madison, Wisc., and London: University of Wisconsin Press, 1989), p. 152.

PERCEVAL'S SISTER: ASPECTS OF THE VIRGIN IN THE *QUEST OF THE HOLY GRAIL* AND MALORY'S *SANKGREAL*

PHILIPPA BECKERLING

T HE French *Queste Del Saint Graal* (*Quest of the Holy Grail*) and Malory's later version of the story, the *Tale of the Sankgreal*, both demonstrate values that deviate from the more secular chivalric outlook that pervades the rest of the Arthurian romance cycle, and nowhere more so than in their attitudes towards women.

The heroines of other Arthurian romances, like Guinevere or Elaine, daughter of the Fisher King, are sidelined in these texts by a relentless focus on the Grail knights' pursuit of spiritual knowledge. Sexually active women are a dangerous temptation to the knight who aspires after good; the Grail mysteries are available to only a few, and in these versions they are always men.[1]

Only one woman, Perceval's sister, plays a major role in the allegorical scheme of the *Queste*. She is necessary to the author's purpose of re-creating, in Galahad, a figure of Christ. She is a virgin; she plays the part of the mother of the Christ figure in the episode dealing with Galahad's initiation. She girds his sword with her hair, and has the divine authority to communicate the holy history that is intended for him, and which has awaited his coming. Within this episode she is granted considerable status in the allegorical scheme. Shortly after this episode, however, she is caught up as a sacrificial victim in an ambiguous episode that is superfluous to the quest story overall, and she dies a pointless death. We see that, in terms of the allegory, her function is limited; once she has served her purpose as Mary figure, she resumes the status of 'ordinary' virgin and minor character, while the main line of the narrative proceeds to its men-only resolution.

I want to look at the implications of this shift in status, but first we must take a look at the subject of virginity in medieval Christian tradition.

The *Queste* author's view of virginity in both men and women has its roots in the teachings of the Church fathers, notably Jerome, Augustine and Ambrose. A great deal of criticism exists on the subject of the virgin[2] but work remains to be done on the aspect that has particular relevance to the *Queste*: the construction of the virgin as virgin for specific reasons, and issues connected with this process. There are many relevant passages in the writings of the Church fathers on this subject, some of the most frank being found in the letters of St Jerome. These writings reveal that the value of the state of virginity in women was located primarily in the psyche of the male. The virgin is prized above all in the fact that she does not represent a carnal temptation to the male; this is her chief characteristic, and the end towards which all the teachings on the subject are directed. As we learn from a study of Jerome and Ambrose, among others, the virgin is ideally a product of a closed environment in which worldly influences are kept to a minimum. She is guided and moulded into physical asceticism from the earliest days and raised on a diet of religious precepts and proscriptions. Her naturally weak nature is never allowed to emerge. Of the many letters Jerome wrote on the subject of the virgin, letter CVII is the most detailed and specific. He makes it clear that the young virgin belongs to Christ, and woe betide a parent who deflects the divine purpose in this regard. He states that

Christians are not born but made, and lists the methods whereby the Christian female baby is 'made' into a virgin. Jerome's chief concern can be seen to be in creating a woman that is not a temptation to men:

> Her very dress and appearance should remind her of Him to whom she is promised. Do not pierce her ears, or paint with white lead and rouge the cheeks that are consecrated to Christ. Do not load her neck with pearls and gold, do not weigh down her head with jewels, do not dye her hair red and thereby presage for her the fires of hell.[3]

Jerome's belief that the virgin is a sign, rather than a generator of signs, to use Roberta Krueger's terms,[4] is expressed in his letter on the virgin's profession, written to Eustochium. He says:

> I praise wedlock, I praise marriage; but it is because they produce me virgins. I gather the rose from the thorn, the gold from the earth, the pearl from the oyster.[5]

The virgin is conceived as an object to be processed by agents of the Church. Her sterility, which carries associations of ornamental artefact in the images of rose, gold and pearl, is the quality that raises her above her source, which is productive wedlock: the inference is clear that her virtue/value lies precisely in the fact that as 'constructed' virgin she is no temptation to men.

Aldhelm's treatise, the prose *de Virginitate*,[6] deals with virginity from a somewhat different viewpoint. In a topos common in discussions of virginity, he speaks of the virtues of the bee:

> The bee, I say, by virtue of the special attribute of its particular chastity, is by the undoubted authority of the scriptures agreed to signify a type of virginity and the likeness of the Church: robbing the flowering fields of pastureland of an ineffable booty she produces her sweet family and children, innocent of the lascivious coupling of marriage, by means of a certain generative condensation of a very sweet juice...

He goes on to identify another essential quality common to bee and virgin:

> This also is to be remembered, I suggest, concerning the harmonious fellowship of the bees, and to be admired as some theatrical spectacle — I mean the spontaneous inclination to voluntary servitude which they are known to exercise in obedience to their rulers.[7]

These views are pertinent to the subject of women in the *Queste* and the *Sankgreal*, which are of two types, both of which are defined by their sexual relationship to the grail knights. There are 'good' women, who are virgins, and diabolical women, who are temptresses. Perceval's sister is unusual, because she is a type of the ideal woman, postfiguring Mary, who combined the roles of mother and virgin while abjuring sexuality.

Caroline Walker Bynum identifies three functions of the mother:

> The female is generative (the foetus is made of her very matter) and sacrificial in her generation (birth pangs); the female is loving and tender (a mother cannot help loving her own child); the female is nurturing (she feeds the child with her own bodily fluid).[8]

It was in only one woman, Mary, that the generally mutually exclusive qualities of maternity and virginity could coexist, obviously, but in the *Queste* author's construction of the later equivalent, Perceval's sister, these qualities coexist metaphorically. As in the case of Mary, Perceval's sister can function as intermediary for Galahad only because she is chaste, and this prescription is made very clear.[9] In bringing Galahad to the ship, giving him his history and girding his sword with her own hair, she is demonstrating qualities of generation and nurturing, which can be seen as a metaphorical equivalent to Mary's giving Jesus flesh. There is a further image of nurturing in the episode in which Perceval's sister, known only as a 'jantillwoman' at that stage, takes Galahad to her castle where he stays a while to eat and sleep.[10]

In the two versions of the grail story, there is a small variation in detail at this point. The French *Queste* speaks of Perceval's sister as the lady of the castle, in a manner which suggests the issue was of some importance to him:

> The maiden was still riding in front when she entered the castle, and Galahad followed after. When the inmates saw her come, they cried out:
> 'Welcome Madam!'
> And they received her with all the marks of joy due to their mistress, which in fact she was.[11]

The primacy of religious values is evident in the *Queste* version; as figure of Mary, Perceval's sister is here constructed as a person of status, and owner of the castle which represents her virtuous qualities. Propriety and inviolability are figured by the strength and admirable construction of the castle:

> ...they came to a castle sited in a valley and superbly furnished against attack, girt with running water and well-built walls, high and massive and deep, steep-sided ditches.[12]

Mary as castle is a motif present in various places, as Roberta Cornelius shows in *The Figurative Castle*, among them a thirteenth-century Anglo-Norman poem, *Le Chateau d'Amour*, attributed to Robert Grosseteste, Bishop of Lincoln:

> the high firm rock is her pure heart; the towers are the cardinal virtues; the baileys virginity, chastity, and holy wedlock; the barbicans are the seven virtues. The four streams from the fountain are the wellsprings of grace.[13]

An aspect of 'putting on flesh', as Mary gave Jesus the means to do, is being given the knowledge of one's placement in history or, in other words, of one's genealogy, and this is

Perceval's sister's chief function in the quest. The knowledge that she imparts to Galahad also gives meaning to the larger pattern of the quest, in the figure of the Maimed King, the broken Sword of David and the Waste Land. Galahad's personal quest for knowledge of the grail will have more general and outward manifestations of success in the healing of the Maimed King, which will supplement his own attainment of spiritual perfection.

The belt of hair which is Perceval's sister's own contribution to Galahad's initiation ceremony is more problematical. Matarasso refers to St Paul's first letter to the Corinthians, 11 and 15, for its explanation:

> Doth not even nature itself teach you, that, if a man
> have long hair, it is a shame unto him?
> But if a woman have long hair, it is a glory to her:
> for her hair is given her for a covering.

For St Paul, the glory and covering are one and the same; the beauty of the hair is in the fact that, as an equivalent to the veil, it covers her head and signifies her inferior status. This is an image consonant with Paul's negative overall view of woman. Inherent in this is the notion that the woman uncovered is a temptress, flaunting her sex to the danger and disadvantage of men. Perceval's sister's explanation focuses on the glory, not the covering, thus demonstrating more of an allegiance to the ideas of Jerome than to Paul. Her explanation, on removing the belt from its casket, begins the author's process of constructing the pliant virgin:

> ...she drew out a belt woven of threads of richest
> gold, and silk, and strands of hair. And the hair was so
> bright and burnished that one could scarce distinguish
> between it and the gold. The belt was encrusted, too,
> with priceless gems and fastened with two gold
> buckles, hard to match for cast and beauty.
> Good sirs, she said, here is the belt that belongs to
> the sword, and be assured that I made it of the most

precious thing I had, which was my hair. Nor was it any wonder that my hair was dear to me, for on the feast of Pentecost, when you, Sir, here she spoke to Galahad, were knighted, I had the finest head of hair of any woman in the world. But as soon as I learned that this adventure awaited me, and this was what I must do, I had my hair shorn in haste and made it up onto the braids you are looking on.[14]

In this passage, the hair is transformed into sacred ornament, equivalent to the gold and precious stones that adorn Church vessels. The hair's value has undergone a transmutation, from being 'the finest head of hair of any woman in the world'. The sacrifice of Perceval's sister's hair represents her rejection of her sexual aspect, and the consecration of her physical person to a spiritual way of life in the service of the Christ figure. Both of these roles, sexual and spiritual, prescribe that she be defined by her relationship to male figures.

Between the incident dealing with the sword, and the one in which she dies, the text includes a brief exposition of the nature of virginity, and, as in the case of the hair/belt, the imagery is once more based on holy artefact. This exposition is placed after the incident dealing with the hart and the lions, in which the hart is metamorphosed into the figure of Christ, and the four lions into his evangelists. At the end of the apparition

They took hold of the seat where the hart was sitting, two to its feet and two to the head, and it was like a throne: and they went out through a window in the chapel, in such a manner that the glass was still entire and perfect after their passing. And when they were gone and lost to the sight of those within, a voice from above made itself heard among the watchers, saying: 'In like manner did the Son of God enter the Virgin Mary, so that her virginity was left entire and perfect.'[15]

The notion of virginity as window occurs in various sources, among them the jongleur Rutebeuf, who writes:

> Just as the sun enters and passes back through a
> windowpane without piercing it, so were you virgo
> intacta when God, who came down from the heavens,
> made you his mother and lady.[16]

It is also found in the *Songe to Mary* attributed to William of
Shoreham:

> Ase the sonne taketh hire pas,
> Withoute breche, thorghout that glas,
> Thy maidenhod unwemmed it was
> For bere of thine childe.[17]

Possibly the most interesting use of this motif is found in the
fourteenth-century *Leys d'Amors*,[18] where, as Bloch points out, the
author produces two entirely contradictory readings from the
same material to illustrate the great gap between the nature of
the virgin and the ordinary woman. He takes the word *femna*,
each letter of which, in his exposition, represents a word. So
femna can mean fenestra — window; enverenada — poisoned;
mortz — death; nostra — our; aparelhada — bringing. So we
have *femna* — woman, poisoned window bringing our death.
The same word applied to the Virgin produces 'fenestra ellumen-
ada mayres nostra advocada — shining window, mother our
defender'.

The central image concerns the closed or open state of the
window, an obvious reference to the presence or absence of the
hymen. In these examples, the presence of the maidenhead is
compared to a 'shining window' and a chapel window, both
presumably decorative, and carrying overtones of being man-
made as aids to worship. Both of these aspects can be applied
to the notion of virginity with some richness of resonance. The
important point, however, is that the virgin in question here,
Perceval's sister, whose affairs both precede and follow this
incident, has been identified in two instances with sacred
artefacts: the belt and, by inference and association, the chapel
window. Metonymically, then, she is herself sacred artefact,
consecrated to the service of the Christ figure, Galahad.[19] It is in

these terms that her apparently meaningless death must be interpreted.

Pauline Matarasso sees Perceval's sister as a figure of Mary, in line with the views of M. Lot-Borodine and F.W. Locke.[20] She suggests that in the light of Perceval's sister's role as a figure of Mary, her voluntary sacrificial death may seem incongruous, but she goes on to justify it. The person for whom she is to die is a leprous lady, and in this regard Matarasso cites St Bernard's association of the will with a 'languid lady covered with ulcerated and suppurating wounds. The members of the body form her court, willing servants of her pleasure, ready to gratify her every whim yet unable, despite their frenzied efforts, to cure her of her affliction.'[21]

Leprosy was a disease of the soul as much as of the body in ecclesiastical tradition, and it was invariably associated with immorality of some kind. Sufferers from the disease were, among other things, fornicators, concubines, the incestuous and adulterers.[22] While it was associated with other sins such as usury, perjury, simony and pride, it was thought to be a venereal disease, and as such was regarded as a result of sexual depravity.

In the literary tradition, according to Brody, the introduction of a leper into a work was done on the understanding that his or her disease was not simply an illness but a punishment sent by God. A leper was a symbol of moral guilt.

Of the many cases of literary leprosy, Hartmann von Aue's Heinrich is perhaps the most comprehensive.[23] In this case, a knight is struck down with the disease as a consequence of excessive pride. His healing is achieved through the intercession of an innocent child, whose superior humility is manifested in her desire to sacrifice herself for him. In the Middle English romance *Amis and Amiloun*,[24] Amiloun's leprosy is similarly cured by innocent children, but with some variations, the most striking of which, perhaps, is that the sacrifice is not voluntary: the suffering is regarded as being Amis's, who is father to the victims. In both of these cases, a substantial mental adjustment is required of the guilty party, after which healing ensues.

In contrast to this pattern is the experience of Henryson's Cresseid, whose affliction with leprosy is the consequence of immoderate sensuality, and indirectly also of faithlessness and betrayal of the hero.[25] In spite of an admission of the justice of her punishment, there is no reprieve for her.

Relevant to the *Queste* incident is the story of Constantine, in which the Emperor's opposition to Christianity is punished by the curse of leprosy. When he hears that his disease can be cured by bathing in the blood of children, he sends for them with the intention of killing them for his health, but is finally unable to do so. This leap in moral awareness signals his readiness to receive the faith, which he does, and is healed.[26]

In most of these cases, and in all in which healing does take place, innocent children or young virgins are involved, and, with the exception of *Amis and Amiloun*, the children are saved from death by a change of heart on the part of the sufferer. In Cresseid's case, it would seem that her past excesses, or 'lustis lecherous', disqualify her from any possibility of healing. With these variations in mind, the leprous lady of the *Queste* and *Sankgreal* makes an interesting case.

On the question of treating like with unlike, Brody notes the following:

> The tradition of healing leprosy by blood, particularly the blood of children, is seen in early Hebrew commentary, Pliny, and many texts of the Middle Ages. In Hartmann, as elsewhere, the moral significance of the cure is apparent. Typically, in clinical practice, the medieval doctor would attempt to treat a condition with remedies containing qualities inimical to the sickness. For example, a man with excess hot and moist humours would be given a cold and dry remedy. Likewise, Heinrich's disease, which stems from moral impurity, can be cured by an antidote of high purity — the blood of a virgin. Elsewhere, as in the Amis and Amiloun story, the blood of innocent children is named as a cure. Thus, for writers who understand leprosy to be a moral disease, the cure by blood can be effective only if the donor is morally pure. The blood cure plays a part in literature because it is symbolically

significant, not because the poets sought to depict actual medical practices.[27]

In the scheme of literary representations of leprosy, Perceval's sister obviously plays the part of the innocent blood-giver.[28] Her death raises a number of questions, because as we have seen, in this scheme, the innocent victim is invariably either reprieved or restored to life, by human or divine agency. The *Queste* author's deviation from this pattern is striking.

In order to justify the apparent pointlessness of this death, Matarasso disengages Perceval's sister's sacrificial act from the consequences for the rest of the court, claiming that they must be seen in isolation from each other. Perceval's sister's sacrifice is voluntary, she claims, and therefore justified in itself.[29] The divine retribution which strikes down the castle and slays its inhabitants is an expression of God's disapproval of the custom of the castle, and punishment for the death of the innocent maidens that predeceased Perceval's sister vainly.

In spite of Matarasso's view, the interconnection of Perceval's sister's death and the consequences for the lady and her castle is stated clearly in the text. When she gives her blood to heal the leprous woman, she says:

> Madam, to give you healing I am come to the point of death. For God's sake, pray for my soul, for my life is at its end.[30]

She then tells Perceval she is dying so that the lady may have health, is given a last communion, and dies. The leprous woman makes a miraculous recovery. As Matarasso has it:

> As soon as she was washed in the blood of the holy maid, she was cleansed and healed of her leprosy and her flesh that had been blackened and hideous to look on recovered all its bloom, to the joy of her own people and of the companions too.[31]

Perceval's sister's sacrifice may be voluntary, as Matarasso believes, in an individual sense, but it cannot be seen as such within the larger context, which is one of external compulsion. She has no choice but to give her blood, as the presence of so many knights against their three makes very clear. She is doomed to die anyway, and her offering of blood is more like a dignified cooperation with an executioner than a real sacrifice. Secondly, the moral and religious context of these various incidents is highly ambiguous; the defending knights state that Galahad, Perceval and Bors will never prevail:

> for were you the best knights in the world you could not stand against us.[32]

The episode is conducted in an environment where mass is heard in the morning, and where a priest is close by and willing to administer the sacraments to the castle inmates. The death of Perceval's sister is mourned but not resented,[33] and more attention is given to a description of her embalming and enshipment for Sarras than to the knights' sentiments regarding her death. She is not mentioned again in this episode, but the retribution visited upon the leprous lady and her court is treated in some detail. The previous episodes in which Perceval's sister played a central role in initiating Galahad into the mysteries of the ship, the sword and his lineage established a certain status for her that is undermined and devalued in this subsequent episode. The message is that in a case involving a woman whose sin is past forgiveness, being inimical to the absolute purity of the virgin victim herself, she does not possess the power to heal, or to restore goodness to the object of her sacrifice, as Mary did for the descendants of Eve. She is constructed as being innocent in more than one sense, for at no time is she shown to be aware that her death is not to be redemptive for the leprous woman herself, or for the members of her court. The success of her sacrifice lies elsewhere, beyond her knowledge, in as far as it brings to an end the practice of taking innocent lives.

The *Queste* author thus creates the figure of Perceval's sister in two simultaneously contradictory ways: the Mary figure blessed with knowledge of divine intention in the first part, and in the second, the naive and innocent virgin/child victim who dies without insight into the nature of her sacrifice.

Perceval's sister compares poorly with the three grail knights in terms of access to the allegorical level. She appears from nowhere immediately prior to the ship episode, and having fulfilled that function she is despatched without much ceremony and buried merely 'as befitted a king's daughter'.[34] She is presented as mere adjunct to Perceval, who initially fails to recognize her and ultimately fails to mourn her, and, most importantly, she is never named. Her power is limited to one role, which is the metaphorical equivalent of giving Christ flesh, when she initiates Galahad into his predestined place, and the blood episode in which she dies is superfluous in terms of the overall quest in all aspects except that in which her ship guides Lancelot to Galahad. She is honoured for one function only, and that is the only one which cannot be performed by a male equivalent.[35]

The superfluity of the episode in the quest as a whole suggests that its function is to remove Perceval's sister from the table of players, for there is no place for her or any woman in the last episodes of the story. The ground for her death is prepared at the close of the episode on the Ship of Faith, in which she girds Galahad with David's sword:

> When she had hung it at his side, she said to him:
> Truly, Sir, it matters no more to me when death shall take me, for now I hold myself blessed above all maidens, having made a knight of the noblest man in the world.[36]

Were Perceval's sister to have been consistently constructed as a Mary figure, restoration to life would have been a logical necessity, because in redeeming the sinful Eve, Mary redeems not only the sin of Eden but also its consequence for post-lapsarian mankind: mortality. The *Queste* author can be seen to be operating in a context which assigns the virgin consecrated to the Church the status of artefact. Her final and ignorant death, in which the author sacrifices allegorical consistency to notions of gender-based exclusivity, confirms this view.

1   The *Queste* author consistently removes all references to women in connection with the appearances of the Grail that are present elsewhere in *The Vulgate Cycle*, and in the *Sankgreal* Malory follows suit. See Malory's versions in his book 5, in which the appearances of the Grail are invariably associated with fair damsels, so much so that Sir Ector, in informing Perceval of the meaning of the Grail, states that

> Hit is an holy vessell that is borne by a mayden, and therein is a parte of the blood of our Lord Jesu Cryste.
>
> [5, p. 817]

All references to Malory's *Morte Darthur* are to the three volume edition, *The Works of Sir Thomas Malory*, ed. Eugene Vinaver, rev. P.J.C. Field, 3rd edn (Oxford and New York: Clarendon, 1990).

2   See especially Marina Warner, *Alone of All Her Sex: The Myth and Cult of the Virgin Mary* (London: Quartet Books, 1976), for summary and bibliography of the subject. For Augustine's and Thomas Aquinas's views on women, see Kari Elisabeth Borreson, *Subordination and Equivalence: The Nature and Role of Women in Augustine and Thomas Aquinas*, trans. Charles H. Talbot (Washington: University Press of America, 1981).

3   *Select Letters of St. Jerome*, ed. and trans. F.A. Wright (London: Heinemann, 1945), p. 35.

4   Roberta L. Krueger, 'Double Jeopardy: The Appropriation of Woman in Four Old French Romances of the "Cycle de la Gageure"', in Sheila Fisher and Janet E. Halley, eds, *Seeking the Woman in Late Medieval and Renaissance Writings: Essays in Feminist Contextual Criticism* (Knoxville: University of Tennessee Press, 1989).

5   ibid., p. 95.

6   Aldhelm, *The Prose Works*, trans. Michael Lapidge and Michael Herren (Cambridge: D.S. Brewer; Totowa, New Jersey: Rowman and Littlefield, 1979).

7   ibid., p. 62.

8   Caroline Walker Bynum, *Jesus As Mother: Studies in the Spirituality of the High Middle Ages* (Berkeley: University of California Press, 1982).

9   Sommer, H. Oskar, *The Vulgate Version of the Arthurian Romances*, edited from manuscripts in the British Museum (Washington: The Carnegie Institution of Washington, 1909), vol. VI, p. 148; P.M. Matarasso, *The Quest of the Holy Grail* (Baltimore: Penguin, 1969), pp. 216–217. The inscription on the holy sword reads: 'It must not be unfastened save by a woman's hand, and she the daughter of a king and queen. She shall exchange it for another, fashioned from that thing about her person that is most precious to her, which she shall

put in this one's stead. It is essential that this maiden be throughout her life a virgin both in deed and desire. And if it happen that she lose her maidenhood, she may be sure that she will die the basest death that can be a woman's lot. This maid shall call the sword by its true name, and me by mine, and never till that day shall there be found a man to name us by our proper names.'

10   Sommer, p. 142; Malory, bk 5, p. 983. *A Songe to Mary*, B.M. Add. 17376, attributed to William of Shoreham, c. 1325, in R.T. Davies, ed., *Medieval English Lyrics: A Critical Anthology* (London: Faber & Faber, 1963), no. 34. Lines 57–58 speak of Mary as 'Emaus, the riche castle,/That resteth alle werye'. Refs also occur in Pseudo-St Bernard, 'Sermo in Antiphorum "Salve Regina"', P.L. clxxxiv, col. 1074, 13th c.

11   Matarasso, p. 211. Concerning Malory's version, Vinaver notes: 'Contrary to his usual practice Malory here adds to the personnel of the story by distinguishing the damsel from the lady of the castle. In the F. they are one and the same.'

12   ibid., p. 210.

13   Roberta D. Cornelius, *The Figurative Castle: A Study in the Medieval Allegory of the Edifice with Especial Reference to Religious Writings* (Pennsylvania: Bryn Mawr, 1930), p. 45.

14   Matarasso, p. 236.

15   Sommer, p. 167; Malory, bk 6, p. 999.

16   Quoted from Rutebeuf, *Le Miracle de Theophile*, ed. Grace Frank, 1925, in Warner.

17   *A Songe to Mary*. The motif is also found in the Sarum Breviary 1, cvi, Matins of the 3rd Sunday in Lent, lesson 6, attributed to St Augustine.

18   Quoted in R. Howard Bloch, *Etymologies and Genealogies: A Literary Anthropology of the French Middle Ages* (Chicago and London: University of Chicago Press, 1983), p. 58.

19   Writing of Augustine's views on the role of woman in the incarnation of Christ, Borreson notes: 'It is significant that Augustine never mentions Eve and Mary's name in most of his writings: he speaks of femina in general. Their part is ancillary and subordinate in relation to the principal actor, Adam, and the new Adam.' (p. 75) 'In the whole history of the human race, a female element in the role of helper and instrument is always involved.' (p. 80)

20   Myrrha Lot-Borodine, *De L'Amour Profane à L'Amour Sacre: Etudes de Psychologie Sentimentale à Moyen Age* (Paris: Nizet, 1961); F.W. Locke, *The Quest of the Holy Grail: A Literary Study of a Thirteenth-Century Romance* (Stanford: Stanford University Press, 1960).

21   Matarasso, pp. 72–73.

22   Saul N. Brody, *The Disease of the Soul: Leprosy in Medieval Literature* (Ithaca: Cornell University Press, 1974).

23 Hartmann von Aue, *Der Arme Heinrich*, eds Erich Gierach and J. Knight Bostock, 4th edn (Oxford: Blackwell, 1965).

24 *Amis and Amiloun*, ed. A. McE. Leach, EETS o.s. no. 203 (London: Oxford University Press, 1937).

25 Robert Henryson, *The Testament of Cresseid*, ed. Denton Fox (London: Nelson, 1968).

26 See Caxton's *Golden Legend*, vol. 1, ed. F.S. Ellis (Hammersmith: Kelmscott Press, 1892), pp. 314 ff.

27 Brody, p. 152.

28 While it is not spelt out, it is implied that her virginity is the inimical and thus curative quality, and it follows from this that the leprous lady's sin is sexual in origin. As in the case of Henryson's *Cresseid*, there is no cure for her.

29 Robert S. Sturges supports Matarasso's interpretation of this incident: 'This adventure provides another example of characters simultaneously living on different levels of meaning: for Perceval's sister her sacrifice is allegorical, whereas for the leper herself it is literal and thus punishable'. *Medieval Interpretation: Models of Reading in Literary Narrative, 1100–1500* (Carbondale: Southern Illinois University Press, 1991), p. 243. While this may be so, it does not adequately take into account the consequences of the sacrifice for the Mary figure.

30 Matarasso, p. 250.

31 ibid.

32 ibid., p. 246.

33 The statement that the companions did not wish to set foot in the castle 'for love of the maiden they had lost there in that fashion' seems to be more to do with physical logistics than moral outrage.

34 Matarasso, p. 281.

35 On the subject of Christ's incarnation, Augustine 'stresses the necessity of female collaboration, in the person of Mary...Christ takes human nature in the form of a man, but this incarnation takes place through the intermediary of a woman.' Borreson, p. 74.

36 Matarasso, p. 237.

BLACK WIDOW: DEATH AND THE WOMAN IN EARLY MODERN ENGLISH TEXTS

ANN CHANCE

> A theory which links death imagery with history must emphasize the struggle to live with the anxiety that death imagery arouses. Men and women can deal with this anxiety by relating themselves to the modes of symbolic immortality which are combined and expressed in constantly changing ways. The struggle is to maintain the meaningfulness of particular expressions of the sense of immortality, or to find new expressions, as historical conditions change.[1]

In his book *The Denial of Death*, Ernest Becker remarks that 'the idea of death, the fear of it, haunts the human animal like nothing else; it is a mainspring of human activity — activity designed largely to avoid the fatality of death, to overcome it by denying in some way that it is the final destiny for man'.[2] Fashions of expressing and coping with death anxiety are not merely culturally determined by historical processes. According to Lifton and Olson, they are also major determinants of cultural change:

In his effort to move forward, man requires symbols of
continuity and flow; these symbols take shape within
the modes of immortality. *From the viewpoint of the
individual* we can say that the life project is to achieve
significant relation to one or more of these modes.
From the broader viewpoint of history we can say that
the collective cultural life project is to maintain the
viability of the modes of immortality so that they will
continue to provide avenues for individual personal
fulfilment.[3]

This essay is concerned with some of the ways in which
individualism and possession related to broad concepts of 'life',
'death' and 'immortality' in early modern England and, further,
some of the psychosocial consequences of these relationships as
demonstrated in various texts. Phillipe Ariäs speaks of a period
in Europe

in which were laid the bases of what was to become
modern civilization, a more personal, more inner
feeling about death, about the death of the self,
[which] betrayed the violent attachment to the things
of life but likewise...it betrayed the bitter feeling of
failure, mingled with mortality: a passion for being, an
anxiety at not sufficiently being.[4]

Such a rise in individualism and separation/death anxiety might
be said to correspond with an intensifying of possessive patri-
lineal practices in early modern England, and both might be
traced to a loss or deterioration of older, more spiritual and communal 'modes of immortality'.[5]

Life and death, at least for the male, were not necessarily
absolute physical states. Particularly among the wealthier classes,
men perceived themselves as extended beyond their biological
life in space (grandeur), time (immortality) and potency, through
their ability to 'possess'. Whatever a man 'possessed' became a
vehicle or extension of his presence, his life. Such possessions
included estates, objects, money, family name and ancestry,
wife, heirs and other offspring. Immortality was perceived not

only as a spiritual possibility but also as an earthly one. A man's potency and presence — or 'life' — could also be extended after biological death by the survival of his personal 'honour' and fame; through monuments, written and oral testament and portraits; through the perpetuation of his name and 'likeness' in the bodies of his descendants, and his 'memory' in the minds of the living.

The individual might invest enormous amounts of money and energy in cultivating and securing his *posterity*, his earthly immortality. Descendants were perhaps the most highly valued form of posterity. Through them:

> thou continuest thy name, thy likeness, and thy Generation walkes upon earth, and so livest in thy similitude, in despight of death, when thou thy selfe art dead, and raked up in dust, and otherwise without remembrance, unless by some ruinous stone or ragged Epitaph, and so (in some sort) makest thy body immortall, like thy soule...[6]

Male descendants were valued more than female, as they represented a better 'likeness' of the father. They also carried the father's name and — being male — greater status. In most parts of England, where primogeniture was practised, the (male) heir was particularly valued, in that he would take his father's place in society, the estate and most of the other possessions. First-born males were likely to be named after their fathers, and greater care and money were spent in arranging their futures for them.[7]

Females were excluded from the forms of symbolic immortality offered by lineage and possession: the 'things of life'. They were, in fact, constructed *as* possessions.[8] However, males — particularly those of the wealthier classes — were also subject to some destructive side-effects of their own self-image. Their relationships with strangers and family alike were soured by the all-pervading competition to be the possessor, rather than the dispossessed or the possession. The struggle was one of life and death. Wherever a man lived — symbolically or physically — he could also die. Loss or diminution of honour/fame/name/

memory, of possessions, or of power — whether sexual, economic or political — all decreased the status of a man, and constituted a kind or degree of death.

After his physical death, a man was impotent to control, maintain and protect the symbolic, earthly extensions of his life. Neither did they rest upon the trustworthiness of God. Rather, they were almost wholly dependent upon the will and actions of the living, particularly the descendants and the widow. No matter how thoroughly their futures were arranged for them, wives and descendants could not ultimately be controlled after one's death, except — to a limited extent — through the conditions of the will.[9] Hence the anxiety and rage manifested in contemplations by 'men of family' on the autonomy of the survivors:

> Compare the loyalty of our times with those of more ancient, and see how they equall thy conscience and carkase breaking, how with thy piled up chestes, they build monuments of remembrances to thy name and memory after death; nay rather observe, but how their ambition, thus heated makes them forgetfull of themselves as well as thee...Who can love those living that he knowes will so soone forget him being dead... yet decease, and such a lethe of forgetfulnesse shall so soone ortake thee as if thou hadst never beene...[10]

The angry cynicism of such writings towards the perceived impotence of these strategies demonstrates not only how real was the drive for immortality, but also how it positioned the individual male in antagonistic suspicion of and competition with all other individuals, *particularly* those who were supposedly his 'nearest and dearest'.

Although primogeniture offered a relatively stable and unified form of posterity, it could be especially destructive in terms of family relationships.[11] Heirs waited impatiently for their fathers' deaths in order to begin their own lives; second and subsequent sons resented both father and heir, perhaps even wishing them dead; wives and daughters competed for the favours of the patriarch and his heir, enslaved by their own dependence and lack of legal status; dowagers and their daughters-in-law lived in competition and resentment over their status within the household; and the patriarch himself lived in suspicion of the sincerity and loyalty of all family members, and in fear of predation from competitive agents, particularly after his own physical death.[12] For one thing, upon his decease he would be subsumed into his heir's ancestry: another status-enhancing form of possession. The more successfully possessive the male became — that is, the more of a *patriarch* he became — the greater was the degree of his isolation and the greater the death-threat posed by all others around him. In particular, he was threatened by that agent with the least to lose and the most to gain: his own woman.[13]

Death and the woman

Traditions equating woman and death are, of course, at least as old as the story of Eve and the worship of Kali, and perhaps as deep in the male psyche as an experience of the omnipotent otherness of the mother. This last, according to Freudian theory, engenders the most basic fears of separation, impotence and/or 'death'.[14] Perhaps it is these fears, and the resultant drive for personal omnipotence, which we see expressed historically through the pursuit of social status and immortality. Given their origin, it would be surprising if such fears and drives were not directed particularly at the female, and if death and the female were not conflated into a single agent or at least perceived as allies. Such a conflation is often exhibited in the writings of sixteenth and seventeenth-century men, whether subconsciously or not.[15] Browne, whose writings display a morbid preoccupation with death and decay coupled with a marked alienation from womankind,[16] says of a friend that:

> certain it is he died in the dead and deep part of the Night, when *Nox* might be most apprehensibly said to be the Daughter of Chaos, the Mother of Sleep and Death, according to the old Genealogy...[17]

Women were perceived as having a particular power over life and death, and an affiliation with these processes which was spiritually, socially and biologically determined. Because women bore and delivered babies, they could also abort or kill or kidnap them. Likewise, because they fed and physicked members of their households (and often other individuals), they might also bewitch and poison them. They also attended the dying and laid out the dead.[18] In death, the male became as vulnerable to the will of the female as he had been as an infant. However, the amount of sensational and cautionary literature about female abuse of these powers appears to have been greatly disproportionate to the frequency of real instances.[19]

It was not only man's *physical* vulnerability to woman that attracted concern. Even while a man remained physically alive, the safety of certain *symbolic* extensions of himself depended upon his woman's self-abnegation. Upon marriage, the woman was subsumed into the man's identity in terms of name and legal status, to become his possession. A man's wife was supposed to be simply a part of himself, and a diseased one at that: 'man is the whole world and the breath of God, woman the rib and crooked piece of man'.[20] According to law and theology, the husband was the 'head' of the woman: that is, the centre of identity and will.[21] Frances Dolan observes that:

> If the husband and wife become a joint subject at marriage, then...popular representations seem to suggest, the wife's enlargement into volition, speech, and action necessarily implicates, diminishes, even eliminates, the husband.[22]

In other words, the extent of the woman's 'life' was proportional to and interdependent with the extent of the man's 'death'. Through actions of self-will — such as disobeying, contradicting, beating, scolding or cuckolding her husband — a wife could very easily compromise her husband's status, thereby 'killing' his honour. In particular, the female tongue was often represented as the cause of male death. According to Rogers, the 'Vicious and Wicked Woman is never like to be silent till she is in the Grave, and she may send him thither first...'.[23] Viscount Shannon tells his female readers that 'ranting governing wives' are guilty of a form of murder: 'the Wife that cuts off the Husbands governing Power, cuts off the Husbands Head...'.[24] Not only so, but a history of rebellion — whether violent, verbal or sexual — was sometimes evidence enough actually to convict and execute a woman for her husband's physical murder. In the cases of Mistress Beast (1583) and Margaret Fernseede (1608), the evidence of guilt seems to have consisted of nothing more than a suspected dislike for the husband or a reputation for disorderly behaviour, particularly that of a verbal or sexual nature. It was proof enough of 'murder' that these women were (according to hearsay) unchaste and/or shrewish.[25] Transgressive behaviour had already branded them as traitors and as murderers of their husbands' name and honour. Their complicity in the physical death either was assumed from this behaviour, as the natural culmination of their paths of sin, or else was simply irrelevant.[26]

Any act of self-enlargement or self-will, and any transference of possession — whether in terms of money, name or body — effected by one's wife could be perceived as an act of betrayal and symbolic murder. To some writers, this applied whether or not the husband was still alive. In this respect, widows presented a special problem. Upon the husband's death, the law automatically accorded the wife status as an entity in her own right, a *femme sole*; and the state of widowhood alone offered this to women.

> Widows could own property and dispose of it as they wished, choose for themselves whether to remarry and whom to marry, and often wielded full authority over their unmarried offspring and the father's estate until the heirs were of age...In addition, the widow was theoretically entitled to a third share of this estate ...The widow of a wealthy man might therefore have access to a good deal of money and power, as well as the freedom to make use of them.[27]

Male writings which concern themselves with death and

posterity, such as those of Niccholes and Browne, display a particular bitterness and anxiety regarding wives: or, rather, widows and wives-as-potential-widows. The threatened territories include the money and estate, the life of the heir, and the widow's body. All of these possessions, these extensions of the dead patriarch, were threatened by the widow's subjective legal and social status, and by what was represented as her female moral 'frailty' — representations of which, of course, commonly occurred over the sites of female *power* to effect the occlusion, dispossession or death of the male. Widows not only represented a threat to individual males and their posterities, but also to the patriarchal system and its general societal structures. Apart from the wider social consequences of dynastic disruption, it was popularly thought that women who were sexually awakened by marriage often became adulterous and promiscuous. Widows, as women unrestrained by male authority, represented the most uncontrollable of these.[28] By functioning as a *femme sole*, a wealthy widow could disrupt the very definition of her gender in terms of woman's role and her 'nature'.[29]

That aspect of widowhood which appears to have been the focus of most concern was the widow's right to choose whether to remarry and whom to remarry. A woman was not supposed to desire, or to function for her own sake and in her own right. If the 'good woman' did desire anything, it was simply to be possessed. As one fictional widow says:

How happily
Might woman live, methink, confin'd within
The knowledge of one husband!
What comes of more rather proclaims desire
Prince of affections than religious love,
Brings frailty and our weakness into question...[30]

A man's widow, therefore, was supposed to be his 'relict'; keeping his memory, honour and name 'alive' in herself.[31] Niccholes gives the moral example of the virtuous widow who turns down an offer of marriage with the assertion that 'My husband ever lives in my thoughts'.[32] The dead husband manifests his presence or life in his widow's thoughts by his continued possession of her mind and body. The widow's bestowal of herself upon another male and her taking of his name were often seen as an outrage. Women were frequently reminded that:

> so much did the wise Emperors of Rome detest all petulancie of Marriage, that they made and ordained Lawes, that Women which within the yeare of mourning for their husbands betake them to wedlocke againe, should be reputed infamous and defamed.[33]

By remarrying, the woman might also put her first husband's heirs, and his accumulated wealth, family history and 'honour', into the hands and, to various degrees, under the *name* of the interloper. Remarrying widows were often figured as traitors, who

> usually upon second marriages, exchange the natural care of their children with the love of their second husbands (for the most part unthrifts or greedy cormorants), that usually make a prey of the children and their estates.[34]

The widow's transfer of possessions through remarriage was often represented as a form of whoredom[35] — or murder. The story of Shakespeare's *Hamlet* revolves around this idea.[36]

In the minds of some male writers, the mere fact of being a widow seems to have proved a woman complicit in her husband's death. Niccholes wrote of widows that:

> [T]hey are...as insatiate as the sea, or rather the grave, which many times the sooner presents them thether: At the decease of their first husbands, they learne commonly the trickes to turne over the second or third, *and they are in league with death, and coadjutors with him,* for they can harden their owne hearts like iron to break others that are but earth; and I like them worse that they will marry, dislike them utterly they marry so soone...[37]

He rather significantly represents the widow's mourning confinement in terms of the customs surrounding birth rather than those of mourning:

> [S]o little a quantity of time shall confine it, that shee [thy widow] shall not lie in her month but shee shall bee Churched againe, and open to another all thy fruitions, with as fresh and plenteous an appetite as the harlot her next sinner.[38]

Shannon similarly regrets 'many of the fine gay young Widows, making the day of their Husbands death, the joyful Birthday of their own freedom' and speaks of the widow as 'she that's newly deliver'd from the bondage of a Marriage confinement...'.[39] Female life depended upon male death.

Apart from the sociopolitical implications of her legal position, the widow's life itself was resented. As the living wife of a dead man, the figure of the widow functioned as a sign of male death and female independence, 'proving' that the two were one. According to Wye Saltonstall, a widow is like 'the last letter of the Greeke Alphabet *Omega*':

> Her rings are so many cheates from severall suters, in one of which shee commonly weares a deaths head, but it is indeed herselfe a better embleame of mortality for memento mori like a Motto to bee written in her forehead. Lastly shee's a canceld bond that has beene long before seal'd and delivered, and is now growne out of date.[40]

No matter how well socialized, the widow's very existence and visibility as a widow were perceived as offensive. Particularly if flaunted in the public eye, her stubborn and unnatural continuance of life after the death of her man was a form of insolence.

Widow control

During the Middle Ages, wealthy widows had been encouraged either to join a convent or to make an institutionalized vow of lay celibacy and seclusion.[41] Although Reformation theology discouraged or prohibited the making of vows of celibacy and seclusion,[42] the widow's vow and her failure to keep it continued to be a major theme in literature.[43] In much of the literature for and about widows, the behavioural guidelines set down for them tend to be stricter than for other women. The widow was forbidden all social intercourse, particularly with men or with unruly women. She was forbidden fine clothes or the use of cosmetics. She was forbidden life outside the home. She was forbidden happiness or physical comfort. She was forbidden any behaviour or practice which called attention to herself, particularly as a possible sexual or marital partner *or* as a contented *femme sole*. She was to 'mortify' herself so totally that she did not even represent an object to living men.[44]

The threatened punishments for transgression included undesirability, ridicule, dishonour, spiritual death, physical death, and damnation. The staging and writing-up of the trials and executions of 'husband-killers' served as justification for male control (and male anxiety), and as a warning to women.[45] In a similar way, the staging and writing of accounts of other kinds of transgressive widows — whether fictional or 'non-fictional' — also provided a means of controlling through threat.[46] Transgressive widows were represented as 'unwomanly' and undesirable: the underlying assumption being that women naturally desire to be desired far more strongly than they desire power. Jokes and comedies about lusty, self-willed or remarrying widows depict the humiliation and dispossession of these symbolic man-killers as comic justice.[47] Tragedies such as *Hamlet* and *Cymbeline* reminded women and the rest of society of the evils inherent in female remarriage — and in the typical nature of widows.

A widow was supposed to be entirely occluded by her dead husband: socially, sexually, economically and — ideally — physically. Timothy Rogers, in his description of *The Character of a Good Woman* (1697), asserts that 'In Health she is active for [her husband's] Service; when sick, he has her Prayers; when she dies, she loves him to the last Breath; and if he be like to die, she would even chuse to die with him'. Elizabeth Dunton (constructed as Rogers's pattern of virtue) is quoted as telling her husband that 'she had rather die than he should be sick', and then, on her deathbed, that 'she desired to live for his sake, and nothing else'.[48] Christopher Newstead catalogues examples of similar wifely perfection:

> It beeing a custom amongst the Indians, that the women should be buried quick [i.e. alive] with their husbands, if the thred of their lives were first cut, they so willingly condiscended unto it, that many times one man having two wives, they would be in mortall strife, who should be interred with him. *Martia*, the Daughter of *Cato*, being demanded when she would surcease from mourning for her deceased husband... When I cease to live...The Wife of *Pompey* slew her selfe upon his dead corps...[49]

Of course, the Christian widow should not actually effect her own death by will or action: the death should represent the natural effect of her lack, frailty and passivity under the circumstance of being separated from her male head and identity:

> [A]las, when she hath lost her husband, her head is cut off, her intellectuall part is gone, the verie faculties of her soule are, I will not say cleane taken away, but they are all benummed, dimmed and dazled, so that they cannot thinke or remember when to take rest or refection for her weake body. And though her spirits and naturall moysture being inwardly exhausted, with sorrow and extreme griefe, she be called and inforced to seeke restauration, by such aliments as life is prolonged by, yet is she nothing desirous of life, having lost a moytie of her selfe, yea the principall moytie now best prised and esteemed, but never best loved...[50]

The agent in this scenario is not the woman herself, but rather grief working upon her. It was only 'natural' that she be *overcome* with grief, *succumb* to the emotional frailties of womanhood, simply *lose* her *will* to live, and gradually fade away. What could be more natural than the death of a headless woman?

In many English texts of the early modern period, the widow is represented as the epitome of female evil. Joseph Swetnam, for instance, concluded his misogynous best-seller with a diatribe against widows, describing them as 'the summe of the seaven deadly sinnes, the Feinds of Sathan and the gates of Hell'.[51] It seems as though allowing one's husband to die, especially if one did not immediately follow him into the grave, could be regarded as an unnatural and transgressive act in itself. The physical murder of husbands represented only the extremity of the threat posed by the advantages of widowhood relative to other female states. It was seen as an enactment of the desire which, it was felt, must burn in the hearts of all women.

Whether or not it was articulated in personal terms towards the husband, female resentment and the urge for freedom remained a threat to the entire social structure. Any display of a desire for power, let alone the outright enjoyment of it given the opportunity, represented a desire for male death. Even if the widow had not physically killed her husband, 'wished him dead', or been guilty of disorderly conduct, the mere fact of her existence was a symbol of the ultimate impotence of the male in the face of oblivion. Her consent to her own life, let alone visibility, was intolerable. Since the presence of the widow denoted the death of the male, it was assumed that the death of the widow would somehow help to safeguard the continued existence of the male. The widow's failure to die a 'natural' physical death demanded at least a social death. Driven more by desperation than logic, man's anger at death was channelled into obliterating what was merely a symbol and a symptom of his personal finiteness.

1   Robert Jay Lifton and Eric Olson, *Living and Dying* (London: Wildwood House, 1974), p. 95.
2   Ernest Becker, *The Denial of Death* (New York: The Free Press, 1973; London: Collier Macmillan, 1973), p. ix.

3   Lifton and Olson, p. 94.

4   Phillipe Ariäs, *Western Attitudes Towards Death: From the Middle Ages to the Present*, trans. Patricia M. Ranum (Baltimore and London: Johns Hopkins University Press, 1974), p. 105.

5   Laurence Stone, *The Family, Sex and Marriage In England 1500–1800* (London: Weidenfeld and Nicolson, 1977), pp. 4–10, 123–269. See also Ariäs.

6   Alexander Niccholes, *A Discourse, Of Marriage and Wiving...* (London: 1615), *Short Title Catalogue of Books Printed...1475–1640* (hereafter STC), ed. A.W. Pollard and G.R. Redgrave (London: Bibliographical Society, 1926), 18514, p. 5.

7   Stone, p. 112. Of course, 'taking the father's place' was a very ambiguous thing to do. The heir could be seen (and could see himself) both as a representative of his father and as a usurper of his place.

8   On the conceptualization of woman as property, see Peter Stallybrass, 'Patriarchal Territories: The Body Enclosed', in Margaret W. Ferguson, Maureen Quilligan and Nancy J. Vickers, eds, *Rewriting the Renaissance: The Discourses of Sexual Difference in Early Modern Europe* (Chicago and London: University of Chicago Press, 1986), pp. 127–142.

9   See Ralph Houlbrooke, *The English Family 1450–1700* (London and New York: Longman Group, 1984), pp. 230–232. Also Susan Dwyer Amussen, *An Ordered Society: Gender and Class in Early Modern England* (Oxford and New York: Basil Blackwell, 1988), p. 77.

10   Niccholes, pp. 26–27.

11   Stone, p. 232.

12   On the consequences of primogeniture, see Stone, pp. 88, 232; Houlbrooke, p. 232; Joan Thirsk, 'Younger Sons in the Seventeenth Century', *History*, vol. 54 (1969), pp. 358–377; and on early modern France, see Natalie Zemon Davis, 'Ghosts, Kin and Progeny: Some Features of Family Life in Early Modern France', *Daedalus* (April 1977), pp. 87–114. Also Sir Thomas Browne, *Religio Medici and Other Works*, ed. L.C. Martin (Oxford: Clarendon, 1964), p. 74. For examples of family histories which exhibit these problems, see Christopher Clay, *Public Finance and Private Wealth: The Career of Sir Stephen Fox, 1627–1716* (Oxford: Clarendon, 1978; New York: Oxford University Press, 1978); G. Davies, ed., *Autobiography of Thomas Raymond & Memories of the Family of Guise*, Camden Third Series, vol. 28 (London: Royal Historical Society, 1973); Alan Macfarlane, ed., *The Diary of Ralph Josselin 1616–1683* (London: Oxford University Press for the British Academy, 1976); and Miriam Slater, *Family Life in the Seventeenth Century: The Verneys of Claydon House* (London: Routledge and Kegan Paul, 1984).

13   On the origins, laws and practice of primogeniture, see also Houlbrooke, pp. 232, 234; Macfarlane, *Marriage and Love in England: Modes of Reproduction, 1300–1840* (Oxford and New York: Basil Blackwell, 1986), p. 62; Joan Thirsk, 'The Family', *Past and Present*, no. 27 (1964), pp. 116–122; and Francis Bacon, *The Elements of the Common Lawes of England* (1630), English Experience Series, no. 164 (Amsterdam: Theatrum Orbis Terrarum, 1969; New York: Da Capo Press, 1969), p. 29.

14   Sigmund Freud, *The Standard Edition of the Complete Psychological Works of Sigmund Freud*, 24 vols, ed. trans. James Strachey (London: Hogarth, 1974). See especially *The Ego and the Id* (1923), in vol. 19, pp. 1–66, and *Inhibitions, Symptoms and Anxiety* (1926), in vol. 20, pp. 75–174.

15   For instance, see *A Discourse of Women, Shewing Their Imperfections Alphabetically* (London: 1667), STC D1611, pp. 124–125.

16   See Michael Stanford, 'The Terrible Thresholds: Sir Thomas Browne on Sex and Death', *English Literary Renaissance*, vol. 18, no. 3 (Autumn 1988), pp. 413–423.

17   Browne, pp. 181–182.

18   Margaret Hallissy, *Venomous Woman: Fear of the Female in Literature* (New York: Greenwood Press, 1987); Amussen, pp. 113–115; Kate Campbell Hurd-Mead, *A History of Women in Medicine from the Earliest Times to the Beginning of the Nineteenth Century* (Haddam, Conn.: Haddam Press, 1938); Thomas Roger Forbes, *The Midwife and the Witch* (New Haven and London: Yale University Press, 1966); Barbara Ehrenreich and Deirdre English, *Witches, Midwives and Nurses: A History of Women Healers* (London: Writers and Readers Publishing Cooperative, 1976).

19   Betty S. Travitsky, 'Husband-Murder and Petty Treason in English Renaissance Tragedy', *Renaissance Drama,* vol. 21 (1990), pp. 175–176.

20   Browne, p. 67.

21   Travitsky, pp. 172–176.

22   Frances Dolan, 'Home-Rebels and House-Traitors: Murderous Wives in Early Modern England', *Yale Journal of Law & the Humanities*, vol. 4, no. 1 (Winter 1992), p. 14.

23   Timothy Rogers, *The Character of a Good Woman, Both in a Single and Marry'd State...*(1697), STC R1846, pp. 70, 77.

24   Francis Boyle Shannon, *Several Discourses and Characters Address'd to the Ladies of the Age. Wherein the Vanities of the Modish Women are Discovered* (London, 1689), STC S2965A, p. 63. Lynda Boose suggests that the ritual shaming practice of carting scolds 'carried the special disgrace of being made analogous to a capital offender, the only other criminal transported by cart to meet his/her punishment'.

'Scolding Brides and Bridling Scolds: Taming the Woman's Unruly Member', *Shakespeare Quarterly*, vol. 42, no. 2 (Summer 1991), p. 190.

25   *A Brief Discourse of Two Most Cruell and Bloudie Murthers, Committed Bothe in Worcestershire...*(R. Warde, 1583), STC 25980; *The Arraignment and Burning of Margaret Fernseede for the Murder of her Late Husband Anthony Fernseede...1608* (London: For H. Gosson, 1608), STC 10826.

26   See Dolan; Travitsky, pp. 171–198; Susan Dwyer Amussen, 'Gender, Family and the Social Order', in Anthony Fletcher and John Stevenson, eds, *Order and Disorder in Early Modern England* (Cambridge: Cambridge University Press, 1985), pp. 118–119.

27   Ann M. Chance, 'Shakespeare's Widow', in Robin Eden, Heather Kerr and Madge Mitton, eds, *Shakespeare and the World Elsewhere*, Proceedings of the Second Conference of the Australian and New Zealand Shakespeare Association (Adelaide: published by the Australian and New Zealand Shakespeare Association, at the University of Adelaide, printed by Flinders Press, 1993), pp. 23–35.

28   See Robert Copland, *The Seven Sorrowes that Women Have When Theyr Husbands be Deade* (London: c. 1568), STC 5734, pp. B2r, B2v; Joseph Swetnam, *The Araignment of Lewde, Idle, Froward, and Unconstant Women...*[Tho. Tel-troth, pseudonym] (E. Allde for T. Archer, 1615), STC 23533, p. 31; and Shannon, pp. 98–100.

29   Amussen, *An Ordered Society*, p. 3.

30   Thomas Middleton, *More Dissemblers Besides Women*, ed. A.H. Bullen, *Works*, vol. 6 (London: John C. Nimmo, 1885), 1.3.3–10.

31   Juan Luis Vives, *A Verie Fruitfull and Pleasant Booke Called the Instruction of a Christian Woman*, trans. Richard Hyde (London: 1592), STC 24863, bk 3, pp. Cc3, Dd6, E; Richard Braithwait, *The English Gentlewoman* (London: 1631), STC 3565, p. 113.

32   Niccholes, pp. 26–27.

33   T.E., *The Lawes Resolutions of Womens Rights: Or, the Lawes Provision for Women*, 1632, English Experience 922 (Amsterdam: Theatrum Orbis Terrarum, 1979), p. 61. See also Father Leonard Leffius, SJ, and Father Fulvius Androtius, SJ, *The Treasure of Vowed Chastity in Secular Persons. Also the Widdowes Glasse*, trans. I.W.P. (n.p., 1621), reprinted in English Recusant Literature 1558–1640, vol. 214, ed. D.M. Rogers (London: The Scolar Press, 1974), pp. 249, 300, 323–324; and Niccholes, p. 25.

34   Quoted in Joel Hurstfield, *The Queen's Wards: Wardship and Marriage under Elizabeth I* (London: Longmans, Green & Co., 1958), p. 332. See also Sir Walter Raleigh, in Louis B. Wright, ed., *Advice to a Son: Precepts of Lord Burghley, Sir Walter Raleigh, and Francis Osbourne* (Ithaca: Cornell University Press, 1962), p. 22; and Vives, p. Dd6v.

35 In fiction, widowhood was often equated with whoredom. The main joke in Middleton's *A Trick to Catch the Old One* relies upon this commonplace: much of the word-play revolves around the expression 'Dutch widow', meaning prostitute (3.3.1–18; 5.2.61–124). New Mermaids Series, ed. G.J. Watson (London: Ernest Benn, 1968). With regard to the general equation of general female transgression with 'whoredom,' see Stallybrass. The act of becoming a widow might rewrite a woman's history, and not only in terms of the moment of the husband's death. Wye Saltonstall's book of 'Characters' asserts that the daughters of the typical widow, 'out of the guilty consciousnesse of her owne youth, are foulded up a nights in her owne chamber for fear of straying...'. *Picturae Loquentes*, reprint from the editions of 1631 and 1635, printed for the Luttrell Society by Basil Blackwell, Oxford, 1946, p. 23. The implication is that only women who are already sexually transgressive become widows, and that the act of becoming a widow proves a woman to have been always transgressive.

36 Chance, pp. 5–6.

37 Niccholes, p. 25. My emphasis.

38 ibid., pp. 26–27.

39 Shannon, pp. 106–108.

40 Saltonstall, pp. 22–24.

41 James Raine, ed., *A Selection of Wills from the Registry at York*, vol. 3, Surtees Society, no. 45 (London: Blackwood & Sons, 1865), pp. 312–374.

42 Stone, p. 43.

43 For instance, see George Chapman's *The Widow's Tears*, ed. Ethel M. Smeak (Lincoln, Nebraska: University of Nebraska Press, 1966); T.E., pp. 376–377; Copland.

44 See Leffius and Androtius; Niccholes, pp. 11–13, 24–28; Vives, p. Bb6; T.E., pp. 376–377; Shannon, pp. 76–77, 99–101; Rogers, pp. 45–46, 77; Christopher Newstead, *An Apology for Women: or, Womens Defence* (London: 1620), STC 18508, pp. 21–26; and Joshua Sylvester, *Monodia. An Elegie, in Commemoration of the Vertuous Life, and Godlie Death of the Right Worshipfull & Most Religious Lady, Dame Hellen Branch Widdowe...*(1594), STC 23579.

45 Catherine Belsey, 'Alice Arden's Crime', *Renaissance Drama*, vol. 13 (1982), pp. 82–102; Dolan; Travitsky.

46 See Charles Carlton, 'The Widow's Tale: Male Myths and Female Reality in Sixteenth and Seventeenth-Century England', *Albion*, vol. 10 (1978), pp. 118–129. 'The attempt by male writers to reduce certain women to laughingstocks in Restoration comedy partly stemmed from fear of female autonomy and the need to staunch it.' Moira Ferguson, ed., *First Feminists: British Women Writers 1578–1799*

(Bloomington: Indiana University Press, 1985; New York: The Feminist Press, 1985), p. 11. See also Linda Woodbridge, *Women and the English Renaissance: Literature and the Nature of Womankind, 1540–1620* (Urbana: University of Illinois Press, 1984), p. 177.

47   Carlton; Beverly DeBord, 'The Stage as Mirror of Society: The Widow in Two Seventeenth Century Comedies', *Selected Papers from the West Virginia Shakespeare and Renaissance Association*, vol. 10 (Spring 1985), pp. 71–78; Saltonstall, pp. 22–24; Swetnam, pp. 59–64; Middleton, *More Dissemblers*; Thomas Betterton, *The Amorous Widow, or The Wanton Wife*, 4th edn (London: 1729).

48   Rogers, pp. 45–46, 143–144.

49   Newstead, pp. 25–26. See also Newstead, p. 24; Niccholes, p. 25; Vives, p. 3:Bb4v; Jacques du Bosc, *The Compleat Woman*, trans. N.N. (London: 1639), STC 18508, p. 15; Thomas Elyot, *The Defence of Good Women* (London: 1540), STC 7657.5, p. 21.

50   T.E., pp. 231–232.

51   Swetnam, pp. 62–63.

JEPHTHA'S DAUGHTER: MEN'S CONSTRUCTIONS OF WOMEN IN *HAMLET*

R.S. WHITE

'Nothing exists that has not been made by man — not thought, not language, not words. Even now, there is nothing that has not been made by man, not even me: especially not me.'[1]

> *Desdemona.* Alas, what ignorant sin have I committed?
> *Othello.* Was this fair paper, this most goodly book,
> Made to write 'whore' upon?
> [*Othello*, 4.2.71–73][2]

There are only two women in *Hamlet*, alongside some nine major male characters and many more minor ones. Since their actions and motives are continually speculated upon by the surrounding men, Gertrude and Ophelia would have ample reason to protest in the words of Leclerc quoted above, all the more so since they have themselves been made by a male dramatist. Furthermore, each is regarded by the men as a 'goodly book' upon which to 'write' or construct some text or other.

Inadvertent touches of sententious language reveal attitudes. Claudius says he has 'taken to wife' (1.2.14) Gertrude, as if she were a chattel in the hands of her husband. Substituting 'taken to market' makes the point graphically. Fortune is a fallen woman, a 'strumpet' (2.2.235 and 487). It is ironic that in a play with so many loquacious men, the act of using language should be imaged as a kitchen wench:

> That I, the son of a dear father murder'd,
> Prompted to my revenge by heaven and hell,
> Must, like a whore, unpack my heart with words,
> And fall a-cursing like a very drab,
> A scullion! Fie upon't! Foh!
>
> [2.2.579–583]

Claudius compares his own hypocrisy to a harlot's trade:

> The harlot's cheek, beautied with plast'ring art,
> Is not more ugly to the thing that helps it
> Than is my deed to my most painted word.
>
> [3.1.51–53]

When Hamlet chooses to reflect on the vanity of human wishes while holding a skull, it is woman he sets up as example:

> Now get you to my lady's chamber, and tell her, let her paint an inch thick, to this favour she must come; make her laugh at that.
>
> [3.1.142 ff.]

Even the image chosen for the disintegration of a body in the grave is female, the chapless 'Lady Worm' (5.1.86), as if death itself is gendered. Above all, in these sententious constructions of woman, man is seen as different. If a man is overcome by grief, he is 'unmanly' (1.2.94). 'Give me that man/That is not passion's slave' (3.2.69–70). When Laertes feels like crying over his sister's grave, he expostulates 'The woman will be out' (4.7.194). Man is above the kind of 'foolery' 'as would perhaps trouble a woman' (5.2.207–209). The compulsive need to construct through imagery negative identities for women is linked to the equally pressing need to construct a positive masculine identity.

> What a piece of work is a man! How noble in reason!
> how infinite in faculties! in form and moving, how
> express and admirable! in action, how like an angel! in
> apprehension, like a god!
>
> [2.2.300–304]

In case we may generously think that here the masculine
stands for humanity, men and women alike, Hamlet specifically
excludes women with a snigger, taking them as simply for the
'delight' of men, worth only a wry smile (308).

It is inevitable that the male act of constructing woman
should be at its most vociferous in the field of sexuality, where
otherness can seem like a danger. Hamlet may have reasons to
question his mother's remarriage, but it is surely premature of
him to conclude that it is solely her doing, and that it is
confirmation of a cliché, 'Frailty, thy name is woman' (1.2.146).
Similarly, he may have reason to be puzzled by Ophelia's
conduct in returning his gifts, but rather than pursue her quiet
reproach that the giver is proving 'unkind' (3.1.101) or to
speculate that she has been 'set up' as Rosencrantz and Guildenstern have been 'sent for', he chooses instead to find more
evidence that women are deceivers and that woman's love is a
byword for brevity. While he spends much time searching
scrupulously for the truth about his father's death, he leaps to
instant conclusions about the nature of women. In particular,
female sexuality must, for its threat to men, be removed, or be
rationalized as mere appetite and lust:

> So lust, though to a radiant angel link'd,
> Will sate itself in a celestial bed
> And prey on garbage.
>
> [1.5.55–57]

Desire cannot exist in the matronly:

> You cannot call it love; for at your age
> The heyday in the blood is tame, it's humble,
> And waits upon the judgement...
>
> [3.4.68–70]

and yet since it seems that Gertrude *does* feel desire, Hamlet must shift his strategy to condemn this original sin of Woman:

> Rebellious hell,
> If thou canst mutine in a matron's bones,
> To flaming youth let virtue be as wax
> And melt in her own fire.
>
> [3.4.82–85]

The contradiction is as blatant as that which simultaneously marginalizes women and makes them the cause of all evil.[3] Although, in men's eyes, women may 'make of them' 'monsters' (3.1.138), yet given the strenuousness and ingenuity of the male constructions of women, exactly the reverse seems to be happening. Men in *Hamlet* make monsters of the women.

Turning now to the women themselves, as constructed by the dramatist, we may ask, do they deserve the glosses, insults and negative constructions imposed on them by the male characters? On this question hangs a very central point for anybody interested in feminist approaches to Shakespeare. Is the dramatist representing an unjust world, implicitly satirizing, parodying and condemning male attitudes, or is he complicit with the misogynistic ideological machinery, not questioning but endorsing it?[4] I cannot pretend to be certain about which way interpretation should move, but I shall sketch out the two lines which are in contention, and offer a tentative opinion.

First, Gertrude. We meet her in Act 1, Scene 2, encouraging Hamlet to terminate his grief for his father, with the unexceptionable advice 'all that lives must die' (72). Her attachment to Hamlet is strong enough to make her urge his continued residence rather than going to Wittenberg (119), and Hamlet 'obeys' her. In the soliloquy that immediately follows, however, we discover that Hamlet's view of his mother is more critical than he has revealed. In his view, she used to 'hang on' the king who has died, 'as if increase of appetite had grown by what it fed on', a rather personal comment, upon which we hear no response from Gertrude. 'A beast that wants discourse of reason/Would have mourn'd longer...O, most wicked speed, to post/With such dexterity to incestuous sheets!' (150–157 passim). All this, it must be said, is supposition, and the audience has no real way of testing Hamlet's construction of Gertrude's motives and conduct.

We find that Gertrude 'shall obey' Claudius (3.1.37) without necessarily venturing opinions of her own. In the scenes of Ophelia's madness, Gertrude's comments are cryptic and sympathetic: 'Nay but Ophelia', 'Alas, look here my lord', 'Alack, what noise is this?'. She is eager for peace, urging 'Calmly, good Laertes' when the young man wishes to attack Claudius, and judging from Claudius's repeated 'Let him go, Gertrude' (4.5.119 and 123), she demonstrates physical strength and courage in restraining the young man. Her set piece on the drowning of Ophelia ('There is a willow grows aslant the brook' [4.7.167 ff.]) is not primarily revelation of character but an authorial intrusion using Gertrude as a mouthpiece to give essential information (which nobody could have witnessed) in lyrical fashion. The scene in which Gertrude would appear to reveal most of herself is the one in which Hamlet addresses her, kills Polonius behind the arras, and proceeds to 'wring' his mother's heart. She begins in assertive fashion:

> What have I done that thou dar'st wag thy tongue
> In noise so rude against me?
> ...
> Ay me, what act,
> That roars so loud as thunders in the index?
>
> [3.4.39–40 and 51–52]

Bludgeoned and steadily silenced by Hamlet's verbal onslaught, it is not surprising that she becomes defensive, but she still does not actually admit (at least in the editions which are normally used) that she has committed any particular fault. She is then astonished by her son's 'mad' speech to a Ghost she cannot see, and ends the scene, still non-committally, asking 'What shall I do?' (180) and swearing that she will keep the conversation confidential. In this scene we do not really find out anything about what Gertrude knows or feels. The male tirade of accusation and construction hardly allows her to get a word in edgewise. It is still going on in critical circles, as there has been vigorous dispute about whether or not she was an accomplice to the murder of old Hamlet.

Judging from the case of Gertrude alone, it is impossible to answer our overarching question about the moral perspective of the play. There is evidence that she has a mind of her own, but she is never given room to express it, so eager are men to tell her what she should think. This might be interpreted as a condemnation of her taciturnity, or equally damagingly as a confirmation of wifely 'obedience'. It could equally be a condemnation of the male characters for their blustering and their domineering assumptions about her character and actions. The least we can say is that readers, actors and directors have genuine options over these matters, and can pursue either direction. Just as the men in the play interpret women's silence or reticence, so do critics.

Ophelia's is a much more complex example than Gertrude's, partly because we hear more from her in different circumstances, partly because she elicits more responses from onlookers, and partly because at one stage she succeeds in wresting control of the play's 'plot' and audience interest away from the principal 'plotters', Claudius and Hamlet. She threatens to change the value system which underlies the court's ethos.

We first see her being lectured to by her brother and next by her father. Both harp on the fact that she must not trust Hamlet's attentions. The men implicitly construct Ophelia as an impressionable and impulsive hero-worshipper, likely to open her 'chaste treasure' to Hamlet's equally impulsive desire. Laertes sees all young women in this light:

> The chariest maid is prodigal enough
> If she unmask her beauty to the moon.
> [1.3.36–37]

Polonius responds to Ophelia's neutral statements about Hamlet's 'affection', revealing that his image of her is one of a child. She gives him enough scope to do this, by admitting her doubt:

> *Polonius.* Affection! Pooh! You speak like a green girl,
> Unsifted in such perilous circumstance.
> Do you believe his tenders as you call them?
> *Ophelia.* I do not know, my lord, what I should think.
> *Polonius.* Marry, I will teach you. Think yourself a baby...
> [1.3.101–105]

Ophelia has her moments of self-assertion directed towards Laertes and Polonius alike. She playfully warns her brother against advising her while being perfectly capable of treading 'the primrose path of dalliance' himself (50), and she seriously repeats to her father that Hamlet's conduct has given no cause for suspicion. He has courted 'in honourable fashion' (111) and has sworn 'With almost all the holy vows of heaven' (114). Both men sweep away scornfully her statements, and like Gertrude she is given little choice other than simply to say, 'I shall obey, my lord' (136). She seems to realize that any more words will provoke more badgering. It should be stressed that in the words given to Ophelia up to Act 4, we can find nothing to confirm the attitudes expressed within the play that she is either impulsive and impressionable or naive. Indeed, she is cautious, distanced and non-judgemental. Epithets like impulsive and impressionable, and even naive, could, however, be applied to Hamlet, at least in his view of women.

We next see Ophelia after she has followed her father's advice to give back Hamlet's gifts, and she is 'affrighted' by the strange change in his conduct. At first Polonius assumes that the woman must have precipitated this 'ecstasy': 'What, have you given him any hard words of late?' (2.1.107), reinforcing the view that while women's judgements are marginal and childish, physically in their beauty they are the cause of all woe for men. When Ophelia points out that she has done exactly what she was advised by Polonius to do, he airily accepts responsibility, admitting his mistake in a tone that makes one feel he wants to take credit for everything, even bad advice. Perhaps Hamlet's cryptic, 'mad' reference to Polonius as old Jephtha, the man who sacrificed his own daughter, is the sharpest comment on this interfering old man.

> *Hamlet.* O Jephtha, judge of Israel, what a treasure hadst thou!
> *Polonius.* What a treasure had he, my lord?
> *Hamlet.* Why —
> 'One fair daughter, and no more,
> The which he loved passing well'.
> *Polonius.* [Aside] Still harping on my daughter.
> *Hamlet.* Am I not i'th'right, old Jephtha?
> *Polonius.* If you call me Jephtha, my lord, I have a daughter that I love passing well.
>
> [2.2.398–408]

The story comes from the Bible (Judges XI.30–40). Jephtha makes a bargain with God that he will sacrifice 'whatsoever' comes out to meet him from his own house when he returns from battle with the children of Ammon. When he returns, unfortunately (but fairly predictably), it is his only daughter who greets him. Like the men in *Hamlet*, he immediately blames her for bringing him 'trouble' and proceeds to carry out his promise to God to kill her.

> 37 And she said unto her father, Let this thing be done for me: Let me alone two moneths, that I may goe up and downe upon the mountaines, and bewaile my virginitie, I, and my fellowes.
> 38 And he said, Goe. And he sent her away for two moneths, and shee went with her companions, and bewailed her virginitie upon the mountaines.
> 39 And it came to passe at the end of two moneths that shee returned unto her father, who did with her according to his vow which he had vowed: and she knew no man: & it was a custome in Israel,
> 40 That the daughters of Israel went yeerely to lament the daughter of Iephthah the Gileadite foure dayes in a year.

Jephtha's daughter can be seen as representative of women whose very lives are sacrificed to the politics and warfaring indulged in by men. Ophelia, too, can be seen in this light. Having unwittingly strayed into the world of courtly *realpolitik*, her life and her virginity are sacrificed like the biblical daughter's, by her father and her lover alike. Many things in Ophelia's 'mad' snatches of songs are explained by this allusion, as she laments the loss not only of her father but also of what Rosalind in *As You Like It* calls her 'child's father', bewailing her virginity in grief.

As one in the audience to 'The Mousetrap' and also in the 'nunnery' scene, Hamlet baits Ophelia with the kind of sexual knowingness that he has constructed in Gertrude and which Laertes and Polonius see in Ophelia. The reason he does it may be explained by Freud's theory about tendentious, sexual jokes, that male power is confirmed by vicariously drawing a woman into sexual banter.[5] If we focus solely on Ophelia's responses in these scenes, we find that she neither condones nor condemns his suggestiveness and salaciousness, neither enters its spirit nor dismisses it. Shorn of all the male interpretation, overlay and obfuscation, her conduct throughout these two rather unpleasant interludes can be seen as respectful, dignified and compassionate, showing none of the impetuousness or sexual vulnerability imputed by her male relatives. She treads a cautious path and maintains her integrity while still being politely responsive. It is ironic that Hamlet, when he feels that Rosencrantz and Guildenstern are attempting to pluck out the heart of his mystery, turns on them angrily: "Sblood, do you think I am easier to be played on than a pipe?' (3.2.33–59 passim), when Ophelia could, equally justifiably, turn the same accusation on him. That she does not muster such anger may be interpreted variously as docility, as social deference, or simply as recognition that this option is not open to a woman in such a dialogue, without precipitating yet a longer and more ferocious tirade from the man.

Far from the adage being true that 'Conceit in weakest bodies strongest works' (3.4.114), it seems that in the actual words and actions of Ophelia and Gertrude, self-restraint and a refusal to give way to imagination, rhetoric and spontaneous feelings are watchwords. Caution rules their speech. These may be admirable moral qualities, or they may be simply strategies for survival, but the corollary risk is that such taciturnity makes the women vulnerable to male assumptions and stereotyping. In Claudius's court, which runs on hugger-mugger secrecy, plots and spyings, espionage and counter-espionage, women are not given a voice, whether or not they want one. This still leaves us, however, with our problem as to whether the play is steering us to challenge the court's male value-system or tacitly to collude with its rhetoric.

There is, however, one episode where a woman, at a cost to her sanity, demands a voice, and demands options, and the effect is devastating on the onstage audience as it can also be on theatre audiences. Ophelia's 'mad' scenes threaten to highjack the whole play, as she wrenches away from the various manipulators of the plot (including the dramatist) the power to dominate the emotional effects and the very line of narrative.

Act 4, Scene 5, is one of the most theatrically self-reflexive in all Shakespeare's works. It lays bare a principle that is fundamental to his assumptions about drama: audiences construct meanings, and each person in an audience constructs a different meaning from every other. The analogy holds with readers. So much is exemplified by the stage audience in their interpretations of Ophelia's conduct, and by inference the same is happening when an audience watches, or a reader reads, *Hamlet*. The point is crucial to a theoretical justification for feminist readings.

> *Gentleman.* ...Her speech is nothing,
> Yet the unshaped use of it doth move
> The hearers to collection. They yawn [gape] at it,
> And botch the words up fit to their own thoughts;
> Which, as her winks and nods and gestures yield them,
> Indeed would make one think there might be thought,
> Though nothing sure, yet much unhappily.
> [4.5.7–13]

Listeners impute or create 'meaning' in what they regard

as fragmentary or coded discourse, reaching for some 'thought', some key which will bring the 'nothing' into coherent meaning. Modern psychiatry works on the same assumption of a 'deep structure' that can be recovered to construct sense and meaning in apparent nonsense. However, the Gentleman makes clear that there can be no presumption of one, single and incontrovertible meaning that can be retrieved. Rather, the listeners create meanings out of their own assumptions, presumptions and preoccupations, 'botch the words up fit to *their own* thoughts' (my italics). We can see this happening in the action throughout *Hamlet*, which on this view is a play showing the world as a lonely place peopled by characters listening for what they want to hear and constantly avoiding true communication. Rosencrantz and Guildenstern are not the only ones trying to make sense out of apparent nonsense, nor the only ones deprived of information in their acts of imputation and construction. In this world of spying, eavesdropping and calculated obfuscation, speculation must rule over truth, which remains ever elusive. Nowhere is this more true than in the case of Ophelia. Horatio thinks her words are a political threat, 'for she may strew/Dangerous conjectures in illbreeding minds' (14–15), presumably by making people suspicious about the hushed up circumstances of Polonius's death, pointing a finger towards incriminating his friend Hamlet. To Gertrude, who, at first, wishes not to speak to Ophelia and rather to push her outside consciousness, the young woman's state is a painful prod to her own conscience, and the dark areas of her 'sick soul'. Perhaps she surmises that her remarriage has unintentionally, through Hamlet's violent responses, led to the death of Polonius — but this is a further gloss on her words. Claudius acts like a psychoanalytic critic, pointing out that Ophelia is making a 'Conceit upon her father' (45), which is not at all certain from the context. He concludes confidently:

> O this is the poison [*or* passion] of deep grief; it springs
> All from her father's death.
>
> [72–73]

This is to ignore material in her songs and comments that uncomfortably implicate men as treacherous lovers, and much else besides. Laertes constructs her presence as a kind of devious revenge on her father's assassin:

> Hadst thou thy wits, and didst persuade revenge,
> It could not move thus.
>
> [165–166]

He realizes 'This nothing's more than matter', interprets his sister's words as aestheticizing unpleasant feelings, 'hell itself' (184), and sees her conduct as 'A document in madness' (175). Many Victorian writers and artists chose to accept this phrase as the 'truth' about her conduct.[6]

To the Gentleman, Ophelia is 'distract' and 'Her mood will needs be pitied'. From another position (the feminist literary critic's?), there is nothing 'distract' or 'to be pitied'. Ophelia's words, it could be argued, have a commanding clarity and force which she lacked or suppressed earlier, and her discovery of new modes of thought and self-expression that break away from the tyranny of male bullying might be seen as far from pitiable and indeed admirable. For once, a woman has more or less silenced, at least marginalized, the men, and this is no mean feat. It could be argued (and there is nothing 'factual' in the text to deny the reading) that for the first time Ophelia has found her own 'legitimate' voice which allows her openly to grieve her father's death and reproach the hypocrisy of her lover who has killed him and deserted her. She can now do without having to confront male taunts, coercive constructions or appropriations. That her voice is not univocal and does not obey linear logic is an advantage in the battle against male constructions, just as Hamlet's 'wild and whirling words' are used, with more calculation, to baffle hearers like Polonius.

What 'matter' we in the audience or as readers make of Ophelia's 'nothing' may be all of these things, or others, or none, and one feminist's reading (for example, that the scene shows a woman finding a 'voice' that subverts male assumptions) will differ from another's (for example, that it shows the final destruction of woman's meaning in a patriarchal society, the final solipsism and eventual silencing, leading to self-destruction). What cannot be underestimated is the disruptive, anarchic theatrical quality of this, pre-eminently Ophelia's, scene. Her intervention snatches attention away from the fate of Hamlet (who was left in 'bloody' mood [4.4.66]), and from Claudius's increasingly desperate cover-ups and machinations. In a strange way, at Ophelia's 'Good night ladies; good night, sweet ladies, good night, good night' (4.5.71), the play itself could have ended, since its whole political, masculine sets of values have been exposed, like Jephtha's war against the Ammons, as callous, destructive and petty, and certainly no fault of the women who, like Jephtha's daughter, die innocently as a consequence. The play does not end here, nor is this Ophelia's true exit line, since she returns even more disturbingly to distribute with disarming self-possession flowers symbolizing thoughts, remembrance and grief to bewildered actors involved in a violent tragedy of blood. A modern analogy might be the archetypal press photographs of a young civilian giving a flower to a bemused soldier in a demonstration against war, or (as in the case of the Portuguese revolution) of an elderly woman giving a flower to a willing soldier. Such gestures not only undermine military display, but they actively ridicule armed conflict and male war games.

The play again goes on past this point, and by now Claudius can claw back the action as a political stage for himself. He retires to do a deal with Laertes about further state security cover-ups and about the assassination of Hamlet (4.7), and after the report of Ophelia's death he can conveniently forget the whole affair. Good night, sweet ladies, indeed, for alternative ethics have no chance of prevailing in this relentlessly political context.

The actual death of Ophelia (4.7.164 ff.) is the real ending of a play that could have been, which we might by now loosely call, the women's play. Her only authentic gesture of self-construction is, necessarily, an act leading to self-destruction, for her words are once again interpreted out of existence. Drowning is like silence in a world of cacophony, and stasis in the element of change. Some redemption comes from her death, in that it precipitates Hamlet's declaration of love and the events that lead to some kind of poetic justice. But this does not bring back from the grave the woman whose structure of values, if less hampered and blocked by male constructions, could have changed the ending of the play. Just as strangely, the death of Jephtha's daughter may in some weird and perverted logic be seen as redeeming the father, at the cost of her young life: 'Lord we know what we are, but know not what we may be' (4.5.41). Or, to be more specific in the context of Shakespeare's invented women: '...what we are not allowed to be'.

Who is doing the disallowing, whether the fictional males or the dramatist himself, seems a question genuinely to be debated. If Elizabethan England is conceived as inveterately patriarchal in its dominant ideology, then Shakespeare can be read as collaborating, or as unusually critical of male values. On the other hand, reading ahistorically (and we can never, after all, *know* what the Elizabethans thought) from a vantage point in the 1990s, there is enough in *Hamlet* to allow us to regard the play equally as uniformly dismissive of women or as satirically subverting male attitudes. We are entitled to botch the words up fit to our own thoughts, at least insofar as we have no alternative, since information is defective, absent, ambivalent or contradictory. In the presentation of women in *Hamlet*, there is no final answer to whether Shakespeare is propping up or savagely satirizing male constructions. What the play presents is an image of such constructions occurring, and therefore the fact that two radical and opposite 'readings' can be made is part of the play's dynamic. Whatever reading we make, it reflects us more than it does the play.

1   Annie Leclerc, *Parole de Femme* (1974), extracts translated by Claire Duchen, reprinted from Claire Duchen, *French Connections* (1987), reproduced in Deborah Cameron, ed., *The Feminist Critique of Language: A Reader* (London and New York: Routledge,1990), p. 74.

2   Quotations from Shakespeare come from William Shakespeare, *The Complete Works*, ed. Peter Alexander (London and Glasgow: Collins, 1951).

3   This theme is developed by Dympna Callaghan in *Women and Gender in Renaissance Tragedy* (New York and London: Harvester Wheatsheaf, 1989).

4   For analysis and illustration of these two positions, see Ann Thompson, '"The Warrant of Womanhood": Shakespeare and Feminist Criticism', in Graham Holderness, ed., *The Shakespeare Myth* (Manchester: Manchester University Press, 1988), pp. 75–88; and Claire McEachern, 'Fathering Herself: A Source Study of Shakespeare's Feminism', *Shakespeare Quarterly*, vol. 39 (1988), pp. 269–289.

5   Sigmund Freud, *Jokes and Their Relation to the Unconscious*, 1905 in German, trans. James Strachey (London: Routledge and Kegan Paul, 1960), p. 141. As a parallel in Shakespeare, compare the scene from *Othello* in which Iago speaks bawdily with Desdemona, who 'beguiles' enjoyment while feeling melancholy (2.1).

6   See Elaine Showalter, 'Representing Ophelia: Women, Madness, and the Responsibilities of Feminist Criticism', in Patricia Parker and Geoffrey Hartmann, eds, *Shakespeare and the Question of Theory* (New York and London: Methuen, 1985), pp. 77–94.

Feminist and Gender Based Studies of Shakespeare—A Selective Bibliography

This listing is in chronological order, and the subheadings are intended to reflect the fact that feminist criticism and gender studies have been and are changing periodically, and to suggest some trends that emerge in hindsight. However, the actual headings have little sanctity and are purely impressionistic. The list is highly selective and does not begin to touch on the massive amount of journal criticism available.

Images of Women and Men

Anna Jameson, *Characteristics of Shakespeare's Women: Moral, Political and Historical* (London: George Bell and Sons, 1879).

Juliet Dusinberre, *Shakespeare and the Nature of Women* (New York: Barnes and Noble, 1975).

Stevie Davies, *Renaissance Views of Man* (Manchester: Manchester University Press, 1980).

Carolyn Lenz, Gayle Greene and Carol Thomas Neely, eds, *The Woman's Part: Feminist Criticism of Shakespeare* (Urbana: University of Illinois Press, 1980).

Coppelia Kahn, *Man's Estate: Masculine Identity in Shakespeare* (Berkeley: University of California Press, 1981).

Simon Shepherd, *Amazons and Warrior Women: Varieties of Feminism in Seventeenth-Century Drama* (Brighton: Harvester Press, 1981).

Irene G. Dash, *Wooing, Wedding and Power: Women in Shakespeare's Plays* (New York: Columbia University Press, 1981).

Linda Bamber, *Comic Women, Tragic Men: A Study of Gender and Genre in Shakespeare* (Stanford: Stanford University Press, 1982).

Marilyn French, *Shakespeare's Division of Experience: Women and Drama in the Age of Shakespeare* (London: Sphere Books, 1983).

Lisa Jardine, *Still Harping on Daughters: Women and Drama in the Age of Shakespeare* (Brighton: Harvester Press, 1983).

Marianne Novy, *Love's Argument: Gender Relations in Shakespeare* (Chapel Hill: University of North Carolina Press, 1984).

Linda Woodbridge, *Women and the English Renaissance: Literature and the Nature of Womankind, 1540–1620* (Brighton: Harvester Press, 1984).

Elaine Showalter, 'Representing Ophelia: Women, Madness, and the Responsibilities of Feminist Criticism', in Patricia Parker and Geoffrey Hartmann, eds, *Shakespeare and the Question of Theory* (New York and London: Methuen, 1985), pp. 77–94.

Patriarchy and Power

Catherine Belsey, *The Subject of Tragedy: Identity and Difference in Renaissance Drama* (London and New York: Methuen, 1985).

Catherine Belsey, 'Disrupting Sexual Difference: Meaning and Gender in the Comedies', in John Drakakis, ed., *Alternative Shakespeares* (London: Methuen, 1985).

Kathleen McLuskie, 'The Patriarchal Bard: Feminist Criticism and Shakespeare: *King Lear* and *Measure for Measure*', in Jonathan Dollimore and Alan Sinfield, eds, *Political Shakespeare: New Essays in Cultural Materialism* (Ithaca and London: Cornell University Press, 1985), pp. 88–108.

Peter Erikson, *Patriarchal Structures in Shakespeare's Drama* (Los Angeles: University of California Press, 1985).

Margaret W. Ferguson et al., eds, *Rewriting the Renaissance: The Discourses of Sexual Difference in Early Modern Europe* (Chicago: University of Chicago Press, 1986).

Stevie Davies, *The Idea of Woman in the Renaissance* (Brighton: Harvester Press, 1986).

Diane Dreher, *Domination and Defiance: Fathers and Daughters in Shakespeare* (Lexington: University of Kentucky Press, 1986).

R.S. White, *Innocent Victims: Poetic Injustice in Shakespearean Tragedy* (London: Athlone Press, 1st edn 1982, 2nd edn 1986).

Jacqueline Rose, *Sexuality in the Field of Vision* (London: Verso, 1986).

Marginalizations: Monsters and Androgynes

Karen Newman, '"And Wash the Ethiop White": Femininity and the Monstrous in *Othello*', in Jean E. Howard and Marion F. O'Connor, eds, *Shakespeare Reproduced: The Text in History and Ideology* (London: Methuen, 1987).

Julia Kristeva, *Tales of Love* (New York: Columbia University Press, 1987).

Phyllis Rackin, 'Androgyny, Mimesis, and the Marriage of the Boy Heroine on the English Renaissance Stage', *Publications of the Modern Language Association*, vol. 102 (1987), pp. 29–41.

Ann Thompson, '"The Warrant of Womanhood": Shakespeare and Feminist Criticism', in Graham Holderness, ed., *The Shakespeare Myth* (Manchester: Manchester University Press, 1988), pp. 75–88.

Claire McEachern, 'Fathering Herself: A Source Study of Shakespeare's Feminism', *Shakespeare Quarterly*, vol. 39 (1988), pp. 269–289.

Jean E. Howard, 'Crossdressing, the Theatre, and Gender Struggle in Early Modern England', *Shakespeare Quarterly*, vol. 39 (1988), pp. 418–440.

Dympna Callaghan, *Women and Gender in Renaissance Tragedy: A Study of 'King Lear', 'Othello', 'The Duchess of Malfi' and 'The White Devil'* (New York and London: Harvester Wheatsheaf, 1989).

Intertextuality and Desire

Marianne Novy, ed., *Women's Re-Visions of Shakespeare: On Responses of Dickinson, Woolf, Rich, H.D., George Eliot, and Others* (Urbana and Chicago: University of Illinois Press, 1990).

Valerie Wayne, ed., *The Matter of Difference: Materialist Feminist Criticism of Shakespeare* (Hemel Hempstead: Harvester Wheatsheaf, 1991).

Philip C. Kolin, ed., *Shakespeare and Feminist Criticism: An Annotated Bibliography and Commentary* (New York and London: Garland Publishing Inc., 1991).

Susan Zimmerman, *Erotic Politics: Desire on the Renaissance Stage* (New York and London: Routledge, 1992).

TEARS AND TUSHES: IMAGES OF GENDER AND POWER IN *VENUS AND ADONIS* AND *THE RAPE OF LUCRECE*

CHRISTINE COUCHE

His ear her prayers admits, but his heart granteth
No penetrable entrance to her plaining
                    [*The Rape of Lucrece*, 558–559]

Being mov'd, he strikes whate'er is in his way,
And whom he strikes his crooked tushes slay.
                    [*Venus and Adonis*, 623–624][1]

I have chosen to start with these two ostensibly unrelated quotations because they show how in Shakespeare's *Venus and Adonis* and *The Rape of Lucrece*, power is represented in terms of one's ability to penetrate and one's penetrability. Furthermore, in both poems this power is distributed according to gender, in such a way that the ability to penetrate is represented as a masculine attribute, and penetrability is represented as a feminine attribute.

Adonis and Lucrece

As the objects of sexual attention, and therefore in a less powerful and more 'feminine' position, Adonis and Lucrece are variously described as fortresses to be breached, tender beauty, soft wax to be imprinted, and food to be consumed by their respective attackers, and the threats that face them are invariably ones of impending penetration. This is expected in Lucrece's case (as she is a woman) but it seems surprising that Adonis, as a male, should be so characterized. This is partly due to the reversal of traditional sexual roles in *Venus and Adonis* and his corresponding status as Venus's sexual prey, but it also derives from the common Renaissance understanding of the nature and status of boys who, due to physical and social characteristics, also share the powerless position of women. As Rosalind puts it in *As You Like It*, 'boys and women are for the most part cattle of this colour'.[2]

The potential manhood of a boy does not seem to have any relevance to his categorization with women, which is based rather on the physiological attributes and power status of his youth. The smooth skin and high-pitched voice of a woman, as well as the feebler frame with undeveloped musculature, identify a boy much more closely with a woman than with a man. Adonis is depicted in images of beauty, frailty, softness and ornamentation, in direct contrast to traditionally masculine qualities like toughness, courage, strength and virility. The main motif associated with Adonis is that of 'the field's chief flower' (8), a paradigm of feminine loveliness, and his 'rose-cheek'd' face (3) is repeatedly described in the red and white imagery which is characteristically used for extolling the beauty of a woman.[3] Adonis's skin is soft and yielding to Venus's touch, '[his] tend'rer cheek [receiving] her soft hand's print,/As apt as new-fall'n snow takes any dint' (353–354).

The other important characteristic that women and boys share is that they are equally considered potential objects of physical attraction and sexual ownership for men, and this shared 'rapeability' stems from other biological similarities between women and boys.[4] To be an object of rape entails not only attractiveness, but also vulnerability to sexual attack: both women and boys are usually physically weaker than men, and lack the personal authority needed to repel effectively any advances or attacks on their persons. The narrator of *Lucrece* makes it clear that defending oneself from such attacks is usually a difficult and even futile task: 'Honour and beauty in the owner's arms,/Are weakly fortress'd from a world of harms' (27–28). Furthermore, in both poems, chastity is seen as something that requires protection from penetration, because it provokes attack.[5] Adonis recognizes his besieged position and the need for defence, for he tells Venus to 'Remove your siege from my unyielding heart,/To love's alarms it will not ope the gate' (423–424), and his 'heart stands armed in [his] ear' (779). The fortress imagery effectively represents Adonis and Lucrece as objects to be breached and reinforces the intent of sexual 'invasion' of Tarquin and Venus, who are correspondingly attributed with other images of enforced penetration. Venus's kisses are likened to the voracious feeding of a starving eagle on its prey, who '[tires] with her beak on feathers, flesh and bone' (56), while Tarquin's hand on Lucrece's breast is a '[rude] ram, to batter such an ivory wall!...To make the breach and enter this sweet city' (464 and 469).

Lucrece's inability to resist penetration is reflected in images of utter helplessness. She is 'the weak mouse' trapped by Tarquin, the 'foul night-waking cat' (554–555), and '[like] to a new-kill'd bird she trembling lies' under Tarquin's hand (457). Adonis is also portrayed as a small bird, but the image of him as a dive-dapper (86) is comic rather than tragic because this situation represents no real threat: at worst, he is only 'tam'd' (560). In *Lucrece*, the threat is terrifyingly real and accordingly the possibility of death is reflected in the images of the helpless, 'new-kill'd' victim, 'trembling' in fear.

The description of the ease with which Tarquin enters Lucrece's chamber, thus inscribing it as a penetrable space, symbolizes and mirrors Lucrece's own penetrability.[6] As Tarquin makes his way to Lucrece's chamber, he breaks through a number of barriers which are 'precisely rendered images [of] the rape, its physical objectification',[7] because each one is symbolic of a kind of chastity belt or hymen that he must penetrate. Tarquin starts with '[the] locks between her chamber and his will,/Each one by him enforc'd' (302–303), and these 'unwilling [portals]'

(309) seem to be personified as rape victims themselves. The final obstacle before Lucrece's chamber door is her glove bearing a needle which pricks Tarquin. The penetrative imagery which elsewhere in the poem indicates power here reflects pathos and emphasizes Lucrece's vulnerability, for the glove is only a part of 'all these poor forbiddings [which] could not stay him' (323). The pricking of Tarquin's finger (319), an image of blood drawn by violent penetration, evokes parallels of hymeneal blood or injury in rape so that although the narrator interprets the needle-prick as a warning to Tarquin, 'the episode reinforces our sense not of Lucrece's resistance but of her penetrability'.[8] Her ability to defend herself is a mere pin-prick against (and in comparison with) Tarquin's sword and strength. The way he opens the final door to her chamber is a displaced description of the act itself: 'his guilty hand pluck'd up the latch,/And with his knee the door he opens wide' (358–359). The only thing separating Tarquin from his prey at this point is the hymen-like curtain around 'her yet unstained bed' (366) — another reference to blood about to be violently spilled.

Despite Adonis's biological maleness, he is also portrayed as a penetrable space, a yielding, feminine receptor, awaiting penetration by a masculine initiator. He is characterized as a potential rape victim by the suggestive and sexually objectifying way the narrative describes his mouth and dimples: 'the ruby-colour'd portal open'd,/Which to his speech did honey passage yield' (451–452) and '[these] lovely caves, these round enchanting pits,/Open'd their mouths to swallow Venus' liking' (247–248).[9] In *Venus and Adonis*, Shakespeare achieves a brief metaphoric inversion not only of sexual roles but of sexual parts, with the male possessing the inviting orifice(s) and the female possessing the penetrating object, here euphemistically referred to as her 'liking'. The inversion of traditional male/female power roles at this early stage of the poem determines the distribution of masculine and feminine characteristics, in such a way that Adonis is depicted as a penetrable space, and Venus the attempting penetrator. This is a significant extension of the kind of characterization Lisa Jardine says targets a male audience:

[submissiveness], coyness, dependence, passivity, exquisite whiteness and beauty compound in the blushing (yet wilful) boy to create a figure vibrant with erotic interest for *men*. Shakespeare's Adonis, though desired prominently by a female god, is alluring deliberately for male readers.[10]

Venus is masculinized by her position as erotically interested observer of Adonis, because she shares it with these hypothetical male readers (remembering that the poem was written for a male patron). This assessment of *Venus and Adonis*'s target audience also marginalizes and trivializes Venus, making her a mere plot device for introducing the figure of the 'blushing (yet wilful) boy', and thus serving purely male purposes.

Venus and Tarquin

Evidence of Tarquin's power abounds. He succeeds in a three-fold penetration of Lucrece: of her chamber as intruder, of her chastity as rapist and of her life as potential murderer and cause of her suicide. Initially, Venus too appears to be powerful, due to the masculine, penetrative imagery that she shares with Tarquin. These images are of aggressive predators and conquerors, characterized by superior strength and driven by their lust. Both are depicted as potential or actual rapists, drawn on by 'the sweetness of the spoil' (*Venus and Adonis*, 553) to penetrate and conquer their passive victims, the prey in their grasp.

The most striking shared images are those of powerful birds of prey, the eagle, falcon and vulture. Tarquin's sword is likened to the falcon, a weapon of war and aggressive sport. The image of the beak, the instrument of penetration and active consumption of the victim, is associated with both Tarquin and Venus:

> Even as an empty eagle, sharp by fast,
> Tires with her beak on feathers, flesh and bone,

Shaking her wings, devouring all in haste,
Till either gorge be stuff'd or prey be gone:
[*Venus and Adonis*, 55–58]

Now quick desire hath caught the yielding prey,
And glutton-like she feeds, yet never filleth.
Her lips are conquerors, his lips obey,
Paying what ransom the insulter willeth;
Whose vulture thought doth pitch the price so high
That she will draw his lips' rich treasure dry.
[*Venus and Adonis*, 547–552]

This said, he shakes aloft his Roman blade,
Which like a falcon tow'ring in the skies,
Coucheth the fowl below with his wings' shade,
Whose crooked beak threats, if he mount he dies:
So under his insulting falchion lies
Harmless Lucretia, marking what he tells
With trembling fear, as fowl hear falcons' bells.
[*The Rape of Lucrece*, 505–511]

Venus is here identified as a powerful and successful bird of
prey, but closer examination reveals that even before Adonis
escapes from her, she is subtly depicted as a *failed* predator.
While Tarquin's '[sharp] hunger' is 'satisfied' (422), Venus is 'an
empty eagle, sharp by fast' (55), and the image of vulture is that
of scavenger not predator.[11] Other images of the phallic penetration and domination of a passive victim associated with Tarquin
include the arrow that kills the gentle deer (579–581) and the
worm that invades and spoils the flower (848). In contrast to this,
Venus is only a caterpillar feeding on 'tender leaves' (798), an
image of peripheral, rather than fatal, damage.

The penetrative ability of the gaze is another common
conceit in these poems, through which the relative potencies of
Tarquin and Venus are contrasted. Georgianna Ziegler points out
the voyeuristic quality of the description of Lucrece in her bed,
which assumes a male reader: '[the] reader's eyes roam with
Tarquin's over the rosy cheeks, dewy hand, marigold eyelids, and

veined breasts of Lucrece...[and] the inclusion of the male voyeur [increases] the pornographic effect of [the] scene'.[12] Just as Venus's observation of Adonis (mediated by a male narrator) reflects her aggressive position as sexual initiator, so the same power distribution of subject/object, dominator/dominated, is established by the narration of Tarquin's observation of Lucrece. The penetrative gaze is here another metaphoric phallus, for such is Tarquin's superior strength and ability to penetrate that he is attributed with 'a cockatrice'[s] dead-killing eye' (540) that pierces and kills with a mere glance, narratively pinning Lucrece to her bed as effectively as his hand and sword.

However, Venus's gaze is not so unambiguously powerful, for she is herself trapped by Adonis's beauty.[13] Voyeurism entails a potentially ambivalent power relationship between observer and object, which is reflected in the ambivalent power status of Venus as 'masculine' aggressor *and* woman (and therefore defined as both powerful and disempowered). While the voyeur may be said to be in the dominant position as consumer of the observed goods, so can the observer be 'captured' by the object, trapped and obsessed by his/her desire to continue viewing. Whereas Tarquin possesses a cockatrice's eye, Venus has her gaze swallowed by Adonis's dimples: she is prisoner of her own gaze, unable to choose not to love (79). Shakespeare here inverts not only the usual power distribution of the voyeur's gaze, but also Venus's status as the goddess of love. Instead of Venus being in control of love and able to manipulate its power over others, Adonis's effect on Venus, via her gaze, subjects her to him, rather than the reverse. The following lines reinforce the nature of her situation:

> Being mad before, how doth she now for wits?
> Struck dead before, what needs a second striking?
> Poor queen of love, in thine own law forlorn,
> To love a cheek that smiles at thee in scorn!
> [249–252]

Furthermore, the 'ill presage' of Adonis's unkind looks strikes her 'like the deadly bullet of a gun' (457 and 461). In the male-privileging logic of the penetrative imagery of these poems, 'looks kill love' (464) and Venus is love (see 328 and 610), so it is Adonis who, in effect, has the cockatrice's eye.

A comparison of the effects of desire on Venus and Tarquin also reveals a contrast between their effective power. Initially, they seem to be equally affected by lust, or desire. Tarquin is described in the first stanza as 'lust-breathed' (3) and driven on by a sexual appetite that has a 'bateless edge' (9). Similarly, Venus is associated with Adonis's 'lusty courser' early in the poem (31) and 'desire doth lend her force/Courageously to pluck [Adonis] from his horse' and push him to the ground (29–30 and 41–43). However, despite occupying the position of sexual initiator and active desirer, Venus is represented as powerless in the face of her own desire, in a way that Tarquin is not.

Venus is not just a desiring woman, she is the personi-fication of desire itself (547), and, therefore, as the narrator tells us, 'she cannot choose but love' (79).[14] Although Tarquin is '[by] reprobate desire thus madly led' (300), there is a sense in which he has chosen to be so led. At the end of his lengthy internal debate about whether he will rape Lucrece or not, Tarquin chooses the inclination he will follow and declares that '[desire] my pilot is' (279). The use of the phrase 'unresisted lust' several lines later (282) also implies that Tarquin potentially could control the lust that drives him. Later in the poem, desire is tentatively imaged as master over Tarquin, only so that the primacy of his own will can be re-emphasized:

> While lust is in his pride no exclamation
> Can curb his heat or rein his rash desire,
> Till, like a jade, self-will himself doth tire
> [705–707]

Moreover, Tarquin's capitulation to desire in this situation is imaged in terms of feminine weakness in the following passage. In his search for a female scapegoat, Tarquin personifies his guilty and stained conscience as a 'spotted princess' (721), effectively distancing his higher male self from the lower passions that constitute a female character. In a cruel irony, Lucrece's discovery by her servants is prefigured in (and implicitly equated with) Tarquin's remorse:

> Besides, his soul's fair temple is defaced,
> To whose weak ruins muster troops of cares,
> To ask the spotted princess how she fares
> [719–721]

The 'victim's' response that follows, while reflecting Renaissance theories of the government of the lower (feminine) passions by the higher (masculine) soul, effects a form of self-justification:

> She says her subjects with foul insurrection
> Have batter'd down her consecrated wall,
> And by their mortal fault brought in subjection
> Her immortality, and made her thrall
> To living death and pain perpetual:
> Which in her prescience she controlled still,
> But her foresight could not forestall their will.
> [722–728]

Tarquin's solicitous care for himself mocks the despair and anguish of Lucrece, while the feminine personification of Tarquin's soul offers him abdication from responsibility through stereotyped female weakness. Because, in this conceit, Tarquin's soul is besieged and violated, it not only reflects both the siege of Ardea and the rape of Lucrece but it also reinforces the gender of defeatedness and penetrability; his soul *must* be a she.

Although Tarquin's guilt is imaged in terms of a pierced soul which bears 'the wound that nothing healeth,/The scar that will despite of cure remain' (731–732), this image is temporary and in direct contrast with the other images of penetration that are associated with him, most notably his impenetrable heart (558–559). The contrast between Lucrece's and Tarquin's different destinies, death and exile, indicate how little Tarquin represents a penetrable space, and how out of character it is for him. The breach of his internal fortress is self-inflicted and displaced onto a female scapegoat, a self-penetration that mocks Lucrece's suicide, and underlines the male gendering of impenetrability and power in the poem.

The siege and battle metaphors are part of '[the] most important figure in *Lucrece* [which] is taken from the activities of war and slaughter [in which] the active metaphors are connected with Tarquin; the passive ones, i.e., of a fort to be conquered, an island to be sacked, of course symbolize Lucrece'.[15] This image of the besieged and conquered fortress used in *Venus and Adonis* and *The Rape of Lucrece* literalizes the conflation of military and sexual conquest. In the latter poem especially, Shakespeare turns this conventional imagery into a fictional reality, so that 'Tarquin's sexual penetration…mirrors the invading army's penetration of the city' and 'given the common association of gates with the vagina, the notion of rape is latent in the image of the attacked city'.[16] Accordingly, the ethos of military conquest informs the words and actions of Venus and Tarquin, where victory over a more worthy or less penetrable opponent, be it human or animal, confers a greater degree of glory and masculinity on the conqueror. Venus articulates this ethos when she tries to convince Adonis of her power over him by describing herself as the conqueror of the great Mars: 'he that overrul'd I oversway'd' (109). Her argued superiority specifically rests in her ability to usurp the phallus, the instrument of penetration, by making Mars change allegiance from war to love, symbolically laying his lance at her altar (103).

In a similar way, Tarquin is attracted to Lucrece because of the status associated with her acclaimed chastity (8–9). The poem's narrator locates the motivation for Tarquin's rape of Lucrece in Collatine's 'boast of Lucrece' sov'reignty' which inspires 'proud' Tarquin to 'envy of so rich a thing' (36–39).[17] In Lucrece's case, 'the power of chastity to arouse desire'[18] exists mainly because Collatine has identified her chastity as a source of male superiority, using it to implicitly raise him above Tarquin in the patriarchal hierarchy.[19] Tarquin vows to destroy this famed chastity as a power play against Collatine and the conflation of the two conquests in Tarquin's mind is made explicit by the narrator: 'Within his thought her heavenly image sits,/And in the self-same seat sits Collatine' (288–289). In Tarquin's eyes, Lucrece's breasts are '[a] pair of maiden worlds unconquered' (408), an image encompassing her desirability as both a sexual *and* political conquest. Collatine's boast '[that] kings might be espoused to more fame,/But king nor peer to such a peerless dame' (20–21) creates and fans Tarquin's desire to 'conquer' her and thereby destroy Collatine's reflected glory from his wife's chastity.

It is therefore no surprise that Lucrece cannot turn Tarquin from his purpose by pleading the honour of Collatine and his family, because '[the] greater those values [of property, status, and symbolic worth], the greater the sense of power their conquest confers upon the rapist'.[20] With such a plea, Lucrece only succeeds in reminding Tarquin of his purpose to dishonour and defeat his rival in both the sexual and political spheres. In this context, the rape is less about the power distribution between Lucrece and Tarquin than about that between Tarquin and Collatine. A good part of Tarquin's power over Lucrece is derived from her position as honour-bearer (and, therefore, also patriarchal status-bearer) for Collatine:

> Tarquin, however, can wield a far greater power over Lucrece and does so with great cunning. This power rests not in his 'Roman blade' but in the nature of his threat against her, which derives its coercive strength from the conditions of Roman marriage, conditions implied in the threat itself...This slander will do irreparable damage to Lucrece's reputation as a chaste wife, but that is not its cutting edge. What matters to Lucrece, as Tarquin knows well, is that it will destroy Collatine's honor [sic] and his family's.[21]

Lucrece's position is that of a pawn, albeit a highly valued pawn. She is the ground of contest between men in the poem, the potentially penetrable object whose value and appeal lie in the challenge of her impenetrability. As such, she is 'incidental to a struggle to power in which only men compete',[22] and it is no accident that parallels are drawn between her rape and the forced entry into Ardea, her chamber, and other inanimate objects.

The only way Lucrece can enter the power politics of the situation and act effectively is to appropriate the use of a metaphoric phallus and use it *against herself* in suicide. Again, effective action that alters destinies is imaged in terms of successful penetration, even if Lucrece's action is self-destroying. (Ironically, it is just after her decision to kill herself that Lucrece declares that she is 'the mistress of [her] fate' [1069].) To fulfil her role as repository and protector of Collatine's honour, Lucrece must enact a second, analogous invasion of her body and self, by 'plunging the phallic knife into the "sheath" of her breast (1723; in Latin, "sheath" is *vagina*)'.[23] It is a bitter and yet logical irony that in the service of the patriarchy, as she understands her position in it, Lucrece '[silences] herself more effectively than had Tarquin with the bedclothes'.[24] Even in the hands of a woman, the penetrative metaphoric phallus manifests its patriarchal function as a weapon against women.

In *Venus and Adonis*, too, the instrument of penetration is either unavailable to Venus, or works against her. Venus initially occupies the 'masculine' position of sexual aggressor, and is accordingly characterized by superior strength, active desire, and persuasive rhetoric that befits a 'bold-fac'd suitor' (6). However, Adonis is immune to her rhetoric and he remains 'obdurate, flinty, hard as steel' (199) — in short, impenetrable.[25] Venus shares with Lucrece the imagery of unsuccessful persuasion as unsuccessful penetration of the heart. Lucrece is powerless to prevent Tarquin from carrying out his threats because '[his] ear her prayers admits, but his heart granteth/No penetrable entrance to her plaining' (558–559), and Venus is unable to penetrate Adonis's defences because '[his] heart stands armed in [his] ear,/And will not let a false sound enter there' (779–780). In contrast with Adonis, Lucrece cannot be her own protector, and although Adonis and Lucrece share the imagery of penetrable spaces, when it comes to the moment of truth, it is Lucrece and Venus who share the imagery of the inability to penetrate. Lucrece's skin is likened to alabaster and ivory, images of hardness and impenetrability, but in reality, she is more penetrable than Adonis, whose skin '[as] apt as new-fall'n snow takes any dint' (354).

Venus's failure to penetrate Adonis verbally or physically is in direct contrast with Tarquin's success, and this contrast demonstrates the striking difference between the power of the refusal of a man and that of a woman: Adonis's refusal to co-operate prevents sexual consummation, while Lucrece's does not. Although Adonis is feminized and represented as a penetrable space in the first half of the poem, in the middle of the poem this reversal of roles is shown to be an illusion. At this point, the traditional power relationship (which has been suggested by the imagery in the poem before the mid-point) is re-established. Venus, earlier pictured as a threatening predator of small birds, is likened to 'poor birds' herself (601 and 604), while Adonis, the prey, becomes a predator of the fearful boar, unencumbered by the trivia of women and love. The balance of power shifts suddenly and decisively at the exact centre of the poem (stanza 100 out of 199) when Venus manages to faint with her arms around Adonis's neck, so that '[he] on her belly falls, she on her back' (594), thus forcing him into position for the consummation of her desire. The scene is set:

> Now is she in the very lists of love,
> Her champion is mounted for the hot encounter.
> All is imaginary she doth prove;
> He will not manage her, although he mount her:
> That worse than Tantalus' is her annoy,
> To clip Elizium and to lack her joy.
>
> [595–600]

Shakespeare here makes explicit the nature of her control over the situation and her ability to force Adonis to make love to her. Her power is shown to be 'imaginary' and this failed coupling is the proof. The importance of these lines is evident, especially lines 597–598, which form the exact middle of the poem: here we have the core reality of the power/gender politics of the poem, with all the rhetoric and complexity pared away. Venus can force Adonis to 'mount' her, but she cannot force him either to an erection, or to penetration. As William Sheidley points out, the vital piece of equipment is missing and Venus can do nothing about it:

> ...rape, a consummating possibility implied by the combination of her power with her desire [and the consummation of unwanted desire in the partner poem

The Rape of Lucrece], is entirely out of the question. In the redistribution of male and female attributes, Shakespeare inevitably ends up with some items left over...The equation that nicely balances for the horses, when drawn up for Venus and Adonis, obviously lacks one crucial factor which, if present, would allow Venus' hopes and those of the sympathetic reader to be fulfilled: that is, simply, an erect phallus, which Adonis will not and Venus cannot provide.[26]

Venus recognizes the problem, and tries to remedy it — '[the] warm effects which she in him finds missing/She seeks to kindle with continual kissing' (605–606) — but without Adonis's cooperation, it is impossible. As the owner of the phallus, Adonis holds the balance of power, the power to control the outcome of the encounter. The narrator confirms the futility of her efforts, addressing both Venus and the reader: 'But all in vain, good queen, it will not be./She hath assay'd as much as may be prov'd' (607–608). Although Venus is characterized by the masculine desire to penetrate, she is given no way to realize that desire, and the poem suggests that the reversal of roles is inevitably unsuccessful and impotent because, in the economy of phallic penetration, the only proper placement of power is with the male. When it is with the female, or she tries to usurp it, the result is impotence,[27] and Venus must be frustrated in her attempts to force Adonis to have sex with her, because she has no way to effect penetration. Instead, Adonis exercises his specifically male power over her by withdrawing consent and withholding the phallus from her use.

The boar

The significance of the ability to penetrate as an index of personal power is emphasized by the boar, the bearer of the only active and effective phallic power in the poem and whom William Sheidley has described as 'the locus of the missing phallic impulse'.[28] Adonis, as the owner of the phallus, controls the outcome of Venus's attempted seduction by remaining passive. In the hunt, however, the boar, as the owner of a greater (because active) phallic power, embodied in his tusks, controls Adonis's destiny and the final outcome of the poem. As the 'conqueror' of Adonis, it could be said that the boar is the most powerful being in *Venus and Adonis.*

Venus admits that she is conquered by Adonis (114) and she is jealous of the boar in a sexual way, competing against him for the penetrable Adonis. She even attributes her own motives and seductive actions to the boar (1110–1118) and, in her grief, imagines that '[he] thought to kiss [Adonis], and hath kill'd him so' (1110). This places the boar in direct competition with her for Adonis's affections, effectively defining the animal as 'a fellow suitor'.[29] However, the only thing that they can possibly be competing for is the penetration of Adonis, and Venus's defeat is complete when the boar succeeds in not only penetrating Adonis but killing him as well.

The way Adonis's relationship to the boar is depicted is particularly interesting in the light of a definition of power as penetration: he is masculine in the hunt of the boar, but his death at the boar's tusk is a physical correlative of the feminizing effect of defeat in battle. Not only is Adonis effectively castrated by the wound, but he is invaginated by the violent phallic tusk, which is suggestively '[sheath'd]…in his soft groin' (1116). Adonis is forcibly made to take on a feminine sexual physiology that graphically and bluntly images his reduced patriarchal power status as failed hunter, and therefore less masculine man. Like Tarquin, Adonis is attracted to the boar as prey because it represents a challenge to and a test of his masculinity, a challenge that is increased because the boar is difficult to penetrate. Thus, Venus only spurs Adonis on rather than dissuading him when she tells him that the boar's 'brawny sides with hairy bristles armed/Are better proof than thy spear's point can enter' (625–626). She undermines her own efforts because she fails to recognize the conquest-by-penetration ethos that motivates Adonis, just as it motivated Tarquin and appeared to motivate her. Because, as a female, she does not fully participate in the phallic penetrative dynamic, like Lucrece she only succeeds in using it against herself, however unintentionally or indirectly.

In *Venus and Adonis* and *The Rape of Lucrece*, images of penetration and penetrability are attributed to both males and females, and each of the four protagonists is characterized by both kinds of images at different times. However, at the basic level of end consequences rather than outward and temporary states, a consistent picture emerges of the power relationship between men and women, and the way that power is represented. Impenetrability and the ability to penetrate characterize the males (Tarquin, Adonis and the boar), while penetrability and the inability to penetrate characterize the females (Lucrece and Venus). Tarquin can vent his desire and Lucrece can do nothing to stop him, but Adonis can refuse to satisfy Venus's desire and she can do nothing to make him.

Finally, Shakespeare makes no narrative judgement in either poem about whether such dynamics are acceptable, for the pairs of protagonists share remarkably similar fates, and none of them are good. Adonis and Lucrece are dead, with the reasons for their deaths left unsatisfactorily resolved. Venus, the 'empty eagle', flees into self-imposed exile on Paphos, in order to make herself invulnerable to further heartbreak and impenetrable to the male eye,[30] while Tarquin, who has 'lost in gain' (730), is sentenced to 'everlasting banishment' (1855). In the end, the phallic instrument of penetration proves to be a double-edged sword.

---

1   All line quotations from the two poems are from *The Arden Edition of the Works of William Shakespeare, The Poems*, ed. F.T. Prince, gen. ed. Richard Proudfoot (London and New York: Methuen, 1960).

2   *As You Like It, The Arden Edition of the Works of William Shakespeare*, ed. Agnes Latham, gen. eds Harold F. Brooks and Harold Jenkins (London: Methuen, 1975), III, ii, l. 403.

3   Compare the extended description of Lucrece using this conceit (ll. 54–71).

4   Lisa Jardine uses the phrase 'rapeable boy' when discussing Adonis
        in *Still Harping on Daughters: Women in the Age of Shakespeare*
        (Brighton: Harvester Press, 1983), p. 18.

5   Venus and Tarquin share the experience that the more Adonis or
        Lucrece pull away, the more inflamed with desire they become
        (Venus at ll. 569–570 and Tarquin at ll. 468–469 and ll. 645–646).

6   See Georgianna Ziegler, 'My Lady's Chamber: Female Space, Female
        Chastity in Shakespeare', where she discusses this imagery of invasion
        (*Textual Practice*, vol. 4 [1990], pp. 73–90). She argues that Lucrece
        is 'closely associated with the chamber in which she is ravished' and
        concludes that '[the] whole process of the actual rape of Lucrece is
        thus prefigured in these details of Tarquin's approach through the
        house' (p. 80).

7   Joel Fineman, 'Shakespeare's *Will*: The Temporality of Rape',
        Representations, vol. 20 (Fall 1987), p. 40. Fineman sees this section
        as simultaneously a displacement of the actual rape, and a kind of
        rape in itself.

8   Katharine Eisaman Maus, 'Taking Tropes Seriously: Language and
        Violence in Shakespeare's *Rape of Lucrece*', *Shakespeare Quarterly*,
        vol. 37 (1986), p. 79.

9   Tess in *Tess of the D'Urbervilles* is portrayed in a similar way which
        makes explicit her status as object of consumption for the author and
        reader, as well as hinting at her rapeability. Penny Boumelha
        comments on Hardy's rape-like narrative: 'The narrator's erotic
        fantasies of penetration and engulfment enact a pursuit, violation and
        persecution of Tess in parallel with those she suffers at the hands of
        her two lovers. Time and again the narrator seeks to enter Tess,
        through her eyes...through her mouth...and through her flesh...The
        phallic imagery of pricking, piercing and penetration...[satisfies] the
        narrator's fascination with the interiority of her sexuality, and his
        desire to take possession of her.' Penny Boumelha, *Thomas Hardy
        and Women: Sexual Ideology and Narrative Form* (Brighton:
        Harvester Press, 1982), p. 120.

10   Jardine, p. 18.

11   See Elizabeth Truax, 'Venus, Lucrece, and Bess of Hardwick: Portraits
        to Please', in Cecile Williamson Cary and Henry S. Limouze, eds,
        *Shakespeare and the Arts: A Collection of Essays from the Ohio
        Shakespeare Conference, 1981, Wright State University, Dayton, Ohio*
        (Washington: University Press of America, 1982), p. 39.

12   Ziegler, p. 82.

13   This unusual arrangement, in which *male* beauty is irresistible and
        inflames desire, is echoed in the young man sonnets, especially 20
        and 24. It also derives from the Ovidian version of the story of
        Salmacis and Hermaphroditus which forms part of the source material

of *Venus and Adonis*, where Salmacis is utterly overcome by Hermaphroditus's beauty and becomes the sexual initiator (bk IV, ll. 382–481).

14 In Ovid's *Metamorphoses*, the main source for this poem, Venus falls in love with Adonis because she is scratched by one of Cupid's arrows. The wound which 'Appeered not too bee so deepe as afterward was found' is another image of successful penetration that effects control over women, as well as indicating Venus's lack of control over her desire. For the relevant lines in Ovid, see *The Metamorphoses: Shakespeare's Ovid Being Arthur Golding's Translation of the Metamorphoses*, ed. W.H.D. Rouse, Centaur Classics, gen. ed. J.M. Cohen (London: Centaur Press Ltd, 1961), p. 213.

15 Hereward T. Price, 'Function of Imagery in *Venus and Adonis*', *Papers of the Michigan Academy of Science, Arts and Letters*, vol. 31 (1945), p. 283.

16 Heather Dubrow, *Captive Victors: Shakespeare's Narrative Poems and Sonnets* (Ithaca and London: Cornell University Press, 1987), p. 94.

17 Joel Fineman makes this point, saying that '[the] poem understands Collatine's praise of Lucrece...as fundamental cause of Tarquin's rape of Lucrece' (p. 30).

18 Coppélia Kahn, 'The Rape in Shakespeare's *Lucrece*', *Shakespeare Studies*, vol. 9 (1976), p. 52.

19 Of Lucrece's (and Imogen's) chastity as object of male rivalry, Georgianna Ziegler says, 'Not content to enjoy their wealth privately, [Collatine and Posthumus] publicize it. They do so in order to enhance their own reputations among their male friends' (p. 78).

20 Catharine R. Stimpson, 'Shakespeare and the Soil of Rape', in Carolyn Ruth Swift Lenz, Gayle Greene and Carol Thomas Neely, eds, *The Woman's Part, Feminist Criticism of Shakespeare* (Urbana: University of Illinois Press, 1980), p. 58.

21 Kahn, p. 58.

22 ibid., p. 61.

23 Maus, p. 72.

24 ibid.

25 Tarquin wastes little time contemplating an attempt at persuading Lucrece to choose to love him. He recognizes that, as a woman, Lucrece may resist persuasion, but cannot prevent him raping her. Therefore, he can bypass such a potentially fruitless strategy because a surer means of achieving his end is available to him: force.

26 William E. Sheidley, '"Unless it be a boar": Love and Wisdom in Shakespeare's *Venus and Adonis*', *MLQ*, vol. 35 (1974), pp. 9–10.

27 'The dislocation of phallic potency predicates the frustration of Venus and brings about the destruction of Adonis. Properly placed, in Adonis, if that were possible, it might have rendered all well'

(Sheidley, p. 11). Despite my ambivalence about the unreflective and sexist understanding of this statement about the proper placement of power, I am indebted to this article, as it contains the most (and really only) satisfactory explanation of the function of the boar in the poem, as well as the clue to the importance of 'the phallic implications of the Boar' (p. 11).

28   ibid., p. 10.
29   ibid., p. 11.
30   The eye to which I am referring is that of the patron to whom this poem is dedicated. In a purely practical sense, Venus does become invisible to the reader, here male, because the poem finishes after her stated intent to 'not be seen' (l. 1194). In a nice touch of self-reflexiveness, the (male) poet too is prevented from further seeing or pen(etrat)ing Venus by the end he himself has created.

SPACE, TIME AND PASTORAL
IN ELIZABETH GASKELL'S
CRANFORD AND *COUSIN PHILLIS*

D.W. COLLIN

LIZABETH Gaskell wrote to Ruskin in 1865, the year of her death: 'The beginning of "Cranford" was *one* paper in "Household Words"; and I never meant to write more, so killed Capt Brown very much against my will'.[1] If her accuracy of recall after thirteen years is trustworthy she planned a fictional space and time much briefer than that eventually occupied by the Cranford papers. The first paper is confined in all its anecdotes and in the story of Captain Brown to the little town of Cranford and does not explore the country-side beyond. It is not straightforward, however, to reconcile her remark to Ruskin with her jolly pre-Christmas letter of 1851 written very close in time to publication of the first Cranford paper: 'I've written a couple of tales about Cranford in House-hold Words'.[2] Captain Brown was hatched and despatched entirely within the first paper, which was published in the number dated 13 December 1851 under the title 'Our Society at Cranford'. The second paper, published in the number dated 3 January 1852,[3] deals with new and largely unconnected material and, in fact, performs the same offices for Mr Holbrook, the yeoman farmer, thus moving to the countryside beyond Cranford. The letter written in December 1851 yields sense if one may assume that the second paper was written only after Elizabeth Gaskell received acceptance of the first and a request for more of the same from Dickens, as editor of *Household Words*, and that on that December Sunday when, wearing blue ribbons, she wrote of having composed two tales, she had already reopened the Cranford time and space which she had at first deemed closed. Her letter to Ruskin suggests also that authorial intention about the close of the first paper was settled, even though she later continued beyond the second paper and developed the work so far as to produce the novel we know as *Cranford*.[4] Such firm authorial intention about the length of the proposed fiction may be compared to her plans for the closure of *Cousin Phillis* which, at a late stage in composition and publication, was adjusted to comply with the space available in the *Cornhill Magazine* where the novella was serialized in four parts between November 1863 and February 1864.[5]

The phrase which seals up Elizabeth Gaskell's intentions in the writing of *Cranford* is: 'killed Capt Brown very much against my will'. Was this an internal conflict or is it, to speculate, another instance of direction from Dickens as editor of *Household Words?* This essay does not pretend to break open the seal but proposes a connection in *Cranford* and *Cousin Phillis* between the effect on women of male death, absence or desertion, the locational and temporal spaces accessible to female and male, and the thread of pastoral which runs through both works.[6]

The author of *Cranford* has been frequently taken to task and forgiven for inconsistencies in the political and personal narrative calendars, but there are qualities in the work which emphasize the thematic dependence on certain kinds of time. Narrative time in the novel is recessive and processive. Retrospection carries the reader more deeply into the past with each of the first three papers and the temporal distance lengthens as the function of recall is passed from narrator to character; delving into time past is measured in decades, by lifetimes, and crosses the mysterious boundary into the preceding century. This temporal reversion, a contravention of natural process, is contained within a processive framework with which it has in common seasonal, weekly and daily reckonings. The smallest particles of Cranford time, the quarter-of-an-hour calls to be returned within three days, the early bedtimes, are a well-remembered detail of the novel and relation of this coffee-spoon time to the larger measures of the novel's fictional time is worthy of study. In *Cousin Phillis* also we find both strict hourly and daily schedules and the slower cycle of the seasons; narrative time is more plainly retrospective.

'Our Society at Cranford' opens with anecdotal retrospection establishing 'elegant economy' (*C*, 42) of time as a controlling trope. The processive calendar begins in November: we hear of a wet Sunday after church and then: 'my friend and hostess, Miss Jenkyns, was going to have a party in my honour,[...]; it was the third week in November, so the evenings closed in about four' (*C*, 45). This part of the tale remains autumnal, perhaps frosty, like Miss Jenkyns's opinion of *The Pickwick Papers*; it is a 'very slippery Sunday' when Captain Brown carries the 'poor old woman's dinner' (*C*, 49). The narrator, Mary Smith, leaves Cranford to return home to the manufacturing town of Drumble and the narration overleaps winter and spring until her return, which occurs within the first paper: 'My next visit to Cranford was in the summer' (*C*, 52). Summer is the season and afternoon the time of day when Captain Brown, 'upwards of sixty' but 'with a springing step, which made him appear much younger than he was' (*C*, 44), is cut down by '"them nasty cruel railroads"' (*C*, 55) while reading the latest number of *The Pickwick Papers*.[7] Within days his elder daughter dies of her 'lingering, incurable complaint' (*C*, 50) and his younger daughter is rescued from a poor and solitary future by the happy return of Major Gordon, the suitor formerly rejected out of filial duty. Again there is a temporal leap, of much greater extent than that between November and summer, to the closure of the first paper years later with little Flora Gordon (not even thought of at the beginning of the paper) reading *A Christmas Carol*[8] to the aged Miss Jenkyns. Effectively, the author has relied upon two seasons, autumn and summer, to frame the central images of the first paper: first, the ossifying society of Cranford and then the fatal railway accident which cuts off the energizing spirit of Captain Brown. The last image of the first paper synthesizes age and youth, the slightly senile Miss Jenkyns and the imperfectly articulated child, while the reference to *A Christmas Carol* reinforces the suggestion of the season of decay containing within itself the possibility of renewal. The possibility of a cycle is suggested but not fulfilled.

In the second Cranford paper the establishment of a seasonal context is at first less certain: the impression is of the season of enclosure and story-telling: initiation of the story depends as does the first paper upon a visit to Cranford by the narrator who tells of a fire in her bedroom, of the kitchen lit by a candle in the evening, of preserved gooseberries and currants for winter dessert, and of Mr Holbrook wishing to buy woollen gloves. This is the contextual season for the visit of the East Indian Jenkynses. The secret and special story to be told — 'And now I come to the love affair' (*C*, 69) — begins with the visit to Mr Holbrook's farm, Woodley, which, woollen gloves or no, takes place in June; the asparagus ferns are in full leaf, the pinks and gilly-flowers are in bloom. Following the excursion by the Cranford ladies, Mr Holbrook pays a call of courtesy upon Miss Matty, to whom he had paid court in youth, and announces that he is going to Paris 'in a week or two', fixing the season agriculturally as high summer: 'as soon as the hay is got in I shall go, before harvest time' (*C*, 78).

The visit to Woodley brings much closer to the surface the sense of pastoral and of the dependence of life outside Cranford town itself upon the cycle of the seasons. Indeed Elizabeth Gaskell uses the epithet 'pastoral' to describe the countryside on the way to Woodley: 'The aspect of the country was quiet and pastoral' (*C*, 72). Of Mr Holbrook the narrator says:

> Altogether, I never met with a man, before or since, who had spent so long a life in a secluded and not impressive country with ever-increasing delight in the daily and yearly change of season and beauty.
>
> [*C*, 73]

The novelist establishes in this paper the richer connection with pastoral as literary form through complicating allusions laid on the surface texture of the tale to Shakespeare, Goethe and, in greater detail, to Tennyson, whose 'Locksley Hall' Holbrook reads in compliment to Miss Matty, who snoozes the while.

After the visit to Woodley the narrator returns to Drumble and during her absence from Cranford processive time again overleaps the slow development of seasons from early summer, the June hay-harvest at Woodley, to the time of her next visit, November, again the time of enclosure, story-telling and retrospect: 'So we talked softly and quietly of old times, through the long November evening'. It is also the season of death for the old: 'The next day Miss Pole brought us word that Mr Holbrook was dead' (*C*, 81). Unlike the youthful Captain Brown, Mr Holbrook was, according to Miss Pole, 'about seventy, I think, my dear' (*C*, 70) and his death when full of years is in accord with the natural season of autumn even as in life he lived in compatibility with 'the yearly change of season' (*C*, 73). Closure, as in the first paper, is again resisted. Holbrook is dead but Miss Matty lives on, though with the beginning of tremulousness. At its centre the narrative turns away from the metaphorical convention of a reconciling marriage as closure, yet opens a byway to continuity with the servant Martha and her follower, Jem. As in the first paper there is ending and no ending.

In both the first and second papers the seasonal cycle for Cranfordians is incomplete, disabled. Only Mr Holbrook, who was snubbed by the quintessential Cranfordian, Miss Jenkyns, and sent packing by her father, the Rector, is a complete being, entering fully into the natural cycle of seasons. Is this because he is a farmer? because he is not contained within the boundaries of Cranford itself? because he delights in the pastoral lyric? or because he is to fulfil the uncompleted life of Captain Brown?

The obviousness of elements of pastoral in the second paper suggests a different emphasis on certain small moments in the tale of Captain Brown. If one may force the argument by asserting that the second paper takes the form of an elegy, then the first paper may be read as its elegiac precursor. The realism of the shocking suddenness of Captain Brown's death masks the more complex elegiac pity evoked on the conventional grounds of the brevity of his life and also the brevity of his elder daughter's life. The response of Miss Jessie, the mourner, is typically elegiac, to beg for the time which is never granted, although in this case it is rather for the reprieve of a period of concealment than for extension of life. The accident which kills Captain Brown is in the mode of realist fiction and reinforces his representation as an appreciative reader of contemporary comedy; but only as reader, not as a true son of the muse. Realism could hardly accommodate the half-pay Captain in the figure of an absent-minded poet wandering onto the railway line. He is, however, represented as a maker, in three kinds: as an engineer with 'facility in devising expedients to overcome domestic dilemmas' (C, 43); as a bard who recites before an appreciative audience the composition of another (C, 47); and as a craftsman who 'endeavoured to make peace with Miss Jenkyns [...] by a present of a wooden fire-shovel (his own making)' (C, 50). To this extent the paper narrates the death of an artist. Elegy as memorial finds its place at the last in the tableau of Miss Jenkyns and the aptly named Flora, the lineal descendant of the Captain-maker, whose youth holds the possibility of renewal of life and who is faithful to the new fiction which led the Captain to his death. Miss Jenkyns, who formerly commanded the field and the funeral, is at the last the means through which the realist narrative, by placing even this formidable woman face to face with dementia and death, mediates the sense that with death comes, ironically, the harmony and absence of hierarchy which are lacking in life.

The second Cranford paper, although more plainly in pastoral mode, is more elusive when read as an elegy. The exquisite pity evoked by youthful death is located not here for the death of a contented elderly bachelor but outside the span of time of this paper and in a more involved form as the prohibition of young love which is implicit in the representation of Miss Matty as a tacit widow. Holbrook, removed from the confined enclosing spaces and manners of Cranford and unlike Captain

Brown, is able to embrace the new poetry and all the literature of his choice without contest. In habits, belongings and tastes, he takes what he pleases from old and new with the important exception of the wife of his desire. There the Cranford conventions defeat him and elegiac irony is inverted: death comes in the fulness of time but without any promise of rebirth at the centre. Holbrook does not belong to the society of Cranford; but neither does Miss Matty's servant Martha, who was precisely 'two-and-twenty last third of October', nor does her Jem, who is 'six foot one in his stocking-feet' (*C*, 82), belong to Cranford society. The comic realism with which the second paper closes is disconnected from any sense of pastoral, and 'The evening of the day on which we heard of Mr Holbrook's death' (*C*, 81) leaves the principal character, Matty, trapped in unacknowledged widowhood without any future course; without any direction in processive time along which she could move forward; and without prospect of pastures new. The narrative now must engage with retrospection to make space for Matty's story; without recessive time there is no space for story-telling to continue.

In the third Cranford paper[9] the narrative moves deeply into the past, receding before the birth of Miss Matty and even before the marriage of her parents. For this, Elizabeth Gaskell evokes the season of story-telling and rehearsal of memories:

> In the winter afternoons [Miss Matty] would sit knitting
> for two or three hours; she could do this in the dark,
> or by fire-light; and when I asked if I might not ring
> for candles to finish stitching my wristbands, she told
> me to 'keep blind-man's holiday'.
>
> [*C*, 84]

In the firelight the narrator hears the story of poor Peter, a story of a spring day: '"it was a very still, quiet day, I remember, overhead; and the lilacs were all in flower, so I suppose it was spring"' (*C*, 95); but in this year the spring flowers become images of the death of youth for Miss Matty: '"poor, withered cowslip-flowers thrown out to the leaf heap, to decay and die there"' (*C*, 97).

In this paper, published under the title 'Memory at Cranford', the novelist uses the narrative strategy of recessive time to explore the moral and psychological dimensions of memory of time past. The innocence of the dying cowslips and other images of spring, by which Matty fixes her recollection, speak for her pain at the loss of her brother Peter and at her loss of innocence as she contemplates the humbling of the autocratic and unjust father. The pathos of the ageing Matty, apparently the lone survivor, is sharpened by the seasonal contrast: memories of spring are relived in winter and burnt in the fire, letter by letter.

The paper forms the fifth and sixth chapters of the novel, in which they bear the titles 'Old Letters' and 'Poor Peter'. The narrative preface to the reading of the old letters lays down a grid of irritating constraints which turn genteel economy into something nearer parsimony: wasted paper, hanks of string, small pieces of butter and candle economy (*C*, 83–84) mark the narrow limits of Cranford's way of life and foreshadow the imprisoning railings behind which Peter plays out his rebellious jape and behind which he is flogged. Cranford is defined in the first paper as a society from which the men have escaped: '"A man [...] is so in the way in the house!"' (*C*, 39). Fleeing from life indoors, they seek and find distant public spaces: the regiment, the ship, Drumble, India. In the narrative which is evoked by reading the old letters Peter too flees, a mere boy, from the confinement of lessons in his father's study and from the railed prison of the rectory garden. Like Captain Brown and Major Jenkyns, he seeks an unfettered existence abroad. The mother and sisters who remain behind are sacrificed in service and obedience to the autocratic and, in my argument, still to be more ruthless father, the Rector: the mother pines and dies; Matty yields up the promise of spacious independence as the mistress of Woodley; Miss Jenkyns denies femininity and adopts the sterile role of a pseudo-male.

The violence of the Rector's flogging of Peter defines the central axis of the Jenkyns family: a struggle for supremacy between old and young males which tosses to the margins of irrelevance the women of the family. And, in its resolution, the flight of Peter is shown as a battle for territory. The scene of the flogging seems at first to be an aberration in the habitually restrained ironic tone of the novel; the frankness of the narration here exercises a judgement far more severe than even the sharpest ironies of Cranford such as those wielded against Miss Pole. There are two aspects to this scene which persuade me that it is far from an aberration in the sense of loss of authorial control; indeed that it is essential to the statement which Cranford makes about women's lives. The boyhood of poor Peter is the only period in the narration when there are two males living in one household; and it seems that there is not space enough under one roof for two males. The women in Cranford do not seem to require for themselves such exclusive territory. Miss Matty and her sister live together; so do Miss Jessie and her sister; even Mrs Jamieson and Lady Glenmire rub along together for a period of time. The second point which enlarges the significance of the flogging of Peter concerns a gap in the narrative and a contest between two males which is omitted from the explicit narrative but which may be detected.

There are three moments in the novel when the narration touches retrospectively on the broken love affair of long ago. In the darkened sitting-room Matty tells of the fruitless search for Peter and her own part in it. She was the only daughter at home:

> '...I had no time for crying, for now all seemed to depend on me. [...] I sent a message privately to that same Mr Holbrook's house — poor Mr Holbrook! — you know who I mean. I don't mean I sent a message to him, but I sent one that I could trust, to know if Peter was at his house.'
>
> [C, 98]

In the seventh Cranford paper,[10] Mrs Fitz-Adam recalls a spring-time moment of Miss Matty's youth:

> '...a gentleman rode beside her, and was talking to her, and she was looking down at some primroses she

had gathered, and pulling them all to pieces, and I do believe she was crying.'

[C, 194]

In the eighth Cranford paper[11] the long-lost Mr Peter, returned from India, stumbles into a revelation of how far the love affair between Matty and Holbrook had really advanced when Peter last visited England and he alludes to one of the incidents which must have surrounded its abortion:

'Poor Deborah! What a lecture she read me on having asked [Holbrook] home to lunch one day, when she had seen the Arley carriage in the town, and thought that my lady might call.'

[C, 213]

The anxious propriety with which Miss Matty takes pains, long years after, to explain that she did not personally send a message to Holbrook suggests the recollection of a stern prohibition against any communication with her suitor, whether or not the prohibition preceded Peter's flight. In the proper course Holbrook would seek the hand of Matty from the Rector, her father. Miss Deborah Jenkyns, whose snobbishness Peter remembers, could not be a central player but surely she was influential. Buried somewhere in a narrative gap is an encounter between two grown males far more formidable than that between the Rector and his son and over a matter far more momentous than Peter's crude joke about an illegitimate baby: no less than an application for a daughter's hand in marriage. Miss Matty remembers her father, after the death of her mother, as 'a changed man': 'Not that he was less active; I think he was more so, and more patient...' (C, 103, 102). How did the Rector reject Holbrook's proposal? Not, I think, with a flogging, although it is not inconceivable that one who could in a moment become 'grey-white with anger, [...] eyes blaz[ing] out under his frowning black brows' (C, 96), might under provocation be aroused from the quiescence of widowerhood to threaten to horsewhip a presumptuous yeoman farmer. Whatever the manner of the encounter, it left a wound sufficiently painful to cause Holbrook to change his market-town from Cranford to Misselton, a momentous step for a farmer. The contest between the Rector and Holbrook was over the lordship of a female, a version of primitive contest having similarities with the contest between Peter and his father in that winner takes all and loser deserts the field. The Rectory was not large enough to contain both Peter and his father; the town of Cranford was not large enough to contain the Rector and young Holbrook. The explicitly narrated flogging of Peter functions also as a vicarious representation of the more significant encounter between the father and the suitor.

Ousted men have or seek other wider territory: Mr Holbrook has his farm and goes to market in Misselton instead of Cranford; Peter makes a life in India. Women who are losers or victims find themselves in narrower spaces. When the Rector died his two daughters, as Miss Matty puts it, 'had to come to this small house, and be content with a servant-of-all-work' (*C*, 103). After the bank failure narrated in the sixth and seventh papers[12] Miss Matty is reduced to a 'sitting-room and bed-room [into which] she had to cram all sorts of things, which were [...] bought in for her at the sale...' (*C*, 200). Even her occupation of the sitting-room is only until a lodger can be found to take it. The narrator, Mary Smith, is 'allowed' by her father to buy in at the auction of Miss Matty's chattels furniture sufficient for 'one tiny bed-room' (*C*, 200) for her own use in case of Miss Matty falling ill.

The retreat to the bedroom in the face of poverty is paralleled by collapse into bed itself in case of illness. The Miss Matty of processive time, neither before nor after the extreme poverty caused by the bank failure, suffers from the degree of illness which felled her mother after Peter ran away; she withdraws on occasion to her bedroom, ostensibly with a headache, but obviously to hide her emotion and she is prescribed 'a warm bed, and a glass of weak negus' (*C*, 213) as treatment for the attack of trembling which Peter's mention of Holbrook brings on. In the recessive time of the novel, however, serious illness seems to afflict Miss Matty on two occasions: in the second Cranford paper she speaks of 'a long, long illness' which the narrator 'dated in [her] own mind as following the dismissal of the suit of Mr Holbrook' (*C*, 81); and in the third paper she tells of an hysterical illness when Peter runs away. In the narrative strategy of *Cranford* these illnesses serve to reveal that which the strict code would conceal.

Illness assists the mechanics of the narrative most plainly in the second paper when Martha writes to the narrator that Miss Matty is '"very low and sadly off her food"' (*C*, 79), thereby bringing the narrator back to Cranford to be a witness to the second part of the story of Mr Holbrook, his illness and death. The reactions both to emotional shock and to poverty signal the powerlessness of the women in the face of the conventions imposed by Cranford society, conventions derived from male hierarchies. The darker irony of the initiating comic image of Cranford ruled by Amazons is that the Amazons struggle to repress and confine themselves to limits imposed on them by an absent phallocracy, which reserves exploration of wider spaces to itself and by its absence denies fertility and future to Cranford society.

The tale of poor Peter sets over against female confinement the male capacity for resolution of distress through escape. His reaction to degrading punishment from his authoritarian father is not illness, not withdrawal, not fight, but flight; flight as a striking out to a new life. The quiet restraint of Peter's manner under his father's whipping is admirable, but this 'five foot nine' boy (who probably towered over his father) knows that it is open to him to leave the confines of the Rectory, 'ma[k]e his way to Liverpool' and join the navy (*C*, 99). In contrast, his sister, at a servant's suggestion that the ponds be dragged in a search for the body of the missing Peter, recalls giving way to hysterical screams: '"(my horrible laughter had ended in crying)"' (*C*, 99). The conflict between the Rector and his son brings loss and grief to the three women of the Rectory and their response is to turn inwards, grouped around Matty's bed: '"[My mother] and Deborah sat by my bedside"' (*C*, 99). The Amazons' reaction to emotional or economic distress is one of withdrawal either into illness, which would now be characterized as psychosomatic, or into stricter gentility and narrower and more private spaces.

The possibility of resolution of the loss of Peter's presence is frustrated as far as his mother and elder sister are concerned by their own deaths. For the survivor Matty elegiac resolution is impossible in the processive time of the novel as long as his death is uncertain:

'I believe he is dead myself; and it sometimes fidgets me that we have never put on mourning for him. And then, again, when I sit by myself, and all the house is still, I think I hear his step coming up the street, and my heart begins to flutter and beat; but the sound always goes past — and Peter never comes.'

[*C*, 103]

In the penultimate Cranford paper the return of Peter diverts the unfulfilled narrative movement towards elegy for youth to a more diffuse sense of mourning for the cumulating losses of Miss Matty's life, which are only partly repaired in old age by the return of an elderly brother. The promise of new life which belongs to classical elegy is patently impossible within the realistic constraints of the novel for Miss Matty and the elderly Cranfordian spinsters and widows, but in a more general way female elegy is denied any route to a new life by the spatial confinement, by class as well as by domesticity, to which female virtue must submit. Marriages which seem on the face of it to be optimistic exceptions do not touch the problems of confinement and sterility which afflict the Cranfordians. Within their social class Miss Jessie Brown's new life and motherhood, a state which depends upon the happy return of her former suitor, is located beyond the boundaries of Cranford in its origin and course of life. The marriage of the widow of the Scotch peer and the Cranford surgeon offers no truly regenerative promise; it is an interlude of comic irony which serves to uncover briefly the unquenched aspirations of the Cranford spinsters: '"Two people that we know going to be married. It's coming very near!"' (*C*, 166)

The author's intentions and method in the composition of *Cousin Phillis* are dissimilar to the erratic evolution and publication of the Cranford papers. First publication was in a periodical, the *Cornhill Magazine*, where the four serial parts came out regularly in successive monthly numbers and were, from the first, interdependent. The appearance of structural strength conceals the facts that publication began before the work was finished and that at a late stage alternative endings were under consideration. In spite of this, the firmness of the foreshadowed span of fictional time permits articulation of a more violent emotional conflict than any explicitly narrated in *Cranford*, one which leaves Phillis, still a young woman, as bereft as the young Matty. In *Cousin Phillis* the contrast between the narrow immobility and confinement of the female against the free range of the male is sharp and symbolic of moral discrepancies. The life-threatening illness of the heroine in response to her father's denial of her adult freedom to love, superimposed upon news of the marriage of the man she thought would return to seek her hand, is the turning point of the narrative. At stake is not only Phillis's life but the re-education of her father, Minister Holman, about the rights of daughters. The anecdotal tone and indeterminate timing of the first Cranford paper are replaced in *Cousin Phillis* by an exposition establishing the narrator, Paul Manning, at some fixed point of fictive composition during his later life from which he looks back to relate a sequence of events which have reached completion.

Bounded by these firm temporal limits, the potential for irony appears to lie between the older Paul as narrator and the callow subject-self, in a manner closely resembling the method of *Great Expectations*. Whereas Paul comes to recognize his intervention in Phillis's life (assuring her that Holdsworth loves her) as a 'want of wisdom' (*CP*, 291), a reading of the novel as *Bildungsroman* places the tardy recognition by her father, the minister Holman, of his daughter's sexual maturity and her right to leave the parental home as the central moment of male enlightenment. In *Cranford*, we are shown by the incorporation of deeply recessive time into processive time that the consequence of the Rector's dismissal of Matty's suitor leads to her lifelong want of husbandly companionship and her unfulfilled yearning for children. In *Cousin Phillis* lack of husband and children is again laid at the door of a misguided father, even though within the more tightly controlled time-span of the novella as published the reader is not shown Phillis in old age and the conviction that her life will remain solitary comes through the retrospect of a maturer narrator at some unspecified later time.

The overarching retrospective narration of *Cousin Phillis* moves steadily forward from a point early in the first part when the narrator 'came to know cousin Phillis' (*CP*, 222), except for a few instances when the currently narrated layer of time is peeled back to hint at some earlier event. Such is the undeveloped reference to the Holmans' having lost a child in infancy. The power of the novella depends, however, on a strategic management of concealment and suggestion operating on two scales of time: within the total time-span measured retrospectively from the present of the controlling and knowing narrator to any one of several points within the tale he has to tell of cousin Phillis, when the manner is ominous; and, secondly, within the day-to-day time-scale of life at Hope Farm, when knowledge in the possession of one character or of the narrator-character is concealed from others.

One of the deprivations suffered by the ladies of Cranford is the urbanization of daily life; gentility isolates them from the productive rural life which should sustain the town of Cranford. Allusions to literary pastoral thus subvert the genteel economy which is the ground of their morality. In the novella, *Cousin Phillis*, Elizabeth Gaskell deploys pastoral to advance the action, to elevate Phillis and conversely, as I shall suggest, to wield irony against the minister. Cousin Phillis herself, daughter of a minister-farmer, enjoys free movement, apparently, within the limits of the farm and free access to a selection of scholarly, literary and practical books. She is closely engaged in her daily tasks on the farm with the seasonal cycle of agriculture, whereas Miss Matty and Miss Pole decline to take a walk around the farm with Mr Holbrook for fear of 'damp, and dirt' (*C*, 75). Miss Matty confuses Tennyson with Dr Johnson but cousin Phillis reads Latin and

Greek and responds with educated sympathy when, in the first part of the novella, her father quotes 'a line or two of Latin', presumed to be a descriptive passage from the *Georgics* (*CP*, 233). Connection with literary and agricultural pastoral in *Cousin Phillis* is made directly by and through the characters even when it works ironically to undermine them; it is accessible without distinction according to gender and is locked into the very tasks which order the productive life of the farm.

There are three particular references to the *Georgics* in *Cousin Phillis* as well as an underlying web of allusions. At the time of the minister's first reference to Virgil, Phillis is unawakened, a contented daughter of protective parents, and dressed in pinafores which belie her seventeen years. His second reference to Virgil, specifically to the *Georgics*, occurs in the fourth part and functions ironically; he reflects upon the narrow-mindedness of a brother minister who has reproved him for quoting the *Georgics* and finds that he has himself been guilty of similar narrow-mindedness in his attitude to the 'quick wits, bright senses, and ready words of Holdsworth' (*CP*, 290), the young engineer whom Phillis loves. The story of the attraction between Phillis and Holdsworth is at this point far advanced; Phillis's love for Holdsworth is not known to her parents but, taught by Paul, she believes that it is returned and it must be presumed that her spirits would rise to hear her father's acknowledgement of Holdsworth's qualities. The narrator's next words reverse the optimistic tone and take up metaphorically the weather-language of the *Georgics*:

> The first little cloud upon my peace came in the shape
> of a letter from Canada [where Holdsworth has gone],
> in which there were two or three sentences that
> troubled me more than they ought to have done, to
> judge merely from the words employed.
>
> [*CP*, 290]

These sentences warn the narrator (and the reader) that Holdsworth has turned away from Phillis. Paul's alertness to the undertones of human communication draws attention to the

selectivity of the minister's interest in the *Georgics*. The passages
which catch the minister's fancy are those concerned with
practical farming, which he quotes with delight in their relevance
to his own farming, saying:

> 'Again, no Scotch farmer could give shrewder advice
> than to cut light meadows while the dew is on, even
> though it involve night-work.'

[*CP*, 296][13]

This, the third reference to the *Georgics* is, like the second,
initiated by the minister-farmer, and occurs later in the fourth
serial part after Phillis has been told by Paul that Holdsworth is
to marry a French-Canadian but before she faces the severer test
of the tearing of bonds between father and daughter as her
father is forced to acknowledge that his daughter is no longer a
child, but sexually mature, and that she has been loved and
given love in return. As Phillis and her mother listen to the naïf
minister reading and translating from the first *Georgic*, 'the
monotonous chant' of the Latin causes Phillis to snap her sewing
thread and for the first time her misery breaks out into words:
'The thread is bad — everything is bad — I am so tired of it all!'
(*CP*, 296).

The ill-educated brother ministers who chastise Phillis's
father for the catholicity of his reading and in particular for its
'profane heathenism' (*CP*, 290) have some justice on their side;
for his preoccupation with the aptness of the agricultural
admonitions in the *Georgics* is maintained in seeming blindness
to the incompatibility of the Latin poet's pagan morality with his
own fervently evangelical Christianity. For the novelist's purpose
the minister's reading of the *Georgics* as an agricultural textbook
is inscribed as misreading on other grounds. It is rather the
minister's blindness to the warning signs of his daughter's
maturity which make ironic and tacit connection with some of
those passages in the *Georgics* from which he does not quote. A
few lines after the passage which the minister admires as 'living
truth in these days' (*CP*, 296), Virgil's text catalogues the storms
of all seasons against which the farmer must take guard, even

that storm which strikes as the farmer leads his men to harvest.[14] In the third part of *Cousin Phillis* the sultry weather leads Holman to forecast 'rain before the morning' (*CP*, 268) and to hasten to get in the hay. Although he is alert to such signs of the physical universe, he perceives not the imminence of storm in his daughter's life, a storm which breaks in July of the year following the downpour at haymaking, and catches up father and mother in its violence.

The selectivity of his reading of the *Georgics* is matched by selective awareness of the passage of time. His apportionment of daily and weekly time to farmwork and religious duties is strict and economical, as is the Cranfordians', in more trivial matters; he rises at three and orders his intercessions by a weekly diary. A thin but threatening symbol at Hope Farm is the ticking of the household clock. Holman's farmwork keeps time with the seasons and he takes a period of relaxation in winter as the *Georgics* recommend.[15] He fails to observe, however, the passage of years which has brought his daughter to womanhood. It is his refusal to grant her the freedom to love as a sexually mature woman, coming on top of the loss of love, which causes Phillis's collapse into a nearly fatal brain fever. The crisis destabilizes a household which has been regulated by clock and calendar within and without.

As with Miss Matty in *Cranford*, Phillis's illness is represented as drawing the family inwards, confined to the bedroom of the sufferer. In *Cousin Phillis* the father also, unlike the Rector of Cranford, forms part of this group, shedding the masculine duties of farming and, apparently, of tending his congregation in order to '[share] the nursing with his wife' (*CP*, 311). More particulars are given of the symptoms and diagnosis of Phillis's illness than of Miss Matty's after the flight of Peter. Matty could recognize those around her: '"I knew by the looks of each that there had been no news of Peter"'; and she was in a '"dull state between sleeping and waking"' (*C*, 99). Phillis falls to the ground crying, '"my head! my head!"'. The narrator continues: 'We raised her up; her colour had strangely darkened; she was insensible'. She remains 'unconscious', is 'slightly convulsed' (*CP*, 309), and later develops more 'unfavourable' symptoms (*CP*, 311). Allowing for the novelist's difficulty in having Matty recollect events concerning the flight of poor Peter had she, like Phillis, become quite unconscious, the illnesses of Matty and Phillis are similar with some loss of consciousness as the most striking, and arguably symbolic, symptom. Margaret Hale, in *North and South*, loses consciousness after telling the lie which protects her brother who has returned to his exile, whereas her mother, who suffers great pain, does not lose consciousness;[16] nor does Miss Brown in *Cranford* become unconscious from her 'incurable complaint'.

How is one to read Elizabeth Gaskell's deployment of loss of consciousness as a reaction to emotional trauma? A common contributing cause of the shocks received by Matty, Phillis and Margaret Hale is loss of a male, either suitor or brother, not by death but by a departure in which the male has exercised his unhindered freedom of travel. In contrast the deserted female lacks, for one reason or another, the power to follow and reacts as though she had indeed lost consciousness through beating her head against her prison walls. More conservatively, unconsciousness seems to represent the extremity of withdrawal. The notorious internal contradictions in *Cranford* make it uncertain whether Matty suffered two emotional illnesses or one: the illness consequent upon Peter's flight is stated with some detail; the cause of the other, if it is another, is only by the inference of the narrator attributed to the dismissal of her suitor. If the contest between the Rector and Peter is regarded as a simulacrum of the unutterable contest between the Rector and young Holbrook, the precipitating causes of the described illnesses of Matty and Phillis are loss of lover and sexual closure. Marriage is denied to each of them at the close of each tale, but whereas Matty's life is confined to Cranford Phillis's recovery is achieved through a conventional change of scene: 'Only for a short time, Paul. Then — we will go back to the peace of the old days. I know we shall; I can, and I will!' (*CP*, 317)

This is an unsatisfactory ending. Clocks drive forward without regard to human maturity, yet even thus Phillis has learned a little: her emphatic statement of the power of will marks her recovery from the physical inertia and emotional withdrawal which followed her illness. *Cranford* and *Cousin Phillis*, however, are both concerned with societies which are being overtaken by industrial change and both works deny the possibility of keeping the old days untouched. Turning to a letter in which Elizabeth Gaskell gives a résumé of a dénouement of *Cousin Phillis* extending beyond that which was published enables a reading which is more satisfying, affirming female access to pastoral space and androgynous control of fertility.

Composition of the novella was not complete when publication began, as a letter dated 10 December [1863] from Elizabeth Gaskell to George Smith, editor of the *Cornhill*, shows.[17] At this time the third serial part had been despatched to Smith and he had written in terms which made her uncertain of how much space he would allow for the conclusion of the novella. Her letter summarizes alternative endings, one being only 'a few lines in addition to the Proofs'. Her summary of her preferred ending, the 'two more nos in [her] head', extends beyond the published ending of the fourth part. She describes a scene 'years after' during a typhus epidemic, which would be developed as the final recollection of the narrator, Paul:

> I find her making practical use of the knowledge she had learned from Holdsworth and, with the help of common labourers, levelling & draining the undrained village — a child (orphaned by the fever) in her arms another plucking at her gown — we hear afterwards that she has adopted these to be her own.

This scene, which denies Phillis the conventionally normal future of the Victorian heroine with a husband and children of her own and which, in its narrative strategy, denies the convention of marriage as closure, might have made a fifth number showing a strong and outgoing woman rather than one timid and confined like Miss Matty. Phillis uses skills learnt from her farmer-father and her engineer-lover and exercises them in public open space. No code of gentility prevents her from engaging in men's work in the

fields; she does not fear damp and dirt like Miss Matty; indeed, she
is fulfilling one of the tasks of the cautious farmer of the *Georgics*:

> ...makes
> A gravel sump to collect and drain the standing damp,
> Especially if in the doubtful months the river has
> flooded
> And covered the water-meadows with a film of mud
> So that the moisture steams in a warm mist up from
> the bottoms.
>
> [I, 113–118]

Here Virgil hints at the uncertain months, the months which
bring the destructive storms. Minister Holman, who was alert to
weather warnings but blind to warnings of emotional events, is
surpassed by his daughter Phillis whose insight unifies physical
and agricultural warnings and tasks with responsiveness to
human needs. In an even more resounding victory over the
sterility which her lover's desertion might have imposed upon
her she gathers children to herself in a trope which affirms that
the absent or deserting male cannot deny creative power to the
female and thus avenges Miss Matty's unfulfilled longing for a
child. The picture is not of Phillis achieving two separate roles as
farmer-engineer and as guardian of children but rather of a
woman of total regenerative and creative power which is both
given to and taken from the pastoral.

Cranford's documentary precursor, 'The Last Generation in
England', states its purpose unambiguously: 'to put upon record
some of the details of country town life' where 'the phases of
society are rapidly changing'.[18] *Cranford* itself is a volatile text,
uncertain whether women benefit or suffer from these changes.
Cousin Phillis also deals with a society which is passed or
passing but appears to say that although women are still at the
mercy of a phallocracy and remain more confined than men, the
pastoral offers them understanding of the future, larger spaces,
and undeniable power and fertility.

1   J.A.V. Chapple and Arthur Pollard, eds, *The Letters of Mrs Gaskell* (Manchester: Manchester University Press, 1966) p. 748.

2   Chapple and Pollard, p. 174. In *Household Words*, 13 December 1851, pp. 265–274; 3 January 1852, pp. 349–357.

3   Dated by the present writer as [21] December. Further details may be found in Dorothy W. Collin, 'The Composition and Publication of Elizabeth Gaskell's *Cranford*', *BJRULM*, vol. 69 (Autumn 1986), pp. 59–95.

4   London: Chapman and Hall, 1853. Page references in this essay are to Elizabeth Gaskell, *Cranford/Cousin Phillis*, ed. Peter Keating (Harmondsworth: Penguin, 1986), and are given within the text in the form (*C*, 49) for *Cranford* and (*CP*, 233) for *Cousin Phillis*.

5   *Cornhill Magazine*, November 1863, pp. 619–635; December 1863, pp. 688–706; January 1864, pp. 51–65; February 1864, pp. 187–209.

6   Martin Dodsworth, 'Women without Men at Cranford', *Essays in Criticism*, vol. 13 (April 1963), pp. 132–145, is a milestone in *Cranford* criticism. *Cranford* and *Cousin Phillis* are perceptively discussed in S. Hunter, *Victorian Idyllic Fiction: Pastoral Strategies* (London: Macmillan, 1984).

7   Dickens substituted references to Hood's poems for references to his own fiction for publication in his own magazine. This essay discusses the novelist's preferred text as published in 1853; Captain Brown's reading at the November party 'out of this month's number' (*C*, 47) of *The Pickwick Papers* is from part XIII, published April 1837; the final double part was published in November 1837.

8   Published 1843.

9   *Household Words*, 13 March 1852, pp. 588–597.

10 'Friends in Need, at Cranford', *Household Words*, 7 May 1853, pp. 220–227.

11 'A Happy Return to Cranford', *Household Words*, 21 May 1853, pp. 277–285.

12 *Household Words*, 2 April 1853, pp. 108–115; 7 May 1853, pp. 220–227.

13 *Georgics*, I, ll. 289–290:

> By night it's best to mow light stubble, by night a meadow
> That's parched, for a clammy moisture is always present at
> night-time.

All translations from the *Georgics* are from *Virgil: The Eclogues; The Georgics*, trans. C. Day Lewis, introduction and notes by R.O.A.M. Lyne (Oxford: Oxford University Press, 1983).

14 *Georgics*, I, ll. 311–334, and particularly ll. 316–321:

> Well, often I've seen a farmer lead into his golden fields
> The reapers and begin to cut the frail-stalkes barley,

> And winds arise that moment, starting a free for all,
> Tearing up by the roots whole swathes of heavy corn
> And hurling them high up in the air: with gusts black as a
>   hurricane
> The storm sent flimsy blades and stubble flying before it.

15   *Georgics*, I, ll. 299–301:

> Plough and sow in the warm months, in your shirt-sleeves.
> Winter's an off time
> For farmers.

16   Elizabeth Gaskell, *North and South* (Harmondsworth: Penguin, 1970), ch. 34, p. 346; ch. 16, p. 171.

17   National Library of Scotland, MS Acc. 6713, Box 2/4; published J.A.V. Chapple, 'Elizabeth Gaskell: Two Unpublished Letters to George Smith', *Études Anglaises*, T.XXXIII (1980), pp. 183–187 (183–184).

18   Published in *Sartain's Union Magazine of Literature and Art*, July 1849, pp. 45–48.

'LOVE'S CITADEL UNMANN'D': VICTORIAN WOMEN'S LOVE POETRY

HILARY FRASER

THE project of recovering the rich tradition of women's poetry which has for centuries transgressed, appropriated, colluded with, and been occluded by the hegemonic male poetic tradition has for some years now been under way. Modern female poets now have access to those elusive 'grandmothers' that Elizabeth Barrett Browning could not find in her own literary heritage. Several excellent anthologies of women's poetry have appeared and new editions of less well known female poets are currently in preparation. In the area of nineteenth-century women's poetry, critics such as Isobel Armstrong, Nina Auerbach, Sandra Gilbert, Susan Gubar, Margaret Homans, Cora Kaplan, Angela Leighton and Dolores Rosenblum have offered characteristically intelligent feminist critiques which explore the ways in which women have variously subverted or negotiated with male conventions and intervened as speaking subjects in a male tradition which had them typecast as silent objects of desire and inspirational muse. Not surprisingly, it is the radical texts, such as Elizabeth Barrett Browning's *Aurora Leigh* and Christina Rossetti's *Goblin Market*, which have appealed to most feminist critics and which have been most vigorously taken up. Women's love poetry, like women's devotional poetry, has been relatively neglected, and does not at first appear to lend itself so readily to feminist analysis.

In a perceptive article published over a decade ago, Dorothy Mermin addressed the problem of the 'embarrassed reader' of Browning's *Sonnets from the Portuguese*,[1] opening the way for a feminist reappraisal of Victorian women's love poetry, but this has yet to happen, although Angela Leighton's book *Victorian Women Poets: Writing Against the Heart* (1992) includes some fine discussions of excellent examples of the genre as part of her brilliant larger study. But most feminist critics fight shy of approaching the heterosexual love poetry of nineteenth-century women. Are we still embarrassed readers of poems like Browning's 'How do I love thee? Let me count the ways'? Or do we still feel the need to dissociate ourselves from the romanticizing, sexually partisan and deeply ideological literary criticism of her work which predominated from the turn of the century until recently and which privileges *Sonnets from the Portuguese* over her radical social and political poetry for all the wrong patriarchal reasons? Or is it simply that a generation brought up on Dorothy Parker ('And love is a thing that can never go wrong;/And I am Marie of Roumania') feels uncomfortable with the sentiments of a poem like, say, Christina Rossetti's 'My heart is like a singing bird', which, for all Woolf's sense of the ludicrousness of the thought of women humming it at luncheon parties before the war, nevertheless 'excites one', she says in *A Room of One's Own*, 'to such abandonment, such rapture', because 'it celebrates some feeling that one used to have (at luncheon parties before the war perhaps)'?[2] There are certainly very few Victorian women represented in the recently published *Virago Book of Love Poetry*. And yet it seems to me important that we attend to Victorian women's love poetry, not only because they wrote so much of it, but because, as Ann Rosalind Jones points out in her book on women's love lyric in sixteenth-century Europe, 'love poetry centralizes socio-sexual differences as no other literary mode does', because the speaker in erotic poetry is always marked by gender. As she argues:

> If women are disempowered by their placement in a
> visual and symbolic order structured around men's
> fantasies, and if worldly as well as verbal power is
> always at stake in reigning love discourses, then a
> woman love poet is certain to disarticulate and remobil-
> ize the sexual economy of her culture.[3]

I want to begin my examination of how the Victorian
woman love poet does this by looking at some of the best
known and boldest examples of the kind of women's poetry
which explicitly challenges and appropriates the male tradition,
sanctioned and fathered by Dante and Petrarch, from which the
female poet is excluded. It was in defiance of that poetic
tradition as well as of the social and sexual mores of her own
day that Christina Rossetti conceived her brilliantly subversive
sonnet sequence, *Monna Innominata*.[4] In a brief prelude to the
fourteen-sonnet sequence, Rossetti contextualizes her own poetic
enterprise. Beatrice and Laura, she says, 'have come down to us
resplendent with charms' (if 'scant of attractiveness'), but what of
that 'bevy of unnamed ladies "donne innominate" sung by a
school of less conspicuous poets', and might not the ladies who
were sung have themselves had poetic talent?

> one can imagine many a lady as sharing her lover's
> poetic aptitude...Had such a lady spoken for herself,
> the portrait left us might have appeared more tender,
> if less dignified, than any drawn even by a devoted
> friend.[5]

Rossetti resurrects such a 'donna innominata' and enables her to
speak across the centuries. The intertextual complexities of the
sequence are fascinating. First of all, the poem both takes as its
subject Italian Renaissance love poetry and formally models
itself on the traditional sonnet sequence. Epigraphs from Dante
and Petrarch appear at the head of each of the fourteen sonnets
in the sequence, and the author's knowledge of early Italian
poetry informs the whole poem. However, the female poet is

well aware of the sexual politics of the centuries-old sonnet tradition, and she deliberately trespasses on a male domain by authoring a sonnet sequence herself and by speaking from the position of the woman, conventionally the silent object of the male poet's desire.

Throughout *Monna Innominata*, Rossetti invokes her illustrious poetic predecessors only to contest or undercut them. The epigraph to Sonnet II, for instance, from Petrarch, 'Ricorro al tempo ch'io vi vidi prima', conjures for the reader the poet's traditional celebration of his dearly recalled first meeting with his lady, yet the sonnet opens

> I wish I could remember that first day,
> First hour, first moment of your meeting me...

and the sestet again begins, 'If only I could recollect it'.[6] Elsewhere, the epigraphs point up the contrast between the fame of the poets whose words are quoted and the obscurity of the women who cannot speak in their own voice across time. After quotations from Dante and Petrarch ('"Vien dietro a me e lascia dir le genti." Dante. "Contando i casi della vita nostra." Petrarca.') follow the lines

> Many in aftertimes will say of you
> 'He loved her' — while of me what will they say?
> [Sonnet XI][7]

In Sonnet V, the speaker refers to the traditional elevation of the man to a state of perfection through his noble love of a woman, then shifts her perspective in the sestet:

> So much for you; but what for me, dear friend?
> To love you without stint and all I can
> Today, tomorrow, world without an end;
> To love you much and yet to love you more,
> As Jordan at his flood sweeps either shore;
> Since woman is the helpmeet made for man.[8]

In Sonnet VII, she demands equality in love, and an equal right to speak her love:

> 'Love me, for I love you' — and answer me,
> 'Love me, for I love you' — so shall we stand
> As happy equals in the flowering land
> Of love, that knows not a dividing sea.[9]

In this way only, to quote Rossetti out of context, is 'love's citadel unmann'd' (Sonnet VII)[10] and woman empowered as both lover and love poet.

In her preface to *Monna Innominata*, Rossetti speculates

> had the Great Poetess of our own day and nation only been unhappy instead of happy, her circum-stances would have invited her to bequeath to us, in lieu of the 'Portuguese Sonnets,' an inimitable 'donna innominata' drawn not from fancy but from feeling, and worthy to occupy a niche beside Beatrice and Laura.[11]

Elizabeth Barrett Browning's *Sonnets from the Portuguese* certainly deviates from tradition in celebrating a love that is happy and fulfilled, and to this extent it is also unlike Rossetti's sequence. And yet there are clearly important parallels between what these two poets attempt in the face of a poetic tradition which is overwhelmingly male.[12]

It is not insignificant that the fictional male lovers who are addressed in their poems are themselves poets, and whilst it is of course true that Robert Browning *was* a poet, Elizabeth Barrett had in an earlier dramatic monologue, like Rossetti, given a male poet's silent lover a poetic voice in a way that reveals her similarly acute consciousness of the sexual politics of love poetry. The speaker in the poem 'Catarina to Camoens'[13] is not a 'donna innominata' but a woman, like Beatrice and Laura, whose beauty inspired the love of a Renaissance poet. Camoens's poem on the sweetness of her eyes is poignantly and ironically referred to throughout Catarina's poem, composed as she lies 'dying in his absence abroad'. The fact that her lover is a poet, with an assured place in a male tradition, is crucial to this poem, as it is in the case of *Monna Innominata* and *Sonnets from the Portuguese*. In the former, following the epigraphs to Sonnet IV ('"Poca favilla gran fiamma seconda" — Dante. "Ogni altra Cosa, ogni pensier va fore,/A sol ivi con voi rimansi amore" — Petrarca.'), the speaker states

> I loved you first: but afterwards your love
> Outsoaring mine, sang such a loftier song
> As drowned the friendly cooings of my dove...

and asks, 'Which owes the other most?'.[14] In *Sonnets from the Portuguese*, the male object of love is depicted as 'My poet', 'chief musician', 'Most gracious singer of high poems'.[15] Both women are apparently self-deprecating about their poetry, and both refer to the silence that is traditionally the woman's lot: 'the silence of my womanhood', 'A silent heart whose silence loves and longs'.[16] And yet Browning, like Rossetti, glories in the evident power of her own poetic voice to count the ways she loves:

> ...And when I say at need
> *I love thee*...mark!...*I love thee* — in thy sight
> I stand transfigured, glorified aright,
> With conscience of the new rays that proceed
> Out of my face toward thine.
>
> [Sonnet X][17]

Through her own utterance, she transforms herself into the heroine of a courtly romance. The language deliberately recalls Beatrice, Laura, and the other silent ladies of Renaissance tradition, but this woman is empowered by her pen: she has constructed herself in this poem, is the speaking subject as well as the object of desire, the mistress of her situation, not merely the mistress and muse of a male poet.

Another woman who draws attention to the fact that she is a female poet addressing a male poet is Alice Meynell. Two of her poems, 'The Moon to the Sun' and 'The Spring to the Summer', are subtitled 'The Poet sings to her Poet'. In the former, she addresses her poet-love, the sun to her moon, as 'my secret glory-giver!' but ends the poem with a powerful claim for her own creativity:

Yet to earth which thou forsakest
I have made thee fair all night,
Day all night.[18]

The poet addressed in 'The Spring to the Summer' may
not be male, for this is a love poem for 'A Poet of the time to be'
who will inherit her lyre. The interesting thing about this poem
is that it makes the female poet the source of a poetic tradition:
'thy thoughts unfold from me', she maintains, 'And I have set thy
paths, I guide/Thy blossoms on the wild hillside'.[19] Meynell's
female personas are confident of their power to speak, and it is
the male addressees of her love poems who are associated with
silence. Her poem 'To the Beloved' begins:

Oh, not more subtly silence strays
Amongst the winds, between the voices,
Mingling alike with pensive lays,
And with the music that rejoices,
Than thou are present in my days.

My silence, life returns to thee
In all the pauses of her breath.
Hush back to rest the melody
That out of thee awakeneth;
And thou, wake ever, wake for me!

Thou art like silence all unvexed,
Though wild words part my soul from thee.
Thou art like silence unperplexed,
A secret and a mystery
Between one footfall and the next.[20]

In her lament 'To the Beloved Dead', the beloved becomes
'Thou silent song, thou ever voiceless rhyme', whilst in 'Regrets'
he is a silent empty pool waiting to be filled up by the full tide
of her love:

I would the day might come, so waited for,
So patiently besought,

When I, returning, should fill up once more
Thy desolated thought;

And fill thy loneliness that lies apart
In still, persistent pain.
Shall I content thee, O thou broken heart,
As the tide comes again,

And brims the little sea-shore lakes, and sets
Seaweeds afloat, and fills
The silent pools, rivers and rivulets
Among the inland hills?[21]

In this poem, it is the speaking woman who is agent, the broken-hearted male who passively waits to be replenished by her love, usurping the role conventionally assigned to the woman in so much Victorian poetry and painting.

Interestingly, Meynell herself (who, for a period when she bore eight children, edited several periodicals and contributed to numerous journals, wrote no poetry) was celebrated by the two male poets who adored her precisely for her silence. Both Francis Thompson and Coventry Patmore are really happier with the idea of the silenced female poet, of woman as herself a poem. Thompson wrote, 'Yea, in this silent interspace,/God set His poems in thy face!', while Patmore, typically, elaborates the idea further:

A girl, you sang, to listening fame,
    The grave that life might be,
And ceased when you yourself became
    The fulfilled prophecy.
Now all your mild and silent days
    Are each a lyric fact,
Your pretty, kind, quick-hearted ways
    Sweet epigrams in act.
To me you leave the commoner tongue,
    With pride, gaily confessed,
Of being, hence, sole theme of song
    To him who sings the best.[22]

And yet, throughout her poetry, Meynell alludes to and significantly modifies the poetic tradition which figures woman as the love object constructed and defined by the male poet. Her sonnet 'The Garden', for instance, draws on the convention epitomized by Thomas Campion's song 'There is a garden in her face/Where roses and white lilies grow' of comparing the woman to a garden (with all its associations with Eden and the Hesperides), in a way that at first seems orthodox, but finally subverts that tradition quite radically:

> My heart shall be thy garden. Come, my own,
> Into thy garden; thine be happy hours
> Among my fairest thoughts, my tallest flowers,
> From root to crowning petal thine alone.
> Thine is the place from where the seeds are sown
> Up to the sky enclosed, with all its showers.
> But ah, the birds, the birds! Who shall build bowers
> To keep these thine? O friend, the birds have flown.
>
> For as these come and go, and quit our pine
> To follow the sweet season, or, new-comers,
> Sing one song only from our alder-trees,
> My heart has thoughts, which, though thine eyes
>   hold mine,
> Flit to the silent world and other summers,
> With wings that dip beyond the silver seas.[23]

The woman's imagination enables her to escape from the 'hortus conclusus' within which such myths would contain her. Such refusal to be circumscribed by masculine prescription characterizes all Meynell's representations of the female poetic imagination and informs her reworking of other myths. And so in her poem 'Pygmalion: The Poet to his Poetry', Pygmalion wonders of his sculptured creation, somewhat uneasily, 'How do I know what the mouth will say', and concedes:

> I know not what the voice will sing.
> I only made the quiet breast,
> And white throat with much labouring.

I only wrought and thought my best,
And lo, a new voice shall out-ring.[24]

Meynell's own voice sings and out-rings nowhere more resoundingly than in her love poetry, even when that poetry tells of how the loss of love renders the female poet inarticulate, as in the sonnet 'A Shattered Lute':

I touched the heart that loved me as a player
Touches a lyre. Content with my poor skill,
No touch save mine knew my beloved (and still
I thought at times: Is there no sweet lost air
Old loves could wake in him, I cannot share?).
O he alone, alone could so fulfil
My thoughts in sound to the measure of my will.
He is gone, and silence takes me unaware.

The songs I knew not he resumes, set free
From my constraining love, alas for me!
His part in our tune goes with him; my part
Is locked in me for ever; I stand as mute
As one with vigorous music in his heart
Whose fingers stray upon a shattered lute.[25]

Love is so closely identified with its own articulation in the love poetry of Victorian women staking their claim to speak that silence constitutes a kind of failure. The speaker in Louisa S. Guggenberger's 'Love and Language' berates her incommunicative lover:

Love that is alone with love
Makes solitudes of throngs;
Then why not songs of silences, —
Sweet silences of songs?

Parts need words: the perfect whole
Is silent as the dead;
When I offered you my soul
Heard you what I *said*?[26]

Her urgent insistence upon her own voice speaking in this short, powerful poem is doubly stressed by the critical metrical placement of the emphatic '*said*'. It is a terse and ironic statement of her frustration, and of her resistance to the equation of perfect harmony in love with silence. 'Parts need words': if she is to have a part in this love relationship she must have the capacity to speak and must equally be heard. The love and language of the title are crucially interconnected.

Very often in Victorian women's poetry, the declaration of love is also a declaration of poetic ambition. Charlotte Brontë's poem 'Master and Pupil' not only functions in *The Professor* as a plot device, informing William Crimsworth that the plain young woman of whom he had just asked himself 'what had she to do with love?' and concluded ' "Nothing," was the answer of her own sad though gentle countenance; it seemed to say "I must cultivate fortitude and cling to poetry..." ' was in fact passionately in love with him. It is also the occasion for the revelation of Frances Henri's poetic aspirations, for in it she constructs a scenario in which not only is her love for her 'master' reciprocated but also the highest poetic accolade is gained:

> At last our school ranks took their ground,
> The hard-fought field I won;
> The prize, a laurel-wreath, was bound
> My throbbing forehead on.
>
> Low at my master's knee I bent,
> The offered crown to meet;
> Its green leaves through my temples sent
> A thrill as wild as sweet.
>
> The strong pulse of Ambition struck
> In every vein I owned;
> At the same instant, bleeding broke
> A secret, inward wound.[27]

Although this poem is given to a fictional heroine, an earlier version of it appears in an exercise book used by

Charlotte Brontë in Brussels in 1843. It is well known that *The Professor*, like *Villette*, incorporates fictionalized aspects of her own experiences in Brussels, including her attraction for Constantin Heger. 'Master and Pupil' might well be seen, like the novel in which it appears, as, in Margaret Smith's words, 'a transcript of the author's experience rather pathetically brought to a happy conclusion by a piece of wish-fulfilment'.[28] Indeed, it is a common fate of women's love poetry that it is assumed to be personal and autobiographical. Dorothy Mermin points out that even Christina Rossetti, in a preface implicitly disavowing any autobiographical element in *Monna Innominata*, takes it for granted that Elizabeth Barrett Browning's *Sonnets from the Portuguese* constitutes a sincere, spontaneous and true testimony of her love for Robert.[29] But Christina Rossetti herself is not immune from the assumption that her poetry is based on her own life experiences (we all know of her scrupulous rejection of James Collinson and Charles Cayley) and neither are the other Brontë sisters, or indeed *any* Victorian women writers of love poetry, even those of whom no biographical details are known. This is arguably precisely because women's love poetry has no established universalizing conventions upon which to draw, and therefore appears to come straight from the heart.

Women poets adopt various strategies in an endeavour to displace the personal in their love poetry. I have already referred to some of the ways in which they allude to and subvert male traditions and rewrite male myths. Other ways of circumventing the autobiographical implications of the genre are to write in a ballad-like narrative mode (as Charlotte Brontë does, for instance, in 'Lord Edward and his Bride' and as Augusta Webster does in her early experiments in the ballad romance, 'Blanche Lisle' and 'Lilian Gray'), or in dialogue form (as Browning does in 'Lord Walter's Wife'), or in a dramatic mode, adopting fictional or historical personae (the Brontë sisters' Gondal poems are an example, Augusta Webster's dramatic monologues are another). Particularly interesting are those female-authored love poems that are written in a male voice. In some cases, parallels may be drawn with the strategy adopted by many Victorian women of publishing under a male pseudonym, although the most spectacular example among poets, 'Michael Field', whose work was a product of the collaboration of Katherine Bradley and her niece Edith Cooper, spoke in a most emphatically female, Sapphic voice. Two novelists who wrote under male pseudonyms, Charlotte Brontë and George Eliot, also wrote love poems in the voice of their fictional heroes, respectively 'Rochester's Song to Jane Eyre' and 'Will Ladislaw's Song'. On the whole, Eliot was not drawn to the genre. She did, though, write a poem called 'How Lisa Loved the King', based on a story by Boccaccio, which throws light on woman's place in the tradition. The poem tells of a young woman named Lisa, living 'in Dante's time', who dreamt of loving 'some hero noble, beauteous, great,/Who would live stories worthy to narrate', and fell for the king. She longed to speak her love, but was debarred by her sex from so doing, for

> Modest maidens shrank
> From telling love that fed on selfish hope;
> But love, as hopeless as the shattering song
> Wailed for loved beings who have joined the throng
> Of mighty dead ones...Nay, but she was weak —
> Knew only prayers and ballads — could not speak
> With eloquence save what dumb creatures have,
> That with small cries and touches small boons crave.

And so, 'inward-wailing' with 'songs unsung', she has no means of communicating her love: 'my dumb love-pang is lone,/ Prisoned as topaz-beam within a rough-garbed stone'. She falls into a decline, and seems certain to die, but then she hits upon a scheme. She summons a male singer to her bedside, and explains her dilemma to him:

> That death, her only hope, most bitter were,
> If when she died her love must perish too
> As songs unsung and thoughts unspoken do,
> Which else might live within another breast.

The singer goes to a poet friend, and asks him to write

...a canzon divinely sad,
Sinlessly passionate and meekly mad
With young despair, speaking a maiden's heart
Of fifteen summers.[30]

And so at the centre of this narrative poem written by a woman, from Boccaccio's story, about a maiden who has no means of speaking her own heart, is a love song performed and written by men who have both access to the literary conventions which are denied to the young woman herself and a right to speak of such things.

The gender of the voice in this love song is equivocal, as it is in a number of love poems in the period. Dora Greenwell's 'A Picture', for instance, is addressed to a woman, but the speaker's sex is unspecified:

It was in autumn that I met
Her whom I love; the sunflowers bold
Stood up like guards around her set,
And all the air with mignonette
Was warm within the garden old;
Beside her feet the marigold
Glowed star-like, and the sweet-pea sent
A sigh to follow as she went
Slowly adown the terrace; — there
I saw thee, oh my love! and thou wert fair.

She stood in the full noonday, unafraid,
As one beloved of sunlight, for awhile
She leant upon the timeworn balustrade;
The white clematis wooed her, and the clove
Hung all its burning heart upon her smile;
And on her cheek and in her eyes was love;
And on her lips that, like an opening rose,
Seemed parting some sweet secret to disclose,
The soul of all the summer lingered; — there
I saw thee, oh my love! and thou wert fair.[31]

Greenwell's erotic poem draws on traditional figurative

representations of female sexuality in this celebration of a woman's beauty (there is no tradition of celebrating the male body in heterosexual love poetry).

The gender of the speaker in Greenwell's poem is ambiguous, but there are numerous poems by women in which the persona is calculatedly male. Edith Nesbit's 'Among His Books', for instance, is spoken by one who, having been jilted, has retreated from love into his books, for

> They do not flatter, change, deny, deceive —
> Ah no — not they!
> The same editions which one night you leave
> You find next day.
>
> You don't find railway novels where you left
> Your Elzevirs!
> Your Aldines don't betray you — leave bereft
> Your lonely years.

But he confesses that his most precious book is a Book of Common Prayer, 'Because the names upon the fly-leaf there/Are mine and hers':

> It's a dead flower that meks it open so —
> Forget-me-not —
> The Marriage Service...well, my dear, you know
> Who first forgot.

The book recalls to him the flush of young love:

> Kisses? A certain yellow rose no doubt
> That porch still shows,
> Whenever I hear kisses talked about
> I smell that rose!

But it is in the end an ironic reminder:

> No — I don't blame you — since you only proved
> My choice unwise,
> And taught me books should trusted be and loved,
> Not lips and eyes!

And so I keep your book — your flower — to show
How much I care
For the dear memory of what, you know,
You never were.[32]

But there are further layers of irony in this poem, directed at the speaker himself, whose womanly ideal, it is strongly implied, is derived from books, which makes it entirely appropriate that he should feel more comfortable in the sterility of his library than with a real woman with lips and eyes. She never was, indeed, the woman he constructed her as: the 'happy and good' little woman, the pinnacle of whose existence was to accompany him to church, sing in the choir with him, and hold hands through sermons.

Edith Nesbit seems, nevertheless, not unsympathetic to her withdrawn and desiccated speaker, and, like Christina Rossetti, Elizabeth Barrett Browning, Charlotte Mew, and all three Brontë sisters, all of whom wrote poems from the male point of view, was clearly exercised by the notion of love as a construction upon which there are many perspectives. There are, however, some very distinctive poems which take a markedly more cynical view of the power politics of sexual love. Browning's 'A Man's Requirements' underlines the sexual inequities of the day by giving ten stanzas to a catalogue of male requirements —

Love me, Sweet, with all thou art,
Feeling, thinking, seeing;
Love me in the lightest part,
Love me in full being…

Through all hopes that keep us brave,
Farther off or nigher,
Love me for the house and grave,
And for something higher —

and concluding with the single stanza:

> Thus, if thou wilt prove me, Dear,
> Woman's love no fable,
> *I* will love *thee* — half a year —
> As a man is able.[33]

Charlotte Brontë presents a more sinister view again in her poem 'Gilbert', in which the male speaker reflects with sadistic satisfaction upon his former love's abasement to him:

> ...'She loved me more than life;
> And truly it was sweet
> To see so fair a woman kneel
> In bondage at my feet.
>
> There was a sort of quiet bliss
> To be so deeply loved,
> To gaze on trembling eagerness
> And sit myself unmoved;
> And when it pleased my pride to grant
> At last some rare caress,
> To feel the fever of that hand
> My fingers deigned to press...
>
> Her youth, her native energy,
> Her powers new-born and fresh —
> 'Twas these with Godhead sanctified
> My sensual frame of flesh.
> Yet, like a god did I descend
> At last to meet her love;
> And, like a god, I then withdrew
> To my own heaven above.'[34]

You will be pleased to hear that Elinor has her revenge, and that Gilbert comes to a bad end.

The male speaker in Emily Brontë's well-known poem 'The Prisoner' takes similarly sadistic pleasure in holding a woman in bondage. The captive, an angel in the house, with her face 'as soft and mild/As sculptured marble saint or slumbering unwean'd child', 'so sweet and fair', seems emblematic of the middle-class Victorian woman, imprisoned within her domestic stronghold by her 'master', whose 'voice is low, his aspect bland and kind/But hard as hardest flint, the soul that lurks behind'. The submissive wife is figured as captive to her husband's/master's desires. Freedom will come only with her death, and therefore she longs for death and welcomes the suffering that must precede it. The original final lines of the poem assert the justness of her masochistic embrace of suffering:

> Her cheek, her gleaming eye, declared that man had
>   given
> A sentence, unapproved, and overruled by heaven.

Brontë later added two further stanzas in which the male speaker confronts the dilemma of the despotic lover:

> ...ruth and selfish love, together striving, tore
> The heart all newly taught to pity and adore;
> If I should break the chain, I felt my bird would go;
> Yet I must break the chain, or seal the prisoner's
>   woe.[35]

The chains which bind a woman to her man are perceived in a more sympathetic light by Adelaide Anne Procter. In a poem entitled 'A Chain', she writes of 'The bond that links our souls together', and asks:

> Will it last through stormy weather?
> Will it moulder and decay
> As the long hours pass away?
> Will it stretch if fate divide us,
> When dark and weary hours have tried us?

— and begs 'Oh if it look too poor and slight/Let us break the links tonight'.[36] Nevertheless, a bond can easily become a kind of bondage. Her poem entitled 'Fidelis' begins:

> You have taken back the promise
> That you spoke so long ago;
> Taken back the heart you gave me —
> I must even let it go.

Where Love once has breathed, Pride dieth:
So I struggled, but in vain,
First to keep the links together,
Then to piece the broken chain.

But it might not be — so freely
All your friendship I restore,
And the heart that I had taken
As my own for evermore.

No shade of reproach shall touch you,
Dread no more a claim from me —
But I will not have you fancy
That I count myself as free.

I am bound by the old promise;
What can break that golden chain?[37]

Procter's love poems are all in a female voice, but they
take up many different positions on love, from the challenging
tone of 'True or False', which begins:

So you think you love me, do you?
Well, it may be so;

and ends, after dispelling some myths about love:

Tell me then, do you dare offer
This true love to me?...
Neither you nor I can answer;
We will — wait and see!

— to the poignancy of 'A Dead Past', in which the speaker begs
her lover, who has taken from her her present and her future, to
spare her past, which is figured as a shrouded corpse.[38]
    Victorian women were, then, by no means silent or of one
mind on the subject of love. It is fascinating to read love poems
by Elizabeth Siddal, for instance, having previously only had
access to Dante Gabriel Rossetti's extensive mythologization of
his love for her, and by Caroline Norton, whose marriage and

affairs were the subject of such intense public scrutiny. It is interesting to look at how women love poets expressed erotic desire in a culture that interdicted sexual passion in decent women. Sometimes it is transposed from the man in question to something inanimate. Alice Meynell, for instance, in her poem 'In Autumn', rolls around in the autumn leaves:

> I lie amongst you, and I kiss
> Your fragrance mouldering.
> O dead delights, is it such bliss,
> That tuneful Spring?
> Is love so sweet, that comes to this?
>
> Kiss me again as I kiss you;
> Kiss me again,
> For all your tuneful nights of dew,
> In this your time of rain,
> For all your kisses when Spring was new.[39]

Elsewhere, she articulates the erotic through dreams. In her sonnet entitled 'Renouncement', she begins the octave with the words 'I must not think of thee', but weakens in the sestet:

> But when sleep comes to close each difficult day,
> When night gives pause to the long watch I keep,
> And all my bonds I needs must loose apart,
> Must doff my will as raiment laid away, —
> With the first dream that comes with the first sleep
> I run, I run, I am gathered to thy heart.[40]

Both Charlotte Brontë and Christina Rossetti use sleep and dreams as occasions for erotic visitation. In the former's poem 'Watching and Wishing', a young man serenades his lover:

> Oh, would I were the crimson veil
> Above thy couch of snow,
> To dye that cheek so soft, so pale,
> With my reflected glow!

Oh, would I were the cord of gold
Whose tassel set with pearls
Just meets the silken covering's fold,
And rests upon thy curls.

Dishevelled in thy rosy sleep,
And shading soft thy dreams;
Across their bright and raven sweep
The golden tassel gleams![41]

In the latter's poem 'Echo', the female speaker invites her lover

Come to me in the silence of the night;
Come in the speaking silence of a dream;...

Come back to me in dreams, that I may give
Pulse for pulse, breath for breath:
Speak low, lean low,
As long ago, my love, how long ago.[42]

But another poet, Edith Nesbit, in her poem 'Villeggiature', brilliantly sends up the idea of the dream as a site of erotic encounters:

My window, framed in pear-tree bloom,
White-curtained shone, and softly lighted:
So, by the pear-tree, to my room
Your ghost last night climbed uninvited.

Your solid self, long leagues away,
Deep in dull books, had hardly missed me;
And yet you found this Romeo's way,
And through the blossom climbed and kissed me.

I watched the still and dewy lawn,
The pear-tree boughs hung white above you;
I listened to you till the dawn,
And half forgot I did not love you.

Oh, dear! what pretty things you said,
What pearls of song you threaded for me!
I did not — till your ghost had fled —
Remember how you always bore me![43]

The control of tone in this poem is superlative. Its lyrical opening conjures for us the speaker's white-draped window, through which she may escape into dream and her lover may enter her. But the symbolic moment of sexual penetration is comically undercut by the bathetic final line of the stanza. The poem achieves its effects by its multiple shifts between the woman's erotic fantasy of a romantic Romeo-lover and the pedantic reality of the man's 'solid self'. The imagined seduction is so much more satisfying than the actual sexual dynamics between them. The ghost-lover finally flees in fear of her sexuality, leaving the man who merely 'bores' her.

One does not expect to find women laughing about sexual matters in Victorian love poetry. In fact it is the *range* of women's experience that these poets seem so urgently to wish to articulate, particularly in those poems which are spoken by a woman. The very diversity of these women in love gives the lie to the monolithic myth of the angel in the house. They speak of their pain and their humiliation, of their desire and their anger, they pine and they jeer and they laugh at their lovers. In short, Victorian women poets make a virtue of necessity and, having no heterosexual female amatory tradition upon which to draw, they take advantage of the freedom this gives them to experiment with and subvert the male conventions which were not made for them and to create their own.

It is not until the end of the century, with the work of 'Michael Field', that they begin to draw on a female tradition of love poetry by recuperating for nineteenth-century women the work and the sexual/poetic ideals of Sappho. Katherine Bradley and Edith Cooper's first joint collection of poetry under their shared pseudonym, entitled *Long Ago* (1889), comprises translation and elaboration of Sapphic fragments, and their subsequent volumes of lyrics celebrate female sexuality with an openness previously unexplored in nineteenth-century women's poetry on the subject of heterosexual love, which is typically characterized by a repressed or displaced eroticism. As Angela Leighton argues, 'Michael Field's best poems are love poems', poems which celebrate Katherine Bradley's and Edith Cooper's love for each other, and which are 'cheerfully defiant both of the literary heritage of the heart and of the heterosexual bargains of the fall'. 'It is as if', Leighton suggests, 'these poems exist in an atmosphere altogether outside the moral and ideological structures of the age'.[44] In that they articulate a love that 'dare not speak its name', even in the 1890s, this is of course true. And yet the claims they make for woman as erotic agent are the claims, albeit more solidly voiced, of a host of other earlier nineteenth-century women who nominated themselves as poets and lovers. I'll finish by quoting one of Michael Field's poems which seems to me to sum up the aspirations of many Victorian women for sexual and poetic empowerment:

> How sweeter far it is to give
> Than just to rest in the receiving,
> Sweeter to sigh than be sighed over,
> Sweeter to deal the blow than bear the grievings,
> That girl will learn who dares become a lover.
>
> The songs she sings will have the glee,
> The laughter of the wind that looses
> Wing and breaks for a forest cover;
> Freedom of stream that slips its icy nooses
> Will be her freedom who becomes a lover.[45]

Acknowledgement: This essay builds on my discussion of the poetry of Christina Rossetti and Elizabeth Barrett Browning in The Victorians and Renaissance Italy *(Oxford, and Cambridge, Mass.: Blackwell, 1992), pp. 159–162.*

1   Dorothy Mermin, 'The Female Poet and the Embarrassed Reader: Elizabeth Barrett Browning's *Sonnets from the Portuguese*', *English Literary History*, vol. 48 (1981), pp. 351–367.

2   Virginia Woolf, *A Room of One's Own* (London, Toronto, Sydney, New York: Granada Publishing Ltd in Panther Books, 1977, reprint 1978), pp. 14–15.

3   Ann Rosalind Jones, *The Currency of Eros: Women's Love Lyric in Europe, 1540–1620* (Bloomington and Indianapolis: Indiana University Press, 1990), p. 7.

4   For an interesting discussion of *Monna Innominata,* see Antony H. Harrison, *Christina Rossetti in Context* (Chapel Hill: University of North Carolina Press, 1988), ch. 5; and Joan Rees, *The Poetry of Dante Gabriel Rossetti: Modes of Self-Expression* (Cambridge: Cambridge University Press, 1981), pp. 152–160.

5   *The Complete Poems of Christina Rossetti,* ed. R.W. Crump, 2 vols (Baton Rouge: Louisiana State University Press, 1979–86), vol. II, p. 86.

6   ibid., p. 87.

7   ibid., p. 91.

8   ibid., pp. 88–89.

9   ibid., p. 89.

10 ibid.

11 ibid., p. 86.

12 On this aspect of Elizabeth Barrett Browning's poetry, see Angela Leighton, *Elizabeth Barrett Browning* (Brighton: Harvester, 1986); Barbara Charlesworth Gelpi, '*Aurora Leigh:* The Vocation of the Woman Poet', *Victorian Poetry,* vol. 19, 1981, pp. 35–48; C. Kaplan, Introduction to E.B. Browning, *Aurora Leigh and Other Poems* (London: The Women's Press, 1978); Mermin, 'The Female Poet and the Embarrassed Reader: Elizabeth Barrett Browning's *Sonnets from the Portuguese'.*

13 *The Poetical Works of Elizabeth Barrett Browning* (London: Smith, Elder, & Co., 1897), pp. 274–276.

14 Rossetti, *Complete Poems,* vol. II, p. 88.

15 Browning, *Poetical Works,* pp. 315, 312.

16 Rossetti, *Complete Poems,* vol. II, p. 93.

17 Browning, *Poetical Works,* p. 314.

18 *The Poems of Alice Meynell* (London: Oxford University Press, 1940), p. 72.

19 ibid., p. 8.

20 ibid., p. 9.

21 ibid., pp. 12, 36.

22 *The Works of Francis Thompson,* 3 vols (London: Burnes Oates & Washbourne, 1925), vol. 1, p. 80; C. Patmore, 'Alicia's Silence', in Viola Meynell, *Alice Meynell: A Memoir* (London: Jonathan Cape, 1929), p. 117. Both poets cited in Angela Leighton, *Victorian Women Poets: Writing Against the Heart* (New York and London: Harvester Wheatsheaf, 1992), p. 251.

23   *The Poems of Alice Meynell*, p. 32.
24   ibid., p. 21.
25   ibid., p. 26.
26   Christopher Ricks, ed., *The New Oxford Book of Victorian Verse* (Oxford: Oxford University Press, 1990), p. 512.
27   Charlotte Brontë, *The Professor*, eds Margaret Smith and Herbert Rosengarten (Oxford: Oxford University Press, 1991), p. 200; *The Poems of Charlotte Brontë*, ed. Tom Winnifrith (Oxford: Blackwell, 1984), p. 238.
28   Brontë, *The Professor*, pp. xvii–xviii.
29   Mermin, p. 357.
30   George Eliot, *Collected Poems*, ed. Lucien Jenkins (London: Skoob Books, 1989), pp. 64, 66–67, 68, 69, 72, 73.
31   J.R. Watson, ed., *Everyman's Book of Victorian Verse* (London: Dent, 1982), p. 200.
32   Ricks, pp. 533–535.
33   Browning, *Poetical Works*, pp. 304–305.
34   Brontë, *Poems*, pp. 32–33.
35   *The Complete Poems of Emily Jane Brontë*, ed. Clement Shorter (London: Hodder and Stoughton, 1923), pp. 13–17.
36   Adelaide Anne Procter, *Legends and Lyrics* (London: George Bell and Sons, 1882), p. 103.
37   ibid., p. 123.
38   ibid., pp. 199–201, 30–31.
39   Meynell, *Poems*, p. 16.
40   ibid., p. 69.
41   Brontë, *Poems*, pp. 216–217.
42   Rossetti, *Complete Poems*, vol. I, p. 46.
43   Ricks, p. 537.
44   Leighton, *Victorian Women Poets*, p. 225.
45   *Underneath the Bough: A Book of Verses by Michael Field* (London: 1893), pp. 131–132. Quoted in Leighton, *Victorian Women Poets*, p. 226.

FIFTEEN SCENES TOWARDS A MELODRAMATICS OF HARDY

TIM DOLIN

A New Version of an Old Story Arranged as a Play for Mummers, in One Act, Requiring No Theatre or Scenery[1]

I. The two Thomases

> Like all new comers to a spot on which the past is deeply graven he heard that past announcing itself with an emphasis altogether unsuspected by, and even incredible to, the habitual residents.[2]

This is the tale of two Thomases. One, old and cantankerous, haunts the heath and woodland of an imaginary province; the other beams and rolls his eyes, and labours happily in the same ideal countryside not so very far away. Are Thomas Hardy and Thomas the Tank Engine such uneasy companions? Is it so difficult to imagine the celebrated author and the Fat Controller arguing over a halfpenny on a platform, or Thomas's crestfallen face and melancholy toot as he ferries some Hardyean hero to their doom? Is it so far-fetched to conceive of Hardy inventing the tragedy of a brightly polished engine that refuses to come out of a tunnel for fear of the rain spoiling its paint, and is bricked up as punishment? Unlikely or not, these two were our companions when we blundered across the on-ramp of the M3 at 6.00 a.m. on a Saturday morning in April. Demented from seventeen hours in a polished capsule called *City of Southampton*, we pointed our rental car, as bright and red as Thomas's friend James, down to Winchester — Wintoncester — the ancient capital of Wessex.

> I am traveling at the speed of time, along the Massachusetts Turnpike.[3]

At the speed of time, yes, but a speed that whispers ill-control. We had come to England, myself, Lucy and Larry, to visit this Wessex, or, at any rate, to visit a curious place — no place, really, because it was partly fiction and partly anticipation — that answered to Wessex. We were, like so many others before us, pursuing the ghosts of ghosts, pursuing them as far west as Lyonesse, and as far north as Christminster. Although, to be accurate, Larry was privately pursuing passions of his own — a passion for Duplo which would take us into every Woolworths in the South-West, but also a silent passion for his grandparents, his *Spot* video, his place. He was, you see, almost two and a half years old then, which explains the second Thomas, and explains too what happened. We had promised ourselves a great adventure, a twelve-week epic of family tourism. But it turned instead into a ridiculous fortnight of delirium and anger and disbelief. Well, what of it? Failed holidays may have their own redolence of shame and absurdity, but it was travel of a kind, and this is a traveller's tale of a kind. To have settled for a cautionary tale now would be churlish, wrong. In its place, I offer you a domestic form, part-melodrama, part-farce, part-something else.

II. Tales of family trips

The following scenes are postcards and performance items. Family journeys can begin as a succession of wonders, but only let scene upon scene fall in beside its unfamiliar neighbour like weary tourists in a bus queue (none of them speaking the same language, but all of them alike) and it shapes itself into a single narrative, each scene imprinted on the bottom right-hand corner with the date and the time, and shuffled into a comfortable sequence. Or this narrative can be resisted; the journey can be broken. Tourism is a theatrical spectacle, comfortable and dangerous, with its novelties repeated and repeated, ever more elaborately and operatically, and its procession of other lives safely rehearsed and abandoned. A double, treble, multiple bill. Or perhaps after all it can be truly melodramatic, involving us, binding us into its dramas of home, its excesses of the ordinary.

> The sentimental tourist...likes to be alone; to be
> original; to have (to himself, at least) the air of making
> discoveries.[4]

Tourism is debased travel, as melodrama is debased tragedy. Tourism, though, like melodrama, is unrealistic, it clears the space for an 'aesthetic transmutation between genres and modes — for a wielding of fantasy, spectacle and realism'.[5] It clears a space in which to indulge illicit emotions, sentimental attachments, illegitimate forms of expression; but also vicariously to appropriate other 'legitimate' experiences (exploration, discovery, originality, or less innocent atavistic gestures — conquest or colonization). Like melodramatic fantasy, tourism 'is fully political and really productive, it helps to produce particular desires, it helps to order social life...it transforms bourgeois culture into universal nature'.[6] As a pursuit of the family, it stages the exorcism of those monsters that threaten the familiar and the familial, and in this, like melodrama, it is openly ideological; indeed it dramatizes the confrontation of bourgeois ideology and its enemies. It is free from the cant of the authentic journey, that sneering distaste for the trooping barbarians which has been, at least since James, the rhetoric of the man who travels alone. Those latter-day pilgrims who so abhor the crass and their cameras (that is to say, you and me) ferry their Romantic clichés in a wide arc around our pusillanimous efforts to read (in English) the neatly packaged and paragraphed sites. They are that species of travel-writer that is always male, always independent, and (like the lonely middle-class boys that mope about youth hostels, bad-tempered and insolent and tired) always prescribing and complaining. The literary criticism of men, too, is so often written as though they were voices alone, unhindered by women and children, and unencumbered by Arthur Frommer, travellers' cheques, and obvious questions. A less obvious question might enquire into the subject-position of the man who is critic: the hermeneutic *mise-en-scène*, the critical spectacle, the *point de belle vue*.

III. The unfortunate consequence

> Make room, make room, my gallant boys,
> And give us space to rhyme;
> We've come to show Saint George's play,
> Upon this Christmas time.[7]

Throughout his life Hardy entertained a passion for the theatre. He was an enthusiastic supporter of the amateur Dorchester company 'The Hardy Players', who adapted a number of his novels for their theatre, and he wrote a handful of pieces for the stage.[8] But Hardy also publicly dismissed drama as low art, and finally only reconciled it with his own more elevated enterprise in the remarkable hybrid of poetry, fiction and theatre that is *The Dynasts*.[9] Significantly, however, his novels, stories and poems are all notably theatrical, drawing on a range of stage effects and dramatic modes: tragedy and comedy; the mummer's play and the pantomime; melodrama and farce.

> He remained at his Weymouth lodgings working at the MS. of *Desperate Remedies*, the melodramatic novel quite below the level of *The Poor Man and the Lady* which was the unfortunate consequence of Mr Meredith's advice to 'write a story with a plot.'[10]

Melodrama characteristically privileges narrative situation over character, the physical over the mental, and action over speech.[11] It presents 'extremes of action, farce, morality, character, and emotion in a framework of fast, short and rapidly changing scenes mounted with a maximum of sensation and scenic effect'. It presents too great a variety of dramatic situations within a rigid pattern and a 'changelessness of form and outlook'.[12] Hardy was an inveterate and accomplished melodramatist, and his work, more than that of almost any other major novelist since Dickens, displays the influence of Victorian popular theatre, and directly invokes a melodramatic mode of narrative situation reminiscent of the fiction of fifty years earlier.[13] These qualities are, in Peter Brooks's words, 'the indulgence of strong emotionalism; moral polarization and schematization; extreme states of being, situations, actions; overt villainy; persecution of the good, and final reward of virtue; inflated and extravagant expression; dark plottings, suspense, breathtaking peripety'.[14]

Hardy's melodramatic imagination has been discussed elsewhere,[15] and his reinstatement in the canon of works studied has been shadowed by the academic reclamation of melodrama:

> From the turn of the century through to the 60s melodrama has been conceived in predominantly pejorative terms. As drama it represented debased or failed tragedy, demarcating an empty period in nineteenth-century dramatic history; in fiction it constituted a fall from the seriousness and maturity of the realist novel, relegating authors such as Dickens and Hardy to the second rank.[16]

Following Peter Brooks, 'I am not making an argument for the direct influence of melodrama proper on [Hardy] (though this influence is in fact discernible), I am rather suggesting that perception of the melodramatic in [his] work can usefully be grounded and extended through reference to melodrama'.[17]

IV. The villainy of reading

> In some way the critic necessarily does violence to the text in the act of understanding it or of interpreting it.

> There is no innocent reading, no reading which leaves
> the work exactly as it is.[18]

Hardy is perhaps most explicitly melodramatic in the lifelong drama
he plays out with his readers. Is there a more theatrical gesture in
all his work than the moment when he renounces novel-writing,
crushed, as he would have it, by the villainy of the reading public?
This response to the publication of *Jude the Obscure* is only one of
several acts in a drama which is enacted at other more fundamental
levels throughout. Melodrama's 'typical figures', 'hyperbole,
antithesis, and oxymoron',[19] while they are invoked in dramatic
situations, plot developments, and variations on the stock
characters of the melodrama, also inform a set of complex
relationships in both the fiction and poetry between narrator-
speakers, protagonists, and readers. The implications of this vein of
melodrama for Hardy criticism, and for the kind of criticism which
Hardy's writing evinces, have not yet been fully explored.

> It is delusive to seek an interior conflict, the 'psy-
> chology of melodrama,' because melodrama exterior-
> izes conflict and psychic structure, producing instead
> what we might call the 'melodrama of psychology'.[20]

Melodrama explicitly appropriates works of all kinds from
high cultural modes — most notably, the tragedies of Shakespeare
— and *makes them melodramatic*. As Elaine Hadley has shown,
this is because the melodrama was forbidden to show performances of spoken plays.[21] It therefore replaced them with what
Brooks calls 'texts of muteness'. This parallel, of texts which speak
and are silent, which are original and paraphrastic, parallels the
relationship between a work and its reading. Melodrama makes
explicit the displacements entailed in the interpretive act of
reading, the act of making a book one's own, rearranging it,
excising parts of it, rewriting it. In the intersections of art and
melodrama, one discovers the reader as arch-plotter, as principal
actor in each culture's methodical melodramatizations of its
repertoires. I do not so much wish to read melodrama in Hardy as
read the melodrama of reading.

V. The melodramatic mode

> In the nineteenth century 'the modality was that of
> melodrama, the dialectic of two absolute forces in
> conflict towards a resolution — the "good" heroine
> against the "bad" villain, Malthus's struggle of
> population against the laws of subsistence, the class
> conflict of Worker against Capitalist of Marx and
> Engels, or Darwin's natural selection of species.'[22]

Melodrama is 'a central poetry'[23] and 'a central cultural paradigm
of the nineteenth century'.[24] It enacts 'the Naturalism of the
dream life',[25] the 'drama of recognition',[26] and the 'drama of
assertion'.[27] The '*melodramatic imagination* is a term that has
become useful for [situating this mode of representation in a
historical and social context and] for signifying this broader
approach. The term suggests that melodrama is a way of
perceiving the world, a response to specific social pressures
which can be located in literature and drama as well as in the
cinema.'[28] The melodramatic imagination is 'an extreme instance
of the Victorian historical imagination'.[29]

> In considering melodrama, we are in a sense talking
> about a form of theatricality which will underlie
> novelistic efforts at representation — which will pro-
> vide a model for the making of meaning in fictional
> dramatizations of existence. The nineteenth-century
> novel needs such a theatricality...to get its meaning
> across, to invest in its renderings of life a sense of
> memorability and significance.[30]

VI. The drama of signs

> [Pixerécourt] declared that he wrote plays for those
> who could not read, and developed a melodramatic
> artistry aimed entirely at an unlettered populace.[31]

In his long and densely argued account of the melodramatic
imagination in the nineteenth century, Peter Brooks proposes that

melodrama is a drama of signs, a mode through which modern Western culture registers and negotiates a 'moral occult', an abyss of inexpressible impulses left by the decline of the sacred. Christine Gledhill defines Brooks's project thus: 'melodrama feeds a demand for significances unavailable within the constraints of socially legitimate discourse but for which there is no other language'.[32] In Hardy the tension between silence and incessant talk is played out, most completely in the poems, as a curse of language. Here a large cast of speakers address their listeners, those dead, absent or indifferent: they are dramas of writing and reading, and the speaking protagonist frequently addresses himselves, those younger or older or elsewhere.

> Hardy's career as a writer was an indirect form of involvement, certainly, but far from annihilating things through forgetful silence it preserved them indefinitely by representing them in words. His work is a verbal repetition and prolonging of reality.[33]

In one sense, Hardy is the most unmelodramatic, because the most clear-sighted, of all artists. If melodrama is a fix, a comfort and an addiction which 'saves us from the openness and hazards of history',[34] then Hardy cannot be accused of indulging it. For, as Gillian Beer remarks, Hardy 'was willing to encounter the activity of forgetting, to let go origins, and to encompass oblivion — with pain certainly, but without panic'.[35] Melodrama indulges a safety in Manichean hyperbole, but Hardy indulges, as Hillis Miller points out, a safety in 'passivity, in secrecy, in self-effacement, in reticence, in the refusal of emotions and of their temptations to involvement'.[36] But it is by no means a complete refusal: 'there is a refusal of direct involvement, but there is also discovery of a means of indirect response. Hardy's preference for such responses may help to explain why he became a writer.'[37] Curiously, this recalls precisely the relationship between writing, politics and melodrama that Christina Crosby posits for Dickens in her chapter on melodrama in *The Ends of History*. Melodrama signals clearly its detachment from the world of power and political machinations, but the ideological energies it conveys are

madder and mushroom air. This is how *The Return of the Native*
begins, with the very earth exuding night. Driving out of Exeter
on the motorway, a blacker Egdon, punctuated with its strange
glowing barrows — the lights of sitting-rooms, the embers of
televisions — sweeps and sweeps past again.

'I travel as a phantom now': the double meaning of this
line[55] — the speaker become bodiless and become a phantom
present, removed from space and time — comes back to me in
the black of the car, with only the voice of our child screaming
and screaming, pressing us back out of this criminal dark,
towards Perth. The night is a sheet of paper with holes in it: see,
look at it, it's like a map with moving points of reference. How
can we be inside a map, be spectator and protagonist, guide and
fool, against the screen and inside the house?

The colours of the evening are fugitive, impermanent; all
is connected with memories, experiences foreign to this place.

Hardy's are the poems of one alone, one voice. Hardy is
childless. We scream back at Larry, we are not left alone with any
phantom.

XIII. Going back to the novels

> The fallacy of the theory of art as an unreal mirror
> image may be experienced most vividly, perhaps, by a
> visit to a place which has been transposed into a
> novel...It is rather to have a curious sense of double-
> ness which might be expressed by saying, '...To
> understand *Tess of the d'Urbervilles* I must go back to
> the novel and read it again with all my attention
> concentrated there. Only in those pages shall I ever
> encounter Marlott, Talbothays Dairy, or Welbridge
> House, or have a chance to understand Tess, Angel, or
> Alec.'[56]

The scene of Jude's first meeting with Sue in *Jude the Obscure*
poignantly foreshadows that novel's distractions of crosses,
crossed lovers, and missed crossings:

they both converged towards the cross-mark at the
same moment. Before either had reached it she called
out to him:
'I am not going to meet you just there, for the first
time in my life! Come further on.'
...They walked on in parallel lines, and, waiting
her pleasure, Jude watched till she showed signs of
closing in, when he did likewise...[57]

The novel's treatment of belief and its relinquishment, its
echoes in Jude's (which is to say the man's plot of the) *via
dolorosa*, the pattern of the lovers' meetings and departings, the
persistent failure of their voices to connect — all of these cross
and uncross in this first fateful encounter. There is something of
this pathos of the crossroads in the melodrama of literary
tourism. The fictional locations and their counterparts promise to
converge, but they pause and fail to recognize one another, they
refuse to meet under such a sign.

We knew no one, had nowhere we could go, it seemed,
but back. Silent and exhausted, we arrived in Plymouth, a city of
no particular importance either to Hardy or to us, with shabby
outer suburbs made from lots of villages mortared into one
mess of a place. It was about six o'clock in the morning. Almost
everything was flattened by the Germans during the war, it
turned out, which accounted for what seemed to be a nervous-
ness about any building being more visible than any other.
Plymouth does not so much rise out of the harbour as shrink
away from it in horror. It is an undulating city, buckled by its
own cowering, full of fear.

We sat foolishly in an empty pay-and-display for half an
hour, then booked into a day sleeper at a five star hotel. We
were led down a long passage with heavy carpet and blondwood
doors without handles that fell shut without a sound. We were
put next door to a room being guarded by two policemen. They
were protecting the witnesses to the sexual assault and murder
of a four year old boy in Plymouth the previous evening.
Nobody slept, we went to find a laundromat, but had given up
by the time we got to the front desk of the hotel, handing over

two bags full of dirty clothes to reception, left to see the sights and protect ourselves from (we were powerless against) the jibes and the looks of hatred levelled by a place sick from disgust at the parents of a two year old child who wouldn't stop screaming for twelve hours. At five in the afternoon we checked out, paid £50 for the empty room and £94 for the washing (individually boxed shirts and individually wrapped baby socks), and drove to London, sleeping in the motorway parking bays. Next day we flew home, back to the novels.

XIV. Letter

Yes I do perceive — I am the male reader who perceives, or valorizes — narratological conundrum and character-centred drive for coherence as incommensurable discursive-ideological positions, and positions which involve my being a man. Are you saying that this desire to sit within this contradiction is in fact in some way a reflection, a condition, of my masculinity? I do think that problems with masculinist ideology are evinced in a direct confrontation between a phenomenology of reading and an account of what I take to be certain textual ideologies. I felt this was my point in fact. The *Jude* reading tries to do what I am now (in between finishing my thesis) trying out more generally in relation to Hardy, and reading him, in Nancy Miller's phrase, as an 'as a': as a white[...]heterosexual man, now, here.[58] That is, Hardy seems to me to represent more fully and poignantly than anything else I have read at length precisely this contradiction between subjectivity and textual ideologies attendant upon interpretation.

The phenomenological model of 'unified consciousness' that Hillis Miller abandoned so freely seems to me to seize on what is so critical in Hardy, without ever really coming to terms with his own interpellation in the model of crossed narrators-speakers-protagonists-plots-readers. The reader emerges from the ideologies of the text, is interpellated and situated and addressed via those ideologies, while at the same time the whole universe of the book is fashioned by an informing critical consciousness in perfect intersubjective relation to author, character, etc., as they are to themselves. Miller's an old formalist at heart, I think, wanting more than anything for the texts to have stable meanings which critics can discover.

What I am trying to do is something which seems, as I think you infer, illegitimate. I want to elicit a drama of reading from the text that includes me as one of its players. Thus, the transgression occurs in both text and myself. Reading Thomas Hardy suggests to me the possibility that somewhere in there, *I* am, not as some kind of constructed reader, but as more. I keep thinking of this process as a melodrama of interpretation, a hyperbolic and unlikely drama of representation that involves the critic. It's a kind of melodrama which at the same time enacts in mask a whole cast of ideological positions re reading and inter-pretation — enacting them in a kind of antagonism, with contra-posing ideological conditions concealed and yet exposed. I think of it as melodrama because it is unsanctioned, illegitimate, lesser, in relation to 'legitimate' interpretation (whatever that is) and because it is at once vividly real and yet contrived; because melodrama, historically (and here the slippage between form and reading is most obvious), develops the idea of an ideologically heterogeneous audience and a hybrid and multiple text, which Hardy really exploits, I think; and because melodrama, and Hardy, present the same conflicts time and time again, but they are not lessened, but rather heightened, by repetition.

But then, perhaps my strategy of using melodrama as a cultural paradigm is itself a form of distancing, and is just another way of keeping the family out of the study.

XV. In the Dorset county museum

There is a vast, quiet hall in the Dorset county museum, a great pail of light. Inside, against the far wall, is its principal exhibit. Like everything else in the hall, it is a glass case filled with objects. But it is also an empty room. It has a darkened glass viewing point which is shielded by a partition, so that when we enter the hall it is as though there is a blank wall facing us at the far end. This glass case is Hardy's study. The bookcases are neatly filled, the chair seems never to have been sat in, so taut and resistant does its leather appear, and the desk is neatly arrayed with blotter, ink bottle, paper. And one other thing — a desk calendar, permanently fixed by Hardy on the date he met Emma Lavinia Gifford, 7 March 1870. Though I press my face to the glass as if to obliterate my importunate reflection, somehow I cannot feel as Adrienne Rich feels, hovering like an insect at the screen of 'that corner room, with its window-light, its potted plants and work table' in Amherst, Massachusetts.[59] Everything is dark and quiet and still. Vacant. 'Everything is destined to persist forever, unredeemed and unredeemable, in a terrifying space which swallows everything in its vacancy.'[60]

> And thus I visit bodiless
> Strange gloomy households often at odds[61]

For Lucy Dougan and Laurence Dolin.

1   Hardy's subtitle for *The Famous Tragedy of the Queen of Cornwall* (1923).

2   Thomas Hardy, *Jude the Obscure*, ed. P.N. Furbank, New Wessex Edition (paperback) (London: Macmillan, 1974), p. 105.

3   Adrienne Rich, 'Vesuvius at Home: The Power of Emily Dickinson', *Of Lies, Secrets, and Silence* (New York: Norton, 1979), p. 158.

4   Henry James, *Italian Hours* (New York: Grove Press, 1959), pp. 4–5.

5   Christine Gledhill, 'The Melodramatic Field: An Investigation', in Gledhill, ed., *Home is Where the Heart Is: Studies in Melodrama and the Woman's Film* (London: British Film, 1987), pp. 5–42.

6   Christina Crosby, *The Ends of History: Victorians and the Woman Question* (New York and London: Routledge, 1991), pp. 90–91.

7   Thomas Hardy, *The Return of the Native*, ed. Derwent May, New Wessex Edition (London: Macmillan, 1974), p. 152.

8   'The Hardy Players' produced versions of eleven works, eight of which were adapted from the prose by other hands. Apart from *The Dynasts*, Hardy wrote the following plays and dramatizations: *The Mistress of the Farm*, c. 1879–80 (from *Far from the Madding Crowd*); *Tess of the d'Urbervilles*, 1894–96 (substantially rewritten for the successful New York production in 1897, revised by Hardy for 'The Hardy Players', produced in London 1925 and 1929); *The Three Wayfarers*, 1893 (from 'The Three Strangers', 1883); *The Play of 'St. George'*, 1921 (adapted for the dramatization of *The Return of the Native*); *The Famous Tragedy of the Queen of Cornwall*, 1923.

9   Thomas Hardy to Florence Henniker, 1 December 1893 (R.L. Purdy and Michael Millgate, eds, *The Collected Letters of Thomas Hardy*, 7 vols [Oxford: Clarendon, 1978–88], vol. 2, p. 43): plays 'are distinctly a lower form of art: what is called a good play, receiving a column's notice in the morning papers, being distinctly in point of artistic feeling and exhibition of human nature no higher than a third rate novel. Consider what a poor novel "Mrs Tanqueray" wd make — I mean, how little originality it wd possess — that sort of thing having been done scores of years ago in fiction.' See also 'Why I Don't Write Plays' (1892), in Harold Orel, ed., *Thomas Hardy's Personal Writings: Prefaces, Literary Opinions, Reminiscences* (London: Macmillan, 1967), p. 139: 'in general, the novel affords scope for getting nearer to the heart and meaning of things than does a play'.

10   Thomas Hardy and Florence Emily Hardy, *The Life and Work of Thomas Hardy*, ed. Michael Millgate (London: Macmillan, 1989), p. 66.

11   See Michael R. Booth, *English Melodrama* (London: Herbert Jenkins, 1965), pp. 38–39.

12   ibid., p. 39.

13   Writing to Lord Lytton, Hardy confessed that had it not been for the peer's championing of cheap reprints, 'I for one should never as a boy have wept over his heroines' (Millgate and Purdy, vol. 1, p. 240).

14   Peter Brooks, *The Melodramatic Imagination: Balzac, Henry James, Melodrama, and the Mode of Excess* (New Haven and London: Yale University Press, 1976), pp. 11–12.

15   Penny Boumelha, *Thomas Hardy and Women: Sexual Ideology and Narrative Form* (Brighton: Harvester Press, 1982); and Joan Grundy, *Hardy and the Sister Arts* (London: Macmillan, 1979), pp. 82–103.

16   Gledhill, p. 5.

17   Brooks, p. 20.

18   J. Hillis Miller, *Thomas Hardy: Distance and Desire* (Cambridge, Mass.: The Belknap Press of Harvard University Press, 1970), p. viii.

19   Brooks, p. 40.

20   ibid., p. 35.

21 Elaine Hadley, 'The Old Price Wars: Melodramatizing the Public Sphere in Early Nineteenth-Century England', *PMLA*, vol. 107, no. 3, pp. 524–537.

22 Louis James (referring to Wylie Sypher), 'Was Jerrold's Black Ey'd Susan More Popular Than Wordsworth's Lucy?', in David Bradby, Louis James, and Bernard Sharrat, eds, *Performance and Politics in Popular Drama: Aspects of Popular Entertainment in Theatre, Film, and Television, 1800–1976* (Cambridge: Cambridge University Press, 1981), pp. 4–5.

23 Brooks, pp. 198 and passim.

24 Gledhill, p. 19.

25 Eric Bentley in Bradbury, James and Sharrat, p. 5.

26 Brooks, p. 27.

27 Louis James, p. 6.

28 Marcia Landy in Landy, ed., *Imitations of Life: A Reader on Film and Television Melodrama* (Detroit: Wayne State University Press, 1991), p. 31.

29 Crosby, p. 75.

30 Brooks, p. 13.

31 Booth, pp. 44–45.

32 Gledhill, p. 37.

33 Miller, p. 71.

34 Crosby, p. 109.

35 Gillian Beer, *Arguing With the Past: Essays in Narrative from Woolf to Sidney* (London: Routledge, 1989), p. 27.

36 Miller, p. 22.

37 ibid., p. 28.

38 Gledhill, p. 33.

39 Louis James, p. 3.

40 James J. Sosnoski, 'A Mindless Man-driven Theory Machine: Intellectuality, Sexuality, and the Institution of Criticism', in Robyn R. Warhol and Diane Price Herndl, eds, *Feminisms: An Anthology of Literary Theory and Criticism* (New Brunswick: Rutgers University Press, 1991), pp. 40–57.

41 Patrocinio P. Schweickart, 'Reading Ourselves: Toward a Feminist Theory of Reading', in Warhol and Herndl, p. 529.

42 Some recent attempts at a personal criticism by men have been only partly successful: Joseph Boone, in 'Of Me(n) and Feminism: Who(se) Is the Sex That Writes?' (Joseph A. Boone and Michael Cadden, eds, *Engendering Men: The Question of Male Feminist Criticism* [New York and London: Routledge, 1990], pp. 11–25), only nearly installs a 'me' into 'men'. Toril Moi observes that Boone's personal self apparently exists largely in the context of the MLA ('Men Against Patriarchy', in Linda Kauffman, ed., *Gender and Theory: Dialogues on*

Feminist Criticism [Oxford: Basil Blackwell, 1989], pp. 186–188). In Paul Smith's 'Vas' (Warhol and Herndl, pp. 1011–1029), the personal-neurological background to Freud remains just that — an anecdotal context which effectively only modifies the tone of the piece.

43   Rich, p. 160.

44   ibid., p. 158.

45   Louis James, p. 6.

46   Hadley, p. 532.

47   Miller, p. 152.

48   On the look in Hardy, see Miller, p. 119.

49   A careful reading of this alternation is undertaken by J. Hillis Miller in 'Topography and Tropography in Thomas Hardy's "In Front of the Landscape"', in Richard Machin and Christopher Norris, eds, *Post-Structuralist Readings of English Poetry* (Cambridge: Cambridge University Press, 1987), pp. 332–349.

50   Hardy and Hardy, p. 213.

51   Kathleen Tillotson, *Novels of the Eighteen-Forties* (Oxford: Clarendon, 1954), p. 94.

52   Lance Butler, 'How It Is for Thomas Hardy', in Butler, ed., *Thomas Hardy After Fifty Years* (London: Macmillan, 1977), pp. 116–125.

53   Miller, *Thomas Hardy: Distance and Desire*, p. viii.

54   ibid., p. 180.

55   Thomas Hardy, 'I travel as phantom now', *The Complete Poems of Thomas Hardy*, ed. James Gibson (London: Macmillan, 1976), p. 458.

56   Miller, *Thomas Hardy, Distance and Desire*, p. 34.

57   Hardy, *Jude the Obscure*, p. 120.

58   Nancy Miller, *Getting Personal: Feminist Occasions and Other Autobiographical Acts* (New York and London: Routledge, 1991), pp. ix–x.

59   Rich, p. 163.

60   Miller, *Thomas Hardy: Distance and Desire*, p. 237.

61   Hardy, 'I travel as phantom now', p. 458.

ANGLED VISION:
D.H. LAWRENCE'S NARRATIVE GAZE

CARMEL MACDONALD-GRAHAME

IN her essay 'Is the Gaze Male?', E. Ann Kaplan links gender assumptions to ways in which women are positioned or fashioned for observation in cultural constructs:

> our culture is deeply committed to clearly demarcated sex differences, called masculine and feminine, that revolve on, first, a complex gaze-apparatus; and second, dominance submission patterns. This positioning of the two sex-genders clearly privileges the male through the mechanisms of voyeurism and fetishism, which are male operations, and because his desire carries power/action, where woman's usually does not.[1]

She summarizes one school of feminist film criticism to suggest that

> eroticization of women on the screen comes about through the way the cinema is structured around three explicitly male looks or gazes: there is the look of the camera in the situation where events are being

> filmed...this look...is inherently voyeuristic and usually
> 'male' in the sense of a man doing the filming; there is
> the look of the men within the narrative, which is
> structured so as to make women objects of their gaze;
> and finally, there is the look of the male spectator that
> imitates (or is necessarily in the same position as) the
> first two looks.[2]

Clearly, these views resist any notion of the camera as passive recipient of unselected material. And they produce interesting possibilities when linked to what Gerard Genette says of literature, that 'essences of narrative and discourse...are almost never to be found in their pure state in any text', and that 'discourse inserted into narrative remains discourse and forms a sort of cyst that is very easy to recognize and to locate'.[3] In other words, it is always possible to identify the presence of judgement within narration which subjectively colours the narrative.

Two aspects of literary narration immediately become significant: firstly, the long-established assertion that 'the most self-evident reality' of a story 'is the fact that it is told by a narrator to an audience';[4] and secondly, the fact that in the telling, the narrative voice '"interpellates" the reader, addresses itself to him or her directly, offering the reader as the position of the *subject in (and of) ideology*', as Catherine Belsey puts it.[5]

'Omniscience', perhaps the most 'self-evident' narrative stance of all, has been formulated as the narrator having 'vision from behind', and has been symbolized 'by the formula Narrator >Character (where the narrator knows more than the character, or more exactly says more than any of the characters knows)'.[6] An effect of this 'knowingness' is the selective privileging of information so that particular meanings appear to have been legitimated. At times, it is complicated by the simultaneous illusion of narratorial non-presence, which is partly the result of access to the internal as well as the external view of character — an effect of indirect free discourse. By this means, values are attributed to characters by the narrator without being 'owned' by the narrator. However, the narrator can never be obliterated by the technique, and is evident in meanings and values which are immanent in the language itself, especially in imagery, and these are usually consonant with privileged values located in characters.

Genette attaches to the illusion of narratorial non-presence the label 'focalization' by means of which the narrative voice slips in and out of characters, or elides with them, nudging us towards a particular view of information. It depends for its success upon a relationship between reader and narrator in literature which is reminiscent of a spectator's primary identification with the camera in film:

> the way in which in narrative cinema the spectator identifies with the camera itself and is seduced into a regime of specularity, caught by the very apparatus itself and then identifying, necessarily, with the positions of desire and sexuality which each individual film puts into play.[7]

The narrative voice might usefully be perceived as a literary apparatus which is designed to 'seduce', and which may carry an illusion of invisibility or non-presence. Although we identify only secondarily with characters, one function of the narrative voice is to make it seem that the 'eye' with which we observe them is our own.

Put another way, narration can be understood as a meta-discourse which 'orders the potentially erratic signifiers of image', as Annette Kuhn phrases it in her comments on documentary film.

Suggesting that 'documentariness' is created through the voice-over, she describes that mechanism and its effects in such a way that it can be likened to the narrative voice as a 'voice from a source outside and apparently "above" the world of the film speaking a discourse which directs the spectator's reading of the film'.[8]

If narrative voice is the reader's primary point of access to story and character, and it is in its subjective colouration that the sexual ideology can be located, then it is a key to understanding the alignment of the gaze at Woman through the gaze(s) at female characters in literature. Observations about women are presented as insights, but are actually 'outsights' for want of a better term. There are obvious drawbacks to any absolute correlation between the narrative voice in fiction and the use of the camera in cinematography, but the analogy can be useful as a way of conceptualizing the process by which representations of women are 'screened' in literature.

Female sexuality and speculation about female desire are so central to the Lawrence novels that they invite the kind of scrutiny which is enabled by the analogy. Such scrutiny supports the view of D.H. Lawrence's novels which argues that, in them, Woman is objectified by phallocentric narratorial positioning of sexual encounters which are themselves phallocentric. I do not mean to suggest that D.H. Lawrence's novels are exceptional in this, obviously, but they are a useful example because what they offer is an appraisal of a perceived social/sexual reality, presenting it as a distortion of ideal sexual relations. The novels illustrate the distortions to which they object by providing a series of object lessons and argue for the ideal by offering a supposed alternative, revised pattern for sexual interaction. It is this, their own imaginary and, most significantly, their equally limited/limiting social reality, which they naturalize. In my view, the re-vision remains phallocentric and, despite the novels' declarations to the contrary, is in fundamental ways no different from the sexual dynamics to which they take exception. Women are held responsible for a perceived failure in male/female relations and it is women who need to arrive at alternative ways of behaving within sexual relationships. Men's participation in heterosexual relationships is viewed as regrettable and they are urged to a kind of sexual apartheid.

It should be acknowledged that to use the phrase 'Lawrence's novels' is to suppress differences between the early and later works which are usually seen to differ in their views of women. I would assert, however, that where difference exists between the novels at the level of their stated arguments, a consistent sexual ideology can be located in the narrative gaze structure through which those arguments are articulated. In the early novels, where the narration is more concentrated on proposing ideal relations, the sexual ideology is implicit in the contrasts between that ideal and the effect of women upon men in relationships. In *Sons and Lovers*, for example, Walter Morel's problems are anchored in the effects of Gertrude Morel upon his more affable nature. And in a cause–effect chain throughout the novel, responsibility for Paul's misfortune is distributed between his mother, Miriam and Clara. In the later novels, the sexual ideology is more often an explicit argument of the narration, as both *The Plumed Serpent* and *Aaron's Rod* illustrate.

Whether the focus is on the sexual encounters of male or female characters, 'the male gaze' operates. (Perhaps 'masculine gaze' is preferable for its skirting of essentialism and generalization.) It objectifies the female in ways that the male is not objectified; when acted upon, his desire carries narratorial approval whilst hers is permeated with dread. And this is equally true whether obvious omniscience is the narrative mode and/or there is an 'intrusive' narrator, or the narration purports to be a series of evenhanded shifts between two or more characters' consciousnesses. It makes no difference to the view of woman. Perhaps this is because these distinctions do not hold in quite the same way when, by means of the analogy with a camera's gaze, the narrator's 'eye' is seen, finally, as the 'eye' through which we view all sexual transactions in the novels.

Elizabeth Grosz's formulation of phallocentrism illuminates my view of Lawrence's narrative strategies. To sum up her definition, phallocentrism may take the forms of gender blindness, expressions of sexual complementarity, and binary opposition.[9] Because sexual difference is the novels' central theme and the worlds constructed within them are viewed almost exclusively in terms of gender, the first category is seldom evident, but the last two describe quite precisely how they operate. Overall, what varies in D.H. Lawrence's novels is merely the form of the phallocentrism — from complementarity to simple opposition — leaving the sexual ideology intact.

Nor is phallocentrism disguised by the centrality of female characters such as Ursula in *The Rainbow* or Kate Leslie in *The Plumed Serpent*. These 'feminine' voices are a function of an ideology which hopes to legitimate for women a particular masculine point of view and system of values. For example, in *The Plumed Serpent*, the most condemning content about femaleness is issued through Kate. Any basis for comparison between the sexes is some element which repels her and can be relied upon to repel most readers, so that maleness emerges in a positive light as/and opposed to femaleness. When womanness is identified with dirt and disease, as it is in this quotation, the character of Kate becomes primarily a vehicle of narrative polemic:

> It was strange to Kate to see the Indian huts on the shores, little holes built of straw or corn stalks, with half naked children squatting on the naked earth floor, and a *lousy woman-squalor* around, a litter of rags and bones, and a sharp smell of human excrement. The people have no noses. And standing silent and erect not far from the hole of the doorway, the man, handsome and impassive. How could it be, that such a *fine-looking human male* should be so absolutely indifferent, content with such a *paltry squalor*.[10]
>
> [*The Plumed Serpent*, 148, emphasis mine]

Women who are not like Kate are, by their otherness to her, explicitly excluded from humanity and made the object of her gaze.

Dread of femaleness is the more usual effect of notions of the 'inhuman'. In *The Rainbow*, when Lydia is in labour, Tom Brangwen makes just such an association:

> There was the sound of the owls — the moaning of the woman. What an uncanny sound! It was not human — at least to a man.
>
> He went down to her room, entering softly...She was beautiful to him — but it was not human. He had a dread of her as she lay there. What had she to do with him? She was other than himself.
>
> [*The Rainbow*, 76]

The operation of the word 'human' is quite explicit here. It is qualified and limited in the first instance, but not to the perception of Tom Brangwen, to the perception of 'a man'. In the second instance there is no qualification. The subsequent flow from Lydia's beauty to inhuman to dread to otherness confirms the suggestion that man is human, and woman, being other than him, is not. Later, in the context of Anna and Will's relationship, we read of the crying baby: 'the very inhumanness of the intolerable, continuous crying arrested him' (*The Rainbow*, 208). The noun 'human' thus begins to mean 'adult male', and the equation between Woman and Nature excludes rather than elevates her. More often than not, when it is applied to female characters, '[n]onhuman nature can be seen as that which is beneath the human, the realm to be controlled, reduced to domination, fought against as font of chaos and regression'.[11] When applied to central male characters, 'non-human' means, by contrast, the 'man created by God' (*The Rainbow*, 493) or some construction of that which is perceived rightfully to do the controlling. As he argues for a 'humanless world' in *Women in Love*, Birkin's distinction between 'Man' and 'the grass, and hares and adders, and the unseen hosts, actual angels that go about freely when a dirty humanity doesn't interrupt them — and good pure-tissued demons' (120) dissolves as the novel progresses into a further distinction between Man and the Sons of God. This in turn is opposed to Woman = Daughters of Men. Sons of men (the miners, for example) are 'mindless, inhuman', and there is a similar association with 'voluptuousness' and sexuality (108). In other words, use of the male universal is usually temporary, selective and unsustained as language is used to suggest a 'chain of being'. If, for Lawrence, the tragedy of the modern world was that it 'had replaced the metaphysical conception of man's place in Nature...by merely illustrative images of Nature', and had become for him 'nothing but a series of free-wheeling meta-phors',[12] then clearly such use of language is more than merely illustrative and metaphorical. At the very least, it sets in place a narrative voice which is identifiably masculine and white.

All this draws attention to the chief characteristic of the

gaze structure; that is, that the dominant and preferred gaze at any point in the text is the gaze which is invested with power. In the above example from *The Plumed Serpent,* Kate Leslie's gaze derives power from ethnocentrism and a particular perspective of social and economic privilege. The phallocentrism results from attempts to align the reader with the specifics of this construction of her as Woman — as opposed to other possible constructions. In the novel as a whole, it also flows from the fact that in any 'contest' of perspectives (always sexual) between Kate Leslie and Don Cipriano or Don Ramon, power shifts either to the perspectives of Don Cipriano and Don Ramon, or directly to the narrative voice. At those moments Kate Leslie is made 'strange' to herself:

> For it was not her spirit alone which was changing, it was her body, and the constitution of her very blood... Yet the process of change within her blood was terrible to her...Her strange seething feminine will and desire subsided in her and swept away...
>
> [419–420]

Such power shifts are used repeatedly to position the reader and legitimate a sexual ideology by offering us an 'angle of vision'[13] which is gender specific, constructs a particular subject position for women, and argues for male hegemony.

A key problem with Lawrence's novels derives from the fact that in the narrative voice, illusion-charged as it is, female characters are declared to be accurate representations of women when they are actually 'mediations, embedded through the art form in the dominant ideology', and what they really signify is 'something in the male unconscious'[14] of their author. Such declarations are generally made at those moments in the text when the narrative voice overtly performs its ideological function and emerges distinct from the voices of the characters. The fact that open articulations of narrative ideology are in harmony with ideology elsewhere attributed to characters makes it clear that character attribution does not explain away the sexual ideology, an explaining away which has consistently occurred amongst apologists of Lawrence's work:

> The fictive life consists in complex interplay between presentation (both dramatic and symbolic), allowing us to see and feel for ourselves, and a struggle to analyse in which both the narrator and ourselves have to be involved...in order to become capable of understanding and sympathy without simplification. But D.H. Lawrence, because he is dramatist, symbolist and narrative ironist, as well as commentator, must never be reduced to the narrator's commentary.[15]

I have argued already that 'allowing us to see and feel for ourselves' is an illusion, but it is also less than useful to consider distinct narratorial commentary as the sole source of sexual ideology. Rather, it can be discerned in the consonance between 'the struggle to analyse', and action, imagery and character. Both modes operate in Lawrence's narratorial style.

In some novels, the alignment of the narrative gaze through character is given immediate impetus by the overt ideological function of the narrative voice. Two which illustrate this in different ways are *The Rainbow* and *Aaron's Rod*. *The Rainbow* opens with an obvious exercise of narrative 'omniscience' in the panoramic, 'wide-lens' presentation of the village of Cossethay and its inhabitants. Gradually the focus draws to the Brangwen family at The Marsh but continues to evoke a sense that time and space are transcended. The separation between women and men and the sense of unbridgeable difference between them are established early:

> Then the men sat by the fire in the house where the women moved about with surety, and the limbs and the body of the men were impregnated with the day, cattle and earth and vegetation and the sky, the men sat by the fire and their brains were inert, as their blood flowed heavy with the accumulation from the living day.

> The women were different. On them too was the
> drowse of blood-intimacy, calves sucking and hens
> running together in droves, and young geese palpita-
> ting in the hand while the food was pushed down
> their throttle. But the women looked out from the
> heated, blind intercourse of farm life, to the spoken
> world beyond. They were aware of the lips and the
> mind of the world speaking and giving utterance, they
> heard the sound in the distance, and they strained to
> listen.
>
> [*The Rainbow*, 2]

The novel continues with this plural, collective use of
'men' and 'women' for a time, and then in a sudden shift,
'women' becomes 'woman', and a single woman becomes representative of her sex. 'Men', however, continue to be described
collectively until the narration introduces them as individual
characters, from which time they do not operate similarly as
representative of their sex:

> The only tangible, secure thing was the woman. He
> could leave her only for another woman. And where
> was the other woman, and who was the other woman?
> Besides, he would be just in the same state. Another
> woman would be woman, the case would be the
> same.
>   Why was she the all, the everything, why must he
> live only through her, why must he sink if he were
> detached from her? Why must he cleave to her in a
> frenzy as for his very life?
>
> [*The Rainbow*, 183]

The narrative 'eye' is evident also in the noticeable dissonance between the elaborate 'omniscient' evocation of these
men as simple, inarticulate folk and the language of their
introspection. Dissonance is also evident between their speech
and thought patterns. The 'vision from behind' becomes self-
evident at such moments. The imperative to urge ideas located in

such characters necessitates having the narrative voice assume greater proportions overall than the characters themselves.

In *Aaron's Rod*, Lawrence pre-empts such a criticism and the reader is gathered up in the narration and openly invited to collude in narratorial assessment of Aaron's rejection of his wife, of his view of the Marchesa, and finally, under the guidance of Rawdon Lilly, of the female sex as a unity. Aaron's inability to 'speak for himself' directly connects the sexual ideology of the Aaron character to the narrative voice. He is 'our acquaintance' (82), and we are addressed as intimate confidants:

> Don't grumble at me then, gentle reader, and swear at me that this damned fellow wasn't half clever enough to think all these smart things, and realise all these fine-drawn-out subtleties. You are quite right, he wasn't, yet it all resolved itself in him as I say, and it is for you to prove that it didn't.
>
> [*Aaron's Rod*, 161]

Of course, the corollary of any assertion that a character is incapable of 'clever' realization is that the narrator is, and this directly places a value on that gaze. This narrative voice offers its own rationale for all elisions of narrative voice with character consciousness:

> If I, as a word user, must translate his deep conscious vibrations into finite words, that is my own business. I do but make a translation of the man. He would speak in music. I speak with words...and it was in his own mode only he realized what I must put into words. These words are my own affair.
>
> [*Aaron's Rod*, 160–161]

An effect of this strategy is direct and obvious access to the persona of a narrator, giving that voice a documentary-style immediacy.

Significantly, such narratorial passages consistently position subsequent formulations of the sex-gender thesis of the novels. In this case, it initiates an extensive consideration of love and marriage, in which the narrator explains on Aaron's inarticulate behalf why it has been 'necessary' (the term used in the novel) for Aaron to leave his family: 'Let a man give himself as much as he liked in love, to seven thousand extremities, he must never give himself away' (161). The narrator arrives at a mode of love which would suit Aaron after deliberations which are critical of perceived sexual mores:

> This is the sacrament we live by; the holy communion we live for. That man give himself to woman in an utter and sacred abandon, all, all, all himself given, and taken. Woman, the eternal woman, she is the communicant. She receives the sacramental body and spirit of the man.
>
> And when she's got it, according to her passionate and all-too-sacred desire, completely, when she possesses her man at last finally and ultimately, without blemish or reservation in the perfection of the sacrament: then, also, poor woman, the blood and the body of which she has partaken become insipid or nauseous to her, she is driven mad by the endless meal of the marriage sacrament, poisoned by the sacred communion which was her goal and her soul's ambition.
>
> [*Aaron's Rod*, 161–162]

The superficial argument for equality of a kind is undermined by the fact that when female desire is given power/action, it is threatening. He is passive, 'the gift', while she accepts and consumes him. Given Christian theologies upon which the sacrament of communion rests, man here either symbolizes or is God. He 'gives himself to woman in an utter and sacred abandon' and becomes saviour, God-made-man, sacrifice and victim. His 'sacred abandon' is evaluated differently from 'woman's' in the use of the heavily emphasized 'all', which praises man's self-sacrifice and denigrates female desire. In receiving the gift, her 'allness' is connotatively negative, an unfortunate excess. 'Sacred', too, resonates positively when applied to the male, and negatively when applied to the female, becoming part of the constant use in this novel of sacramental language to allege the destructiveness of women's inflated power in sexual relations. The 'we' of men and women is unconvincing because the gaze is so strongly invested in aligning the reader's gaze with what it positions as the male side of the negotiation.

The structure of the gaze in this novel is caught up also in the character of Rawdon Lilly, whom past critics have read as a 'mouthpiece for Lawrence's own musings'.[16] This arises from the obvious elision between the narrator's voice and Lilly's. Aaron Sisson is on the run from a marriage based on his wife's desire, and his vision of an ideal relationship is compared in intrusive narration with 'Two eagles in mid-air, grappling, whirling, coming to their intensification of love-oneness there in mid-air. In mid-air the love consummation.' (*Aaron's Rod*, 163) Elision between the narrator and Lilly is clear from Lilly's later use of the same image in dialogue, which otherwise defies logic: 'You want passion to sweep you off on wings of fire till you surpass yourself, and like the swooping eagle swoop right into the sun' (284), and 'Passion or no passion, ecstasy or no ecstasy, urge or no urge, there's no goal outside you, where you can consummate like an eagle flying into the sun...' (285). Thus Lilly guides Aaron towards apprehension of his 'lost illusions' (284), and persuades him that the real necessity is 'deep fathomless submission to the heroic soul in a greater man' (289). Given all that has gone before and the gaze-structure, the word 'man', I would suggest, is used advisedly.

Much of the sexual ideology in *Aaron's Rod* is located in Lilly, who acts as a marker of its implicit preferred reading. Hence the narrator has it both ways. While the greater distance between Aaron and the narrator is less manoeuvrable in some ways than elision, it allows for open narrative assessment of mentor-friend Lilly's ideology, as Aaron metamorphoses under his influence. At the same time, the full range of narrative strategies is at work to support the views expressed by Lilly. The result is that there are two peculiarities to the gaze-structure in *Aaron's*

Rod. Where Aaron and Lilly are in discussion about sexual relations, the female/feminine is subjected to a triple male gaze — the narrator>Lilly>Aaron — and while there is no female character with the status of an Ursula Brangwen or a Constance Chatterley, women are still a central subject of the novel. The result is a retrospective composition of the effect of female desire, rather than a composition of the sexual struggle in progress. Encounters with women merely justify the flight from woman, the only path to selfhood for men. Lilly's argument, the central argument of the novel, that men should eschew love in favour of power, is not only unopposed, it is actively supported by the narrative voice.

For the most part the novels depend on indirect free discourse. The examples above of Kate Leslie's musings and of the elision with the voice of Rawdon Lilly are cases in point. Even in closely focalized exchanges, the narrative voice is always actively aligning the view characters have of each other and inviting the reader to share that view.

In *Sons and Lovers*, the famous consummation scene by the canal shows how the alignment of the narrative gaze positions information given by characters. Most obviously, and therefore most easily resisted, is the way in which Clara is objectified at the level of vocabulary: '*What* was she?' (353), '*something* he loved' (353), and Clara 'looked up at him, frightened, like a *thing* that was afraid of death' (338, emphases mine). As a mechanism for shepherding the reader, this is continual enough for it not to be lightly dismissed. However, it supports and is supported by more subtle 'seductions'.

The sexual encounter is initiated by Paul: 'Be with me now, will you, no matter what it is?' (352). Clara's compliance involves the unlikely perception for a supposed feminist that she has no right to do any less:

> *And she took him in her arms.* After all, she was a married woman, and she had no right even to what he gave her. He needed her badly. She had him in her arms, and he was miserable. *With her warmth she*

folded him over, consoled him, loved him. She would
let the moment stand for itself.

[352–353, emphasis mine]

The italicized lines here are those in which the focalization
through Clara dissolves into explicit narration. They convey
information which a character could not convincingly be
described as giving about herself. The 'eye' which views the
exchange emerges in them from otherwise intimate focalization
— 'the look of the camera in the situation'. The unemphasized
lines have less to do with conveying action and event to the
reader than with setting Clara's consciousness in place. The
reiteration of 'And she took him in her arms' as 'She had him in
her arms and he was miserable' supports this. It has the dual
function of conveying Clara's awareness of Paul's emotional
state, and of conveying her realization of something which we
have already been told in the narrative voice. The voice of the
character has been 'preceded' by the voice of the narrator.

Practitioners of indirect free discourse might describe
these as thoughts directed by Clara to herself. The mode allows
for a narrator who preserves the authorial mode and at the
same time moves 'directly into the experiential field of the
character, and adopts the latter's perspective in regard to both
time and place'.[17] This is hypothetical, of course, since the
character has no pre-existing perspective to be adopted. Inverting
the idea produces a more accurate metaphor: that the character's
perspective is, rather, a product of the narrator's, angled by him
in a kind of ventriloquism. It is most evident when the thoughts
characters have about themselves are inappropriate unless the
reader allows for some voice other than theirs. For instance, in
The Rainbow, Ursula might have significantly less appeal if
material like this were solely attributable to her: 'The dimness
and stillness chilled her. But her eyes lit up with daring. Here,
here she would assert her *indomitable gorgeous female self,*
here.' (301, emphasis mine)

In the series of focalizations distributed between Paul and
Clara in the passage from *Sons and Lovers*, the narrative voice is

also perceptible in its control of what each character cannot know about the other's needs or perceptions if the story is to be plausible. For example: 'She wanted to soothe him into *forgetfulness.*/And soon the struggle went down in his soul, and he *forgot.*' (353, emphasis mine) Here, the close alignment of 'forgetfulness' and 'forgot' disrupts the intimacy of each focalization. Since Paul should not know that his forgetfulness is what Clara wants, the juxtaposition of 'forgetfulness' and 'forgot' not only achieves stylistic flow, it also indicates narrative regulation — unless the two are mind-reading.

So when the paragraph continues to: 'But then Clara was not there for him, *only a woman*, warm, *something* he loved and almost worshipped, there in the dark. But it was not Clara, and *she submitted to him*' (353, emphasis mine), the suspect sexual ideology of the italicized phrases is not explained away by attribution to Paul. The boundaries between character and narrator are blurred, and both the construction of Clara and her submission are presented not only as Paul's way of seeing her but as an appropriate way of seeing her.

As the passage proceeds, there is a relatively even distribution of Paul-assigned and Clara-assigned information with narrative control identifiable in the play of perceptions each has about the other. Balance is attempted in the use of 'otherness' as a factor in the sexual dynamic for both. Clara 'stood clasping him and caressing him, and he was something unknown to her — something almost uncanny' (353). Paul's reaction is similar: 'He lifted his head, and looked into her eyes. They were dark and shining and strange, life wild at the source staring into his life, stranger to him, yet meeting him; and he put his face down on her throat, afraid.' (353) However, the balance exists only in having each in turn look at the other. Much more is made of Clara's strangeness to Paul than of his to her, and her strangeness is specifically equated with non-human, natural phenomena. His deliberations have length and resonance which are not brought equally to bear on hers. A significantly different tone of dread rings through the expression of Paul's perception of Clara, and, as usual in the novels, it becomes crucial to the way that female sexuality is constructed and foregrounded as a subject of speculation. Encompassing statements about both sexes constantly slide and give way to a different result for each.

Clara's 'strange, wild life' is linked with 'cosmic' elements and Paul's dominant gaze is indicated in the 'he wondered' and 'he realized' of the paragraph in which the linkage is made. She is 'manoeuvred into position' also by the sentence sequence: 'What was she? A strong, strange, wild life, that breathed with his in the darkness through this hour. It was all so much bigger than themselves that he was hushed.' (353) These three sentences counteract the mutuality of the subsequent 'they' and 'their', which is Paul's perception of what they have done: 'They had met, and included in their meeting the thrust of the manifold grass stems, the cry of the peewit, the wheel of the stars' (353). Mutuality belongs to Paul and the narrator. The association between sexual release and cosmic forces is not invited on behalf of Clara's consciousness. Even the use of 'thrust' phallo-centricizes the description. All indicators are directing the reader towards making that association on Paul's behalf, and she is so much more 'other' than he that she is subsumed into the image itself by connection and objectified by being made a part of it: Clara>grass stems>peewit>stars. The process of actively inviting us to read Paul's perspective as dominant over Clara's 'gives away' the perspective of the narration despite apparent evenness of attribution. It is often superficial in this way, and contributes to the overall sense that the sexual ideology prevails against women.

Throughout *Sons and Lovers*, such narrative regulation propels Paul's perceptions to the centre so that they have greater weight than those of all other characters. The literary resonance of his perceptions is as heightened as any accompanying unfocalized narrative description, which is why, in the passage which is my example, the characterization of Clara emerges via Paul's 'gaze' — 'the look of the men within the narrative, which is structured so as to make women objects of their gaze', to recall Kaplan's words.

A contradiction inheres between such ideological effects of

the gaze alignment and the necessity of positioning female characters as desirable to male characters, who might otherwise appear irrational for their sexual interest. Where this is addressed by inviting the reader's gaze into rapport with female characters, the invitation is governed by a limited, traditional vision of the power differential between men and women. In particular, compliance and submissiveness to male desire is the chief characteristic of their desirability. This is at the heart of difference between Ursula and Gudrun in *Women in Love*, where the resistant Gudrun is reminiscent of the Ursula of *The Rainbow*, whilst the metamorphosed Ursula is transformed by submission to Birkin. Wherever they are reluctant or resistant to male control of sexual relationships, all Lawrence's major female characters exemplify Nina Auerbach's point that 'the angel can modulate almost imperceptibly into a demon'.[18] Minor female characters, such as Winifrid Inger in *The Rainbow*, Hermione in *Women in Love*, or Bertha Coutts in *Lady Chatterley's Lover*, are a mechanism for articulating the attack on a perceived womanhood and, by comparison, supporting the constructions of femaleness which, in the terms of the narrative argument, are exemplary. This differentiation between two kinds of femaleness reduces the meaning of Woman to two possibilities and femaleness is constructed according to the particular ideological point being made at any moment in the text.

It is in the relationship between narrator and central female characters that the question of whether or not Lawrence's novels champion women arises. The lifting of women's oppression is certainly among their subjects, from Clara's feminism to Kate Leslie's deliberations about whether or not to enter the pantheon, but in my view, the nature of the novels' 'feminism' is encapsulated here by Rosemary Radford Ruether's comment on some 'male feminists':

> they want women to cultivate this male definition of
> the 'feminine' in order to nurture the 'feminine side' of
> men. They purport to understand and sympathize with
> women and, no doubt, sincerely think they do. But

they tend to become very hostile when women suggest that this definition of the 'feminine' is really a male projection and not female humanity. The male ego is still the center of the universe, which 'feminism' is now seduced into enhancing in a new way.[19]

Resistance to the sexual ideology of D.H. Lawrence's novels depends upon understanding this kind of cooptational narrative strategy which is inextricably tied to the narrative voice: 'for the relation of fact to fiction, of the real world to the world of story, is itself a kind of "metaphysical pact", a secret to which the narrator's art is the metaphorical key'.[20]

1   E. Ann Kaplan, 'Is the Gaze Male?', in A. Snitow, C. Stansell and S. Thompson, eds, *Powers of Desire* (New York: Monthly Review Press, 1983), p. 311.

2   ibid.

3   Gerard Genette, 'Frontiers of Narrative', in *Figures of Literary Discourse* (New York: Columbia University Press, 1982), pp. 138–139.

4   Roy Pascal, *The Dual Voice* (Manchester: Manchester University Press, 1977), p. 6.

5   Catherine Belsey, *Critical Practice* (London and New York: Methuen, 1980), p. 57.

6   Gerard Genette, *Narrative Discourse* (Oxford: Basil Blackwell, 1980), p. 189.

7   Jacqueline Rose, *Sexuality in the Field of Vision* (London: Verso, 1986), p. 217.

8   Annette Kuhn, 'Real Women', in J. Newton and D. Rosenfelt, eds, *Feminist Criticism and Social Change* (New York and London: Methuen, 1985), p. 270.

9   Elizabeth Grosz, *Sexual Subversions* (Sydney and London: Allen & Unwin, 1989), p. 105.

10   Because of the interplay of comparisons being made here, details of quotations from Lawrence's writings are incorporated into the text throughout this essay and publication details of those selected appear at the end of these notes.

11   Rosemary Radford Ruether, *Sexism and God-Talk* (Boston: Beacon Press, 1983), pp. 75–76.

12   Brian Wicker, *The Story-Shaped World* (London: Athlone Press, 1975), p. 121.
13   Pascal, p. 6.
14   Kaplan, p. 310.
15   Mark Kinkead-Weekes, 'Eros and Metaphor: Sexual Relationship in the Fiction of Lawrence', in *Lawrence and Women,* ed. Anne Smith (London: Vision Press, 1980), p. 105.
16   W. Tiverton, *D.H. Lawrence and Human Existence* (London: Rockcliff Publishing, 1951), p. 46.
17   Pascal, p. 9.
18   Nina Auerbach, *Woman and the Demon* (London: Harvard University Press, 1982), p. 107.
19   Ruether, p. 190.
20   Wicker, p. 4.

Selected List of D.H. Lawrence's Writings

Sons and Lovers 1911 (London: Heinemann, 1955).
The Rainbow 1915 (London: Heinemann, 1955).
Women in Love 1921 (London: Heinemann, 1954).
Aaron's Rod 1922 (London: Heinemann, 1954).
The Plumed Serpent 1926 (London: Heinemann, 1954).
Lady Chatterley's Lover 1928 (London: Heinemann, 1960).

'THE MOST DIFFICULT LOVE':
EXPECTATION AND GENDER IN BARNARD ELDERSHAW'S *TOMORROW AND TOMORROW AND TOMORROW*

IAN SAUNDERS

I T is difficult indeed to read without expectation. Neither texts nor readers operate free of constraint or context: reading is to bring a text within an operational field. To read, we might say, is to expect a text to perform in a way that is consistent with that field. Or: to read is to expect a text to behave itself.

In the light of expectation, the history of the reading of Marjorie Barnard and Flora Eldershaw's *Tomorrow and Tomorrow and Tomorrow* has been one of disappointment. Expecting a story focused on the domestic and personal, its first publisher was horrified to receive a bulky manuscript that seemed as much devoted to class analysis as to the analysis of love, and wrote to the authors accordingly: 'What we would like to ask you is this: — Are you prepared to risk your reputation as front rank Australian creative writers for the sake of an ideology?'.[1] They were, and did; its 1947 publication was greeted with little enthusiasm, they did not write fiction again, and were quickly forgotten by the literary establishment.

The republishing of the text in 1983 under the Virago

imprint sponsors a different kind of expectation, one that flourishes on the very grounds of earlier disappointment. Here is a publishing enterprise that is unashamedly ideological, unashamedly feminist, embracing a text censored for its politics, and subsequently discarded by the (patriarchal) critical institution of its time as a novel betrayed by 'mental confusion'.[2] And here is a text written in partnership by two women, a double, low blow to that long-standing, masculinist dogma that writing is necessarily singular. Great expectations indeed.

As it turned out, though, even within this apparently more sympathetic universe of expectation, reading remained — unexpectedly, disappointingly — difficult. It is a political novel, but for this new generation of readers it seems disturbingly blind to the fact that gender is itself a matter of politics. Indeed, the sympathetic explorations of female experience in Marjorie Barnard's collection *The Persimmon Tree*,[3] published just prior to the writing of *Tomorrow and Tomorrow and Tomorrow*, seem simply displaced here by an interest in class politics: as Drusilla Modjeska puts it, the situation and experience of women 'is peripheral to the main focus of the novel, the nature of the crisis in capitalism': regretfully, 'there is no suggestion of collective or political action by women against their oppression as women'.[4] Once again, it would seem, the text fails to live up to expectation.

Now to a large extent one would have to concede that class politics, and not gender, is the primary focus of the text; nonetheless there is more to be said, and I want to examine *Tomorrow and Tomorrow and Tomorrow* here in the light of expectation, difficulty and disappointment, and suggest that, whatever its failures, it is of more theoretical interest than may first appear to be the case. In particular, I argue, its structure prefigures in an intriguing way the opposition between accounts of gender identity that highlight social production and those that emphasize the dimension of innate quality, between (that is to say) accounts fashioned according to the dictates of constructivist and essentialist logics.[5]

As the text is not as well read as it might be, a brief recollection of it may be useful. Although not published until 1947, the text was actually written largely in the years from 1940 to 1942, as an outraged response to the war, an analysis of the events that made it inevitable, and an analysis of the catastrophic future to which it was headed. The narrative difficulty of melding the story of the past with one surveying the future is solved by telling both from the point of view of a novelist working in the twenty-fourth century. The text begins with Knarf, having just completed 'his' historical novel about the twentieth century, contemplating the dawn of day which will see him read from it to his friend Ord, an archaeologist, and on which a community vote is planned to test the people's interest in a move to democratize their rigidly controlled society. *Tomorrow and Tomorrow and Tomorrow* traces the events of that day: the public vote, and the private reading. Knarf's novel, *Little World Left Behind*, traces the political and social events that led to the Second World War. There is little doubt about where his sympathies lie. As he explains to Ord:

> Now the salient feature of that world of the twentieth century — and for many years before — was competition. Whether they willed it or not, men lived by profit. From this basis of competitive living, there followed a series of reactions of which war was one. The system gave rise to fiercer, more frequent wars, leading on to war, total and continuous, and the death of civilization.
>
> [139][6]

Or again:

> The really curious thing about the nineteen thirties is that the world was never before, perhaps never since, so aware. The decade began in the depths of the Depression, something calculated to stir the social forces as even the first world war had not done, an object lesson brought into almost every home,

certainly a working-class home. If ever event brought indictment against a social system, the Depression brought one against capitalism.

[135]

For much of the narrative itself, it is precisely a 'working-class home' that offers a focus, as the novel follows the career of Harry Munster, ex-Anzac, from his failing chicken farm, to a job driving a truck in Sydney, from whence he is sacked on account of his unionism and unemployed for five years of the Depression, finally to find tenuous security operating an elevator in a city department store until his death in an air raid in the Second World War. Knarf's novel ranges over the lives of a number of other characters: Harry's family, acquaintances, fellow citizens of Sydney, icons of an entire society. The two novels (both *Little World Left Behind* and *Tomorrow and Tomorrow and Tomorrow*) also attempt an explicit, large-scale historical account of the events. At times, sections of Knarf's novel are dedicated to this, at times he breaks into reading the domestic narrative of Harry Munster, and sketches in the background for Ord's benefit:

> Knarf broke off. 'You know all this as well as I do. The time of unrest, of strikes, and civil violence. The demobilised men who could not adjust themselves to a world that was neither the old one they remembered, nor the new one they hoped for; the uprooted people who remained helpless; the wolf packs of slave labourers; the mass of workers resenting and fighting...'
> [Georgian House: 365/not included in Virago edition]

Both Knarf's *Little World Left Behind* and *Tomorrow and Tomorrow and Tomorrow* end with a kind of failure. Knarf's novel concludes with a revolution that, for all its genuine intent, leaves Sydney destroyed and its participants to wander into the desert, where they perish. The larger narrative ends with the failure of the twenty-fourth century Union of Youth's attempt to mobilize public opinion in favour of a democratic alternative to the ruling Regional Congress. The pilot vote is taken but — despite the best efforts of naive enthusiast Ren (Knarf's son) — can record nothing better than overwhelming indifference.

In each case, though, the ending that the narrative trajectory seeks is supplemented, coda-like, by a change of key, from the discourse of the social to that of the private, and from failure to something like optimism. And in each case the supplement concerns fathers and sons.

The account of the exodus from Sydney ends with Ben Munster — a truck-driver as his father had been — pausing at the top of a rise to allow the truck's boiling radiator a chance to cool. It is late evening. He spots a deserted farmhouse which, the narrative hints through juxtaposition of this with the episode that immediately precedes it, may well be the house his parents left, for the city, on the eve of his birth (readers familiar with David Malouf's *Child's Play* will no doubt begin to sense a precursor here). At any rate, he needs water, and looks for it there, but finds the farmhouse water tanks dry. Seeing an orchard, he is overcome by craving for the 'sweet cleanliness' (422/414) of fruit and, eventually, he finds an apple. Eating the apple, he looks back, surveying the procession of refugees and the burnt-out city behind them. It was the city of his childhood, and its destruction takes him back to the Sydney he had known as a child, when his father was alive. He remembers his father's death, he remembers 'the night his father had eaten the dinner set aside for him when he was a kid selling papers and his father was out of a job, and how crook his mother had been about it' (GH:423/omitted Virago), and he remembers, earlier still, 'the truck his father used to drive':

> It was the first thing he could remember. Just for a moment his mind swung back to being the mind of a child, and the acrid smoky air with its choking fumes became the dust of a sidestreet now lost in rubble and the petrol fumes of a long time ago. The pride and glory of the grocery truck! He saw, he actually saw,

again his father's hands on the driving wheel as he sat
on his knee, his feet among the gears and the steering
wheel alive and vibrant against his chest. He saw
them as he saw his own, sure and steady on the
wheel of his truck down there driving out of the
burning city. He saw them with the eyes of a child and
with his own eyes. He recognised them as kin. Strong
good hands that he couldn't remember, only see.

[423/415]

Ben's meditation on the Sydney of his childhood is literally
of a 'world left behind': no return is possible to either city or
childhood. But that nostalgic recognition of loss is tempered both
by the warmth of the memory and by the inheritance sensed not
by cognition but through direct, sensuous apprehension and a
merging of temporally remote experiences. His mind is also 'the
mind of a child', his eyes at once 'his own' and yet 'the eyes of
a child'; he sees his father's hands 'as he saw his own, sure and
steady on the wheel of the truck'. A sense of necessity is established precisely because the continuity is not constructed within
the realm of the mental, but simply seen; the relation Ben
senses, the text implies, is entirely within the natural order of
things.

The framing novel ends in a way that strongly recalls the
ending of the embedded text. After the disappointment of the
vote, Knarf's son Ren escapes the settlement to the solitude of
'the other world' (451/441), over the river. 'Then there would be
plenty of time and space to think.' As he walks, night falls.
Increasingly exhausted, he loses all sense of direction. He hears
not the twenty-fourth century nightscape but the voices of the
twenty-first century pioneers, heading as he is out west to some
better future. When Knarf realizes that Ren is missing, he sets out
to find him, and eventually does, close to unconscious, his ankle
broken from a fall. It is impossible to move him, so Knarf settles
with him for the night:

Knarf eased Ren's head and shoulders till they rested
on his knees and spread his own cloak as far as it

would go over them both to keep the warmth of their bodies. The boy was wide awake now, stimulated by the spirits, and his foot, released from pressure, was not unbearably painful so long as he kept still. The worst part was the aching of the cold.

Now that the normal walls of their existence were down, moment by moment a new intimacy sprang up between father and son. Each felt a great relief. Ren wanted to talk, and the darkness and the spirits both made it easier.

[462/452]

They talk about the failed vote, about liberty, death, about the past and the future. Ren does not fully understand his father, but his words bring reassurance. 'He felt quiet and almost happy. He had come past a crisis and was relieved. He had not been so safe since he was a child.' (466/456) As dawn approaches, head on his father's knees, he at last falls asleep:

Tired, safe, and a little drunk, he could not keep awake any longer. The long day was over. Sleep unwound its tension. Knarf watched over his son and his heart was wrung with the most difficult love in the world, the love of a father for his son. It has no code and no ritual, no physical release, it must forever stand by and its way is the way of relinquishment.

[466/456]

The novel ends with just two more sentences. 'He saw the first light of another day creep into the eastern sky. He thought "This is the beginning," and "The earth remains."'

Given expectations, it is writing that poses a certain difficulty. To speak within the space of the personal, there is much here that I feel is deeply resonant. I am a father, I am a son, and — or so it seems to me — these fragile moments of emotional intimacy within the text catch something of both experiences. The overwhelming urge to protect, and the recognition that one will fail, inevitably: this rings true, as does the discovery of a kind of security in a sense of inheritance, an inarticulate continuity, at just that moment when the prior security of unmediated proximity is understood as immovably of the past. On the other hand, though, both narratives seem to be celebrating a rite of patriarchal regeneration from which women have been altogether excluded. It is all very well to write of fathers and sons; what, though, of mothers and daughters?

In the light of our expectations, it has to be said, the text behaves badly. There are a number of mothers in the book, but it has little sympathy for any of them. Ren's mother Lin — as her name might suggest — is a cypher, a blank with no internal substance. She simply exists as a provider of meals, of domestic order, as Knarf's wife, as Ren's mother. She is anxious for success, but only for a success measured in external terms: she is concerned that the luncheon proceeds without unseemly disruption, that Knarf behaves with the dignity appropriate to his position, that Ren embarks on an exemplary career in the civil service. She has no interest in Knarf's novel, and considers Ren's political activism a youthful foolishness that could well block his chances for advancement. She is described as being 'hostile' (35), 'irritated' (221), angry (215), 'anxious', obstinate, 'bitter' and with a 'woody and acrid' will (222), fearful and exasperated (455/445), 'harsh and angular' (456/446) and — or so Knarf believes — not even much of a mother:

> Nor was there much that was motherly in Lin, though always now her eyes went past him to Ren and he had seen a dumb greed in them that horrified him. Lin, in a way, had remained immature. Though she was over forty her youth had not left her, it had hardened, so that she was like a fruit turned woody. She was still waiting for heaven knows what improbable spring.
>
> [25]

Expectations might prompt us to see this resentment as symptomatic of the untenable position the social has prepared for her, an outcome of the fact that within its ideology the conjuncture of maturity and ambition is exclusively the provenance of the male; however, that reading is one that the text itself makes, well...

difficult. 'Opportunity, both before and after her marriage, had been as much open to her as to any one else, but she had not risked taking it. She had wanted her husband, home, and children to absorb her, and when it hadn't been like that she blamed Knarf for her inability to deal with her own life in her own way.' (25)

Ben's mother, Ally, is likewise a figure of resentment and bitterness, full of the knowledge of what she has missed, indifferent to the fate of those who have less than her:

> 'I don't care about the people who haven't,' she answered passionately. 'Plenty have. There's good things in the world, lots of them, and I want a share.' She thought of the city, its lights, its amusements, its piled-up plenty. She wanted all the silly things, the things she didn't need, to lord it over them. The people who had were the victors.
>
> [63]

Again, we might be inclined to say, her resentment is well founded, finding herself as she does without power or position, and with little recognized function beyond the biological. As she says, 'Looks like I've got a life sentence. Four kids and no money.' (61) As the novel continues, though, sympathy is progressively withdrawn. She becomes entirely absorbed in the minutiae of the world of petty urban gossip; uninterested in her husband or children, 'slovenly' about the house, as quick to condemn others for their shortfalls or the fact of their mere difference as she is unable to accept responsibility herself, she is portrayed as entirely egotistical, self-indulgent and self-deceiving, focused on nothing more edifying than the consolation of food, the furtive gratification of purchase by lay-by, and 'the small trickle of excitement' to be had in putting bets with the local SP bookmaker (87). The war, and the social turmoil of which it is a part, mean little to her:

> Ally went on as usual. She defied the war, and, come what might, she meant to get her share of everything that was. In a small way she hoarded food, not for her

family, but for herself. The more the public were asked to conserve water, the more she used her tap. For sensation value in the newspapers she found the war far inferior to a good murder or divorce. She put on weight steadily, and when she could get at Harry she nagged him.

[309/305]

Regardless of our hopes, from the novel's point of view it is a decline that can be firmly sheeted home to one person alone, Ally herself.

The difficulty the text represents, then, is that given expectation it seems to behave rather poorly, at once patriarchal and misogynist. Fathers nurture, while mothers remain blind to the real needs of their children; fathers offer a site of security, mothers a bitter resentment; fathers represent continuity, mothers the trivial demands of the present. Disappointing to say the least, and it is beginning to look as if we best scotch expectation, and contend that here is text that tells us more of the dominant discursive formations of the day than it does of the gender of its authors. After all, we know full well that faith in authorship is itself theoretically suspect, the textual analogue of faith in the law of the father. Whatever it was that Barnard Eldershaw felt or truly intended, we might say, the actual text is best read not as simply expressive, but as the manifestation of the ideological context within which it was produced, the patriarchal Australia of the 1940s.

Is there more to it? One might begin by noting that no historical moment is ideologically homogeneous. All are marked by alternatives and resistances, and although these too, we must remember, may well fail to satisfy the appetites and desires of our own conviction, we still could hope for something in addition to the instantiation of the dominant ideology of its historical moment, although we certainly do get just that. On close inspection, I think, the text does struggle towards an alternative construction of gender identity: to begin to see it, it is useful to return briefly to the question of fathers and sons.

I have already suggested that the episodes are imbued with

a kind of resonance, and pointed to the field of personal experience as an explanation. Beyond that, though, there is a doubled narrative resonance, structural and allusive, and it is here that it is possible to see something of an alternative critique emerge. In terms of structure, the passages are constructed on a principle of repetition. Both concern memory, a form of repetition itself. Ben remembers his father's death, the night that his father had mistakenly eaten his dinner, the war memorial, his father driving the truck; each memory-instance is, moreover, itself a textual repetition. Ben remembers what the text has already produced, so the memory takes the form of a textual revisiting. The force of nostalgia is driven, at least in part, by the logic of narrative repetition. That logic is all the more powerful — and all the less related to the psychological texture of character — in the episode that concludes the larger novel, for there the sense of resonance is predominantly underwritten by its structural homology with the episode that concludes Knarf's novel. *Tomorrow and Tomorrow and Tomorrow* ends by repeating the narrative shape of the ending of *Little World Left Behind*; as the titles themselves suggest, nostalgia and the resonance it engenders are grounded in repetition. The upshot is a little unexpected: if these episodes are about patriarchal value, it would appear that it is a value determined as much by the apprehension of the structure of repetition, by the mere fact of the possibility of doing it again, as by anything inherent in the past. What the text calls 'security' is produced within the cool logic of repetition, and in the absence of a substantive ground within the law of the father.

The security of the father, in fact, while real within the moment of apprehension, seems to unwind upon inspection. Ben's introspection concludes by shifting gear:

> Strong good hands that he couldn't remember, only see. They'd meant security, and out of their insecurity all this had come. They were the hands that had let the world drop because it was beyond their power to hold any longer.

[424/415]

There is a retreat from focalization here, from Ben's inarticulate apprehension to the text's articulate knowledge that, finally, the strength of the father was not enough. The last sentence of Knarf's novel is, simply, 'Ben stood on a hillside in the apocryphal night, eating his apple', and one could say that if Ben's night is 'apocryphal', his vision is too, with the force of myth but also — like all myth — built through fiction.

Within the cultural context of this text, the most enduring myths of the father who both secures and yet must give up his son are, of course, biblical: the God that sees his offspring, having eaten from the tree of knowledge, making their own way in the world; the New Testament Father for whom love 'is the way of relinquishment' (466/456). That allusive background helps to fill in the emotional texture of the experience of both endings, but we need not suppose it is indicative of a theological faith the text itself endorses. Far from it. The father as patron is in fact a continual disappointment: Oran, the bureaucrat upon whom Lin pins her hopes for Ren's future, is interested in nothing more than the maintenance of his own power; Olaf Ramsay, the wealthy accountant who secures Harry his job, has the means and inclination of patron-philanthropist, but is incapacitated by a corrosive scepticism about the possibility of any absolute justification or value in the action he takes. And God himself, it turns out, can do no better. In a rather peculiar dream sequence, Olaf, determined to speak to 'some one in authority' (167), visits the first author. Although he is reassuringly familiar — he looks surprisingly like H.G. Wells at first — God has nothing to offer by way of enduring, foundational principle beyond the law of cause and effect. 'I've laid down one plain ruling and I'm leaving it at that.' (168) The point, though, is that in the 'one plain ruling' of causality, there can be no ethical justification, no significant meaning of the type required, and so no security. The logic of causality is the logic of repetition, too. Father he may be, first principle he is not:

A terrible suspicion crossed Olaf Ramsay's mind that God after all might be an Irishman. He certainly had a look of Bernard Shaw. He felt discouraged. 'It's confusing, very confusing,' he muttered.

'Yes, I get confused, too.' God agreed placidly.

'Oh, no.' The cry was wrung from Olaf Ramsay. If God couldn't keep a clear head, who could? God seemed to read his thoughts.

'But you made me in your image, didn't you?' he asked mildly.

'I think it was the other way. I'm sure it was.'

'It doesn't really matter.'

[168]

God is transformed once more — this time, into 'the image of Winston Churchill, but he had a Hitler moustache' (169) — but the situation remains unchanged. If God is taken to exemplify the qualities of security, authority, and foundational value that Ben/Ren sense in their fathers, the text itself makes it clear that the claim is a hollow one. The moment of safety that Ren feels, the sense of inheritance that Ben experiences, are within the world of the text 'real' and yet, it implies, we would be naive indeed to follow them and read the experience as a demonstration of the existence of a genuine, antecedent value. Epistemic conviction does not imply ontological security.

The difficulty the text poses can be, if not resolved, at least somewhat recast at this point. The endings register a strong sense of narrative closure as much as a sense of emotional satisfaction, but the text in fact is reluctant to endorse the ontological and ethical claims bound up in those endings. On the contrary: within the text, they are claims that are seen to be hollow. The *sense* of inheritance is real, but there is nothing of substance to inherit. Feeling safe can be genuine enough, but the foundational order upon which it seems to draw is chimerical. There is a common pattern here, and it recurs through the book: deeply felt needs and obligations imply and (or so it seems) draw upon a fundamental order, but that turns out to be spurious, no more than a repeated pattern of behaviour. The events in Knarf's novel are played out within a context of military and economic imperative: to fight, to work, to play one's part as a consumer, these things are taken seriously by the characters within the book, as if there really was a profound justification informing the struggle, as if the discourse of patriotism, the morality of the work ethic, and the enticing, erotic language of consumption actually meant something more than ways of talking and acting as banal in their form as they are viciously inequitable in outcome. Within the text, discursive formations owe their effectiveness to the conviction they evoke, but not at all to any ground that might in truth justify that conviction. Rather, the conviction is fuelled by their success as discourses, as ways of speaking and acting that become codified, that are constituted in their repetition and in the aura of expectation thus produced. Resonance, the sense that there is a deep order that will somehow make sense of the terrifying emptiness of the everyday, is the byproduct of that aura.

The job Olaf Ramsay secures for Harry can be read as aptly metaphoric in this regard. He becomes employed, he has the pride of the uniform, the comfort of a position within a vast organization, but if it is a narrative of progress it is a progression that (literally) can go nowhere. Up and down in the lift, day in, day out, Harry can do no more than repeat a prior movement, to trace a circuit within the complex system of movement and transaction that constitutes the whole; it is a circuit that — like any codified movement, any ritual — implies an order of significance, for all that it means, alas, nothing at all. Within *Tomorrow and Tomorrow and Tomorrow*, the narrative of repetition and expectation evokes meaning, but the text itself must bear the unhappy knowledge that it may well be a meaning 'signifying nothing' at all.

Knarf feels, you will recall, 'the most difficult love in the world, the love of a father for his son. It has no code and no ritual, no physical release, it must forever stand by and its way is the way of relinquishment' (466/456). Enough of fathers and sons, though; instead, let us ask, if this is 'the most difficult love', what would be the most easy?

In this formulation, difficult love is love that has 'no code and no ritual'. Accepting this, we might say that difficult love is not determined by the structure of a discursive formation, it is not at home within the codified restraints and articulate order of a repetitive system, and does not deal in the currency of expectation. Now if this is so, what then of 'easy love'? The night before the exodus from Sydney could be well taken as exemplary:

> The Botanic Gardens, which for the first time were not closed at sundown, became a grove of Aphrodite. In the darkness of the bushes, on the lawns in the elusive moonlight, lovers sought and found one another. Many had never seen each other by daylight. For this hour they were sufficient to one another, they were nothing but man and woman, they were oblivious of all the other couples. Live and let love. Trees threshed the sky, shadows fleered and struggled on the grass. Up from the earth there came confused and inarticulate cries. The smell of sap and crushed vegetation was carried on the dusty wind. In all the flux only the statues, the fountains, the pagodas, stood firm.
>
> [403/396]

Easy indeed, and yet the activities of the night do not seem to draw on the codes and rituals we were expecting, not at least if by that we meant something systematically codified, the upshot of a structure articulated by regularity and rule. On this night of easy love, no social code regulates or controls; rather than clarity there is darkness and 'elusive moonlight', a world of shadows and confusion, 'inarticulate' and 'in flux'. Amongst the flux, it is only the detritus of civilization, 'the statues, the fountains, the pagodas', that retain distinct form, and thus remain within the space of the readable. Easy love, that is to say, seems less defined in contradistinction from 'difficult' love, as from social love, the love that is determined within the realm of the discursive. Rather than articulate, easy love is confused; rather than social, instinctual: 'the city was reverting to ancient patterns, her people unconsciously bent themselves to old rhythms and were borne, unknowingly, on elemental tides' (403/396). On such 'elemental tides' personal identity is a matter of indifference, as is the moral reading of action; the narrative unfolds according to natural principles, innate and shared.

We might say, then, that within this text, 'difficult' love is not properly paired in opposition to 'easy' love. Rather, difficult love is the *third* term that falls outside a rather different opposition, that between love that is determined within the codified space of the social, and that which is wholly instinctual. To borrow Garcia Marquez's vocabulary, official love versus natural love.[7] Both are 'easy'; it is easy to abandon oneself to sensation, but it is easy, all too easy, to obey the law, too.

Of course, all this talk of 'love' is a little difficult itself. This is not, after all, a term that has been accompanied by much theoretical cachet in recent decades. So, if professional expectation is not to be disappointed, rather than the opposition between natural and official love, let us talk of two different conceptions of gender identity, and two different explanatory spaces within which interactive relations can be understood: essentialist versus discursive, or the innate and instinctive versus the socially produced. On the one hand, one can think of gender identity as natural, as reflecting immovable, elemental qualities; on the other as being 'official', the outcome of particular discursive practices, particular forms of code and ritual. Within this opposition, feminist writing itself has traced a two-part circuit. The first stage was constituted by the welcome critique of essentialist conceptions of gender, and the recognition of the ways in which the socio-linguistic machine produces and determines its subjects. If identity is not natural, it must be constructed, but that means that inequities and injustices so evident have no better justification than the fact of their prior existence in the machine itself, and are thus ripe for attack. The second part of the circuit is to escape the machine altogether, to refuse the identity fabricated within its economy. To act not as a woman produced within the discourse of patriarchy but as a (real) woman. But that, of course, gets us back to where we came from. The circuit seems as inevitable as it is problematic: from essentialism to discursive production, to essentialism once again. If this much be granted, it seems not unreasonable to read *Tomorrow and Tomorrow and Tomorrow* as both ranging across the terms of this opposition and, in the concept of 'difficult' love, testing the possibility of some alternative.

If the night in the Botanic Gardens represents the essential and instinctual, marriage — not altogether surprisingly — is the site in which the social codification and production of gender is at its most powerful. And, one ought to add, within this text marriages are universally unhappy. Marriage is a machine that produces misery (although the misery is not doled out in equal portions, women doing notably worse than their husbands). Like all discursive machines, its mode of operation is repetition: it produces expectation, most of all the expectation of continuity and progression, the expectation that the temporal extension of the marriage will take the form of some inherently satisfying, innately valuable narrative. As Harry puts it, 'Love was a fairy tale told so often that people believed it' (152). Once within the machine, women find themselves wholly determined by its hegemonic reach: they are perceived as wives, and perceive themselves as wives only.

As we have seen, the self-perceptions of the book's married women are projected entirely upon the narrative of conventional familial success and its twin goals: prosperity founded upon the husband's career trajectory, and the marriage of the children. It is always a narrative liable to disappointment. Harry Munster's career is miserable, while Knarf and Olaf seem uninterested in the societal dimension of their respective positions. Most remarkably of all, none of the children marry. The text construes the result for the wives and mothers, as we have seen, in terms of resentment, the growing bitterness of women who have invested in the narrative of patriarchal identity but have in the end nothing to show for it, no spiritual success, and not even something that could function as its material analogue. The family home, the space in which the story is meant to unfold, is profoundly important in their lives, but its importance is as much a reminder of constraint as anything else. For each mother (Ally, Lin, Mrs Ramsay), significant action takes place within it, never beyond it — with the exception of the opening scene of Knarf's novel, but even there Ally's journey to the city is evidence of her inability to function in any space beyond that of the domestic: worn down by the day, the weight of the sick child, the news of her fourth pregnancy, she eventually snaps in the crush of a railway carriage and responds to the infant's yelling by beating it, outraging her fellow passengers and shaming herself. Again, her reaction is cast in terms of resentment:

> She wanted madly to explain that what had happened was not her fault. She'd had an awful day, she was trapped, caught, everything was against her, it was her husband's fault.[...]She looked from face to face, she must make her defence, but that would be the whole story of her five years' marriage. It was his fault that she had disgraced herself in public, everything was his fault.
>
> [54]

In this novel, the 'whole story' of marriage is to be 'trapped' and 'caught'.

Unable to cope with the environment beyond her own home, Ally — like Lin and Mrs Ramsay — feels trapped within it, too. Trapped, but not secure: moments of emotional security — like the scene that ends the novel — are inevitably located outside the walls. Even those few moments of sexual passion within the text (Paula and Archie, Harry and Gwen, the anonymous lovers of the garden) belong outside the architectural and legal space of marriage which itself, in the end, can only look impotent and provisional. 'We only went there temporary', says Ally as she leaves her home of almost twenty years, 'it never was home' (409/401). The tragedy is that nowhere else will be, either, but that nonetheless her own sense of identity is entirely constructed within the machinery of official love, the narrative of which will always expect, but fail to deliver, 'home'.

Neither essentialist nor constructivist paradigms offer tenable solutions in the text. Given the social context, the path of sheer instinct is one that can only be available on the most rare, apocalyptic, of occasions. There is a sense of tautology in this, as the social and the instinctual are constitutively opposed. To act within the social is to act in a way that is something more than immediately instinctual: it is to act within linguistic mediation. For this text, this is precisely the point: we can conceive of essentialist identity, but it is a country to which no return is possible. But if essentialism is impossible, constructivism is painfully unpalatable. The projection of identity onto the narrative of marriage is as easy as it is liable to disappoint, as all characters come to realize. Harry 'supposed that most people's marriages went phut sooner or later' (84), Gwen 'took it for granted that most people didn't get on after they were married' (185), Lin finds that what she had thought had been love for Knarf 'had been a blind alley, leading neither to joy nor to tragedy, only to a dull beating imprisoned pain' (222).

It is against this opposition — natural love, official love — that the text posits difficult love: not that of father for son, but the love of Paula and Archie, and, most significant of all, between Ruth and Sid Warren. Ruth and Sid first walk together of a Sunday in the Domain, and Ruth's younger sister Wanda is quick to read the evidence: 'you went for a walk with him and came back with your dress torn. Don't think I don't know what that means.' (261) The torn dress indeed 'means', but its referent is a struggle that takes place in the space of the political, not the sexual: she becomes caught up in a people's counter-movement against the aggression of on-leave soldiers, outraged by the anti-war sentiments of a socialist speaker. Wanda's misreading has a kind of truth, nonetheless: theirs is a relationship in which the language of courtship tends to indicate, simultaneously, a site of political struggle. 'It isn't any good', he says, 'I'm not free to marry you' (295/292); however, the constraint is not that of being already married, as the phrase ordinarily would imply, but of being committed to a course of political and social revolution which would undermine the machinery of marriage. To Ruth's insistence that she did not need marriage, that she too can be 'hard', Sid is conventionally dismissive:

> 'You're not like that, really,' he accused her. 'You're not rough and tough. It's just a show you're putting on to get your own way. You mightn't know it but it is. All women are the same.'
>
> [296/293]

His claim to knowledge, and the stereotypes he draws upon, are instantly dismantled, though:

> She understood his anger for what it was. She had felt his need. Shaken, she was still reinforced. She couldn't tell him that she wanted this hard difficult love. It was a part of the world opening before them. It was her charter of equality. She accepted it. It was he who was clinging to tradition, gone rotten, from the world he thought he had abandoned. She didn't speak or move.

'Difficult love' here is the love in which gender identity is neither the product of 'tradition', nor yet is it the easy identity of essentialism. Rather, 'difficult love' is the work of production, but it is a self-engendered production, in which identity is discursive, but constructed through a narrative of one's own making. Finally, no longer determined by the codes and rituals that align gender and power, 'difficult love' is a 'charter of equality'.

If it is a liberation, it is a liberation from that tradition of gender stereotypes and, above all, from the codes and rituals of marriage. The other difficult love, that of Paula and Archie, likewise runs its course beyond the space of marriage. Stifled by the family home, Paula leaves to live alone, beyond expectation, unwilling to accept the social narratives available to her within it. The account of the progress of her relationship with Archie is remarkable for its disavowal of the clichés of romance: there is no hint of seduction or of a loss of control; it is a matter of clear-headed decision. In neither this nor Ruth's case is there any narrative condemnation: the novel is as sympathetic to their position as it is impatient to that of married women. Paula and

Ruth find 'difficult' love, but their action is a result of choice: the choice to refuse the impoverishing constraint of marriage. For this text to be produced within the prison of marriage is an outcome of a failure of nerve.

It has to be said, though, that the text is not successful in giving a substantive sense of what would be involved in such a self-engendered narrative. In fact, what more we see of Ruth and Sid suggests a rapid regression to the familiar narrative in which she supplies the human warmth to his cold determination, and in which she becomes the exemplification of her own name to his increasing and complementary ruthlessness. In the end, her confidence fails in the face of the destruction of the fire, as she finds she has gone too far to return to the order of tradition, but can no longer project her own path forwards: 'the past had fallen in, the future did not exist' (414/407). Having countenanced the possibility of a different kind of gender identity, the text is unable to imagine the narrative that might emplot it; it is literally a future that does not exist yet. And, while Ruth cannot return to the past, the text, alas, finds its way back to the exclusions and disappointments of the patriarchal order. Ruth becomes Sid's helpmeet, and Lin keeps the home fires burning while Knarf and Ren share a drink and sanctify the world of fathers and sons.

If this is a failing of the text, it is, I think, one that reveals more than a mere failing of the feminist determination, as indeed it reveals more than the relatively barren ground Australia in the 1940s was for feminism, although it does both these things, too. The crucial feature of the textual logic I have been following is in its complication of the essentialist/constructivist dyad through the introduction of a third term, the 'difficult love' that is other than the easy love of either nature or institution. That third term, however, is a marker of a logical position, a notional pos- sibility, without substantive content. For a brief moment, the text reaches towards the 'charter of equality' in gender identity that the 'difficult love' of a self-engendered narrative might produce, but it fails to hold it. More than a personal failure, though, it may well point to a necessary failure, too, and remind us that while the movement beyond the closed circuit of essentialism and constructivism is the very foundation of any cogent 'charter of equality', it is, paradoxically, a movement beyond the logic of gender identity, too.

Why so? One answer might run like this. Within that circuit, the driving force is the ideological processing of biological fact. The circuit produces meaning through the distribution of power it effects; that is, the economy of gender difference can be read as an economy of power difference, too. This much is axiomatic enough. The question then becomes, though, can gender difference be read as anything other than the outcome of an economy of power? The third term, the 'difficult love' of *Tomorrow and Tomorrow and Tomorrow*, identifies the space of that reading; the space itself, though, remains empty: necessarily so. It is easy to find significance in an operational difference, a difference in the ability to act. But what of non-operational differences? To borrow Wittgenstein's metaphor, what difference is there between two machines that function in precisely identical ways, that are built of precisely the same components, except that one of them has an extra part, quite independent and of no operational effect? Beyond the sheer fact of the part's existence, there is no difference. Or, more simply, there just is no meaningful difference at all — the empirical difference does not signify. Only differences which register a difference in the capacity for action can be read as significant: to be of significance requires substantive, operational difference. A capacity for action, though, is nothing other than a measure of power. Operational differences are power differences. If that is so, then it would follow that difference cannot be read as significant unless, simultaneously, it marks an articulation in the economy of power.

The 'charter of equality' that the text finds in the 'hard difficult love' Ruth wants, in abandoning the inequalities of the gender identity of tradition, necessitates an escape from the economy of power that underwrites those identities. Insofar as gender difference, and thus gender identity, is premised on a differential distribution of power, it is necessarily inequitable. In contrast, our expectation — like Ruth's — is for gender difference not aligned to the economy of power, but difference thus not aligned is not significant difference at all. There is no *gender* identity in the space to which the charter gestures, and the text thus faces a choice between abandoning gender as a marker of significant difference or falling back into one or another of the constructivist discourses that produce it. To escape the circuit of essentialism and constructivism is not a path to a genuine knowledge of gender identity, but an escape from narratives of gender altogether.

Faced with this utopian moment thrown up by its own narrative logic, *Tomorrow and Tomorrow and Tomorrow* fails. Gender identity is not dismantled in the revolution that ends the twentieth century, and the old, bad structure awaits us in the twenty-fourth. One begins to expect disappointment, I suppose, but if it is a failure, it is also an intimation of the fact that there is an uncompromising disjunction between the expectations prompted in the pursuit of narratives of gender identity, and the libertarian ambitions that fuel them. Of course, it is easy to have wished the text to have behaved a little more in line with its status as a newly resurrected classic, but in fact it is most striking in the way it declines to fudge the issue. One cannot have both the security of gender narratives *and* equality, and although one might well wish the text had been able to choose differently, its failure to do so ought to remind us how very difficult, and radically different, the alternative would be.

---

1   Edgar Harris, manager of Georgian House, Melbourne, to Marjorie Barnard, 22 March 1944. Marjorie Barnard papers, Mitchell Library, uncatalogued MS 451, box 4.

2   Anonymous review, 'Past Imperfect', *Times Literary Supplement*, 12 March 1949, p. 165.

3   Marjorie Barnard, *The Persimmon Tree and Other Stories* (Sydney: Clarendon, 1943).

4   Drusilla Modjeska, *Exiles at Home: Australian Women Writers
        1925–1945* (Sydney: Angus & Robertson, 1981), p. 243.

5   Important recent work of relevance includes Denise Riley, *Am I
        That Name: Feminism and the Category of 'Woman' in History*
        (Minneapolis: University of Minnesota Press, 1988); Judith Butler,
        Gender Trouble: Feminism and the Subversion of Identity (New York:
        Routledge, 1990); Rita Felski, *Beyond Feminist Aesthetics: Feminist
        Literature and Social Change* (Cambridge, Mass.: Harvard University
        Press, 1989); Diana Fuss, *Essentially Speaking* (New York: Routledge,
        1989); and Tania Modleski, *Feminism Without Women: Culture and
        Criticism in a 'Postfeminist' Age* (New York: Routledge, 1991).

6   For a great deal of the text, the 1947 Georgian House edition
        (Melbourne) and the 1983 Virago edition (London) have common
        page numbers. Where they differ, both are listed, the Georgian
        House edition first. It is my view, incidentally, that the earlier edition
        is far superior to the latter, which seems to have been constructed
        with little care.

7   Gabriel Garcia Marquez, *Love in the Time of Cholera* (Harmondsworth:
        Penguin, 1989).

MAPPING 'THE LABYRINTH WITHIN US': THE SEARCH FOR NEW ONTOLOGICAL TERRITORY IN ANGELA CARTER'S *THE PASSION OF NEW EVE*

JANE SOUTHWELL

'WE start from our conclusions', states the narrator of *The Passion of New Eve* at the beginning of the final chapter. Not only do we read or perceive our world according to the ideological clues or maps which we take up as we journey through it, but we are formed, often before our beginning, by the social codes which greet our existence. This apparently circular logic looks deceptively imprisoning. The paradox of such a statement is exploited by Angela Carter, however, in order to turn our world inside out, to expose the socially inscribed patterns of our minds and bodies.

Carter's circular structures are more than the uroboric circle that she cites, the mythic snake that eats its own tail; they are characterized by an excess, a spilling over or metaphoric shedding of skin. A visual exploration of such a circle is a möbius strip on which the inside surface is the outside surface, or further, the drawing by Escher entitled *Waterfall* in which the water appears to be flowing down but when we alter our perception the waterwheel seems to be self-generating from water which is circulating on the same level.[1] Within narrative these devices form a 'strange loop' or metalepsis which has the function of appearing to return the reader to the same place but, at the same time, allows the reader to see things differently. This is common as both motif and structural device in much post-modernist fiction, and is especially noted in the short stories of Borges such as 'The Garden of Forking Paths' and 'The Circular Ruins'.

The reader is caught in a labyrinth which we may figure to represent the spiralling and dizzying paths and connections of the unconscious. In Carter's labyrinth of desire it is Ariadne, the woman who is motivated by heterosexual love, who gives to a man the key, the thread to all mythologies. But it is the fate of Theseus to abandon Ariadne, as Evelyn abandons Leilah in *The Passion of New Eve*, until Theseus can become Ariadne and see with a marginal perspective. The eyes, the gaze, and the *trompe l'oeil* effect that unsettle our ideologically inscribed perceptions are frequently used by Carter as devices to refigure our images of self. Misrecognition is foregrounded; illusion is real and reality is illusion. Carter lays bare the devices which give us the illusion that we are who we think we are.

Desire, too, is refigured as production, as process, as giving, as flowing, in the sense in which Deleuze and Guattari use it.[2] Deleuze and Guattari's concepts of process suggest strong metaphoric intersections with the ideas of Julia Kristeva, even though they repudiate the Freudian/Lacanian model of lack. The flux or the flow, the spilling over of desire, may be concep-tualized as an abstraction, as a movement between binary poles such as subject/object, masculine/feminine, human/animal. This movement allows for a breaking down/up of philosophically exclusive categories which are arbitrarily established by the 'desiring-machines', as Deleuze and Guattari rename the patri-archal, the phallogocentric ideological[3] constructs:

> Desiring-machines are binary machines, obeying a binary law or set of rules governing associations: one machine is always coupled with another...And because the first machine is in turn connected to another

whose flow it interrupts or partially drains off, the binary series is linear in every direction. Desire constantly couples continuous flows and partial objects that are *by nature* fragmentary and fragmented. Desire causes the current to flow, itself flows in turn, and breaks the flows. [my italics][4]

The particular use of the word 'nature' in this quotation creates problems for a feminist critique. Although Deleuze and Guattari stress that they 'make no distinction between man and nature'[5] and that this is an instance of the effect of the production of desire breaking down the linear flow between these mechanical categories, the gendered use of the word 'man' and the lack of acknowledgement of the intersection of 'nature' and its cultural connotations remain problematic.

Similarly problematic and, at the same time, extremely useful is the Deleuzian concept of 'le devenir femme' or 'the becoming woman'.[6] Deleuze valorizes process as an end in itself, as opposed to a process which points in a linear fashion towards a goal. The use of the word 'woman' here is not tied to a bodily configuration that is female or to Simone de Beauvoir's famous statement about the social construction of woman as Other to man: that is, the proposition that 'one is not born, but rather becomes, a woman'. 'The becoming woman' is instead an image of the various positions of marginality which offer a perspective other than that endorsed by the dominant and shifting centre. It resembles Julia Kristeva's statement that 'she does *not* exist with a capital "W"'.[7] Thus, 'the becoming woman' is the name for a subject position, in the Kristevan sense, which relates to both men and women. Indeed, it is a particularized 'place' which offers a different way of seeing due to its marginality and can be conceptualized as similar to Virginia Woolf's Society of Outsiders.[8] This is not a biological position. As Alice Jardine states, 'the woman who does not enter into the "becoming woman" remains a Man, remains "molar", just like men'.[9] For Deleuze and Guattari, the term 'molar' signifies 'sedentary' and is used pejoratively to contrast with 'molecular' which signifies speed, the unfettered flow of desires — 'In the unconscious it is not the lines of pressure that matter, but on the contrary the lines of escape'.[10]

Deleuze and Guattari's position has been criticized for its gender-blindness. Despite some of the evident problems with their position, I would like to appropriate the substance of their hypothesis for feminism as a means towards mapping a space for new ways of being. Irigaray has noted the similarity between 'the becoming woman' and the female split subject, who historically struggles for subjectivity and a place in language and history. She sees it as yet another example of the struggle by women to overcome invisibility in an economy of the same.[11] Jardine also alerts us to the dangers of the use of 'woman' as metaphor:

> But to the extent that women must 'become woman' *first* (in order for men, in D+G's words, to 'follow her example'), might that not mean that she must also be the *first* to disappear? Is it not possible that the process of 'becoming woman' is but a new variation of an old allegory for the process of woman becoming obsolete? There would remain only her simulacrum: a female figure caught in a whirling sea of male configurations. A silent, mutable, head-less, desire-less, spatial surface necessary only for *His* metamorphosis?[12]

Despite the problems for feminist criticisms which are inherent in the terminology used by Deleuze and Guattari, many of the key ideas relating to process, flight, escape and flow are particularly useful for a reading of *The Passion of New Eve*. Equally problematic, but no less necessary, is access to a vital and unbounded collection of Surrealist representations of the unconscious. Carter edited and wrote the commmentary for a work of selected paintings by Frida Kahlo and is known to have had a passionate attachment to the films of Luis Buñuel, who collaborated with Salvador Dali in the early 1930s. The ambivalence of the male Surrealists towards women, and at times their outright misogyny, cause tensions in Carter's work where the artistic debt to this disparate group is evident. Of great importance to this reading of *The Passion of New Eve*, however, is Carter's use of the Surrealist device of the representation of the interchangeability of surfaces. The definition of an inner versus an outer space is deliberately confused such that the outer is merely a representation of the inner field. The works of Leonora Carrington provide an example of some of the areas of concern to women members of the Surrealist Movement. Drawings from Carrington's *Down Below* offer the image of a hand and a glove which depicts the proximity of one to the other and the oneness with each other. At one and the same time, they are separate and in contact.[13] The Surrealist technique, too, of the literal exploration of a linguistic image informs a reading of a text which pursues the materiality of 'the becoming woman' when the protagonist is forcibly changed from a man into a woman.

Although the plot nearly defies explanation and is, thus, a challenging example of the extreme divergence between *sjuzet* and *fabula*, an attempted rendition is necessary for an introduction to the rupturing of logocentrism and time and space employed by Carter. We are embroiled in and transported through the extraordinary mathematical and fantastic possibilities of a journey to discover the muse, Tristessa. After an opening apostrophe to this simultaneously ageing and ageless film star, the plot moves to an indeterminate apocalypse in New York where Evelyn, a young middle-class white man, encounters Leilah, a seventeen year old black prostitute. When Leilah becomes pregnant, Evelyn makes a hasty exit ('go west young man'), leaving Leilah sterile due to a botched abortion. During his journey Evelyn is captured in the desert by Mother and her female guerrillas who surgically and psychically change him into a woman now known as Eve. She escapes, only to be captured and raped by Zero, the misogynistic keeper of a harem. On the road again, Eve finds Tristessa, the object of her/his screen idolizing, and discovers that she is really a he. Zero and his sex slaves force Eve (him/her) to marry Tristessa (her/him) and the resulting progeny is transported across the Pacific Ocean to a nameless destination. This only happens, however, after we discover that Leilah is now Lilith, one of the black guerrillas and the daughter of Mother. And Mother now languishes in a nostalgic gin haze on the beach. So nothing is as it seems and all is read according to the many and varied intertextual allusions that we as culturally inscribed beings bring to the text.

Despite Carter's deliberately dizzying plotting, it seems possible to construct a model of emplotment. The body of the text resembles a spiral that opens outwards and expels its protagonist at the end, giving birth literally and metaphorically to the next generation, *Nights at the Circus*. Evelyn 'isn't in Kansas any more' but neither is there 'no place like home'. The new Eve has to begin from scratch. The plot itself is revolved by the movement from one place to another and one time to another. If the plot itself is confusing, it is meant to be. We are plunged into chaos, but it is a chaos that is ordered in its disorder. As readers, we attempt to impose order on the disorder, only to find that there is, in fact, a pattern in the chaos, if only we look hard enough for it. The key to the puzzle of the structure, the 'enigma',[14] of the text, is uncovered in the figure of the motor which drives Tristessa's revolving glass house in a spiralling movement of centrifugal rather than centripetal force. As central symbol or *mise-en-abîme* of the text, this helix mirrors the movement of the plot as well as reflecting its inhabitants in its glass structure. The reflective surface of the dark glass also provides opportunities for Tristessa and Eve to reflect upon the nature of the construction of self. Carter rarely misses the opportunity to use the full effect of puns.

Carter generates a text that revolves about and evolves from the huge number of intertextual references employed. We first meet Evelyn in a flea pit, watching an ancient rerun of Tristessa as Catherine Earnshaw in *Wuthering Heights*, a text which is alluded to on numerous occasions. The Gothic forms a strong component of the imagery and plot devices of *The Passion of New Eve*, as has been evident also in many of Carter's earlier texts. Evelyn loses faith in his image of Tristessa as the 'ethereal Madeline' (6) from Poe's 'The Fall of the House of Usher' when he is sent another contrasting and contradictory manufactured photographic image of Tristessa, the golfer. Evelyn bemoans the loss, the lack of nostalgia in this image, and desires a return to a time other than one when the prevailing ideology is 'Body, all body, to hell with the soul' (7). Investigations of the social constructions and inscriptions of the body are developed by comparisons with the journeying through time and space in Virginia Woolf's *Orlando* and L. Frank Baum's *The Wizard of Oz*. Roland Barthes describes the intertext as 'a circular memory'[15] since the intertext recognizes:

> the impossibility of living outside the infinite text — whether this text be Proust or the daily newspaper or the television screen: the book creates the meaning, the meaning creates life.[16]

Julia Kristeva is credited with the coinage of the term 'intertextuality' and refuses the interpretation frequently used of 'the influence by one writer upon another, or with the sources of a literary work'.[17] Kristeva privileges the definition that it 'involve[s] the components of a *textual system*'. Roudiez gives as its origin *La Révolution du langage poétique*, where it is defined as 'the transposition of one or more *systems* of signs into another accompanied by a new articulation of the enunciative and denotative position'.[18] What Kristeva tends to use instead of the misappropriated 'intertextuality' for references to other texts is Bakhtin's term 'polyphony', particularly in terms of the polyphonic novel. The text is then ambivalent or dialogical — that is, it talks to itself, and to the temporal, geographical and connotative spaces which it constructs and by which it is constructed. Thus, Kristeva says that:

> The writer's interlocutor, then, is the writer himself, but as reader of another text. The one who writes is the same as the one who reads. Since his interlocutor is a text, he himself is no more than a text rereading itself as it rewrites itself. The dialogical structure, therefore, appears only in the light of the text elaborating itself as ambivalent in relation to another text.[19]

Barthes's reference to 'a circular memory' reflects accurately this movement of a dialogic or polyphonic text such as *The Passion of New Eve*. As a site for the playing out of the struggle to elide the differences between cause and effect, to allow a filtering through or a folding back on itself, this novel pushes to the limits the nature of the circle. It both encloses and allows infinite progression. Tristessa acts as a referent for this very process. He/she is a fleshy example of the uroboric circle since he/she lives out his/her female-preferred existence by removing his/her memory of maleness and taping his/her penis to his/her anus. Carter prefigures and echoes this image of the circle defining our identity and determining the boundary of our existence when she inserts into the text the titbit — or more correctly, the bumbit — that Evelyn averts the failure of his journey west by taping his money to the hollow of his crotch. Evelyn begins his journey with the comment 'down the freeways in fine style, like a true American hero, my money stowed between my legs' (37). Evelyn/Eve functions as an example of the trace of recognition that there must be between men and women in order to cause, in a patriarchal system, such concern to maintain the differences between the sexes.

By creating a being that is physically female with some reconditioning of the psyche from masculine to feminine as well, Carter plays a 'before and after' game. Whilst investigating the different social treatments meted out to women and men, Carter also examines the part played by the memory contained in the body as well as the mind. To the extent that there is some residual conditioning, it is sufficient to blur the socially constructed differences between masculine and feminine behaviours and to underline the commonality between women and men. A system based upon similarities rather than differences must produce newness out of the resulting entropy. Although some will interpret this development as chaos, it can just as easily be seen as order. Disorder and order are merely different perspectives on the information that we receive and, given more information, they start to look very similar. The world is turned on its head or, more appropriately, on its sex.

Carter uses parodic devices and strategies to challenge our acceptance of the culturally constructed differences between genders as 'natural'. In the English language we are restricted to the use of only two genders compared with the wider range of three in many other European languages, unless we employ the distancing and class-specific pronoun 'one'. Maintaining the differences or mapping the territory between the genders so that they do not collapse back into one, or fragment into many variations, requires the constant repetition and performance of the naturalized behaviours that have been attached to each gender. In her analysis of feminism and identity entitled *Gender Trouble*, Judith Butler recognizes the performative acts which must be engaged in in order that societies continue to subscribe to the belief that there are only two genders and that they are immutably attached to their corresponding sexes.[20] Following a Foucauldian line, Butler argues too for the social construction of sex. If the philosophical division between nature and culture is culturally determined and nature is named by culture, then Butler would argue that our gendered society constructs our sexual identities too. The 'nature is to culture as sex is to gender' paradigm is undone. It follows similarly, then, that the constructedness of our sexual identities must be reinforced by repeated performative acts. We are accorded female or male status at birth and become by definition one and not the other. The ideological belief in an ordered society is threatened by any categories which exist beyond those bounds. They are literally out of bounds.

In Irigaray's reading of Freud, a woman achieves 'femininity' — that is, she becomes a woman who is regarded as 'normal' psychoanalytically — by entering into the 'masquerade of femininity'. Irigaray argues that 'the female Oedipus complex is woman's entry into a system of values that is not hers, and in which she can "appear" and circulate only when enveloped in the needs/desires/fantasies of others, namely men'.[21] The character Leilah appears to construct herself nightly before the mirror in order to transform herself into a prostitute for the purpose of earning enough money to feed herself and Evelyn.

However, Evelyn, now at the end of his/her journey and with the perception of the new Eve, looks at Lilith and sees her as a 'different person' with the residual traces of the earlier Leilah:

> ...the slut of Harlem, my girl of bile and ebony! She can never have objectively existed, all the time mostly the projection of the lusts and greed and self-loathing of a young man called Evelyn, who does not exist either. This lucid stranger, Lilith, also known as Leilah, also, I suspect, sometimes masquerading as Sophia or the Divine Virgin, seems to offer me disinterested friendship, though in the past I *might* have caused her pain...[my italics]
>
> [175]

While he cannot trust his eyes, Evelyn 'knows' that Leilah is projected desire:

> And, in my heart, I knew it was my own weakness, my own exhaustion that she had, in some sense, divined and reflected for me that had made her so attractive to me. She was a perfect woman; like the moon, she only gave reflected light. She had mimicked me, she had become the thing I wanted of her, so that she could make me love her and yet she had mimicked me so well she had also mimicked the fatal lack in me that meant I was not able to love her because I myself was so unlovable.
>
> [34]

And so Evelyn searches for 'that most elusive of all chimeras, myself' (38) in the desert, a landscape that most closely represents the state of his heart. 'The postmenopausal part of the earth' (40) becomes, paradoxically, the site for the fecundity of Eve. In an interesting similarity to the paintings by Dali which depict the complex and infinite and yet barren and finite unconscious, the desert landscapes which hide or repress the underground labyrinths provide an a-mazing journey for the reader. Presence is absent and absence is present. We give

ourselves the illusion of movement forwards. In the hypnotic
language of a trance we are urged to:

> Descend lower, descend the diminishing spirals of
> being that restore us to our source. Descend lower;
> while the world, in time, goes forward and so presents
> us with the illusion of motion, though all our lives we
> move through the curvilinear galleries of the brain
> towards the core of the labyrinth within us.
>
> [39]

We are led by Ariadne's thread into Beulah, a labyrinth
resembling the uterus and echoing with resonances of Bunyan and
Blake. This structure is home to Mother, a large, black, four-
breasted woman, vision of all-consuming Phallic Mother.[22] Together
with her band of merry young 'priestesses of Cybele', Mother
changes Evelyn physically and psychologically into Eve. 'In
Beulah, myth is a made thing, not a found thing' (56) and this
setting becomes the site for an exploration of the consolatory and
dangerous power of mythology to keep us culturally bound in a
place which takes no cognizance of historical change. Mother
attempts to create her own mythology by gestating the semen of
Evelyn in the uterus of the Newly Born Eve, thereby creating the
first creature of the Year One. The community of Beulah, the
practices of reproductive technology and the Phallic figure of
Mother are savagely parodied by Carter in a heteroglossia of
genres, a polyphony of voices where the collisions of the changing
tones create laughter. Mother is 'as big and black as Marx' head in
Highgate Cemetery' and, below her 'false beard', 'she was fully
clothed in obscene nakedness' (59), 'her nipples leap[ing] about
like the bobbles on the fringe of an old-fashioned red plush
curtain at a french window open on a storm' (64). Her female
followers chorus the incantation 'Ma-ma-ma-ma' and offer up the
song of mythic images to 'Our lady of the cannibals' (62) who is:

> Ineradicable vent of being, oracular mouth
>
> absolute beginning without which negation is impossible
>
> [61]

Evelyn is raped in what is, if we are to accept the Freudian and Lacanian models of identity formation, an enactment of the ultimate return to the womb, the union of the Son with the Mother, by which the identity of the son is fused with the mother and therefore ceases to exist separately. Instead of the weapon that Evelyn had made of it, his 'pretty little virility' becomes 'just darling, harmless as a dove, such a delight! A lovely toy for a young girl.' (66)

Mother intends to create a new being to subvert the valorized dichotomy of the sexes since 'woman has been the antithesis in the dialectic of creation quite long enough' (67). However, Mother's closed Platonic circle, in which the male and female halves are absolutely joined together again,[23] is broken apart by excess and flight. Just as Evelyn's 'tribute of spermatazoa' to Tristessa in the very first sentence of the narrative spills over, escapes the bounds of allowability, and functions as the desire which produces, which will not be contained, so too the excess of sperm, the 'snailtrack' which Sophia scoops up to freeze for later use, runs beyond the economy of heterosexual reproduction. Eve runs, escapes, keeps moving away from one site of attempted closure to another. Her flight, like the fast-moving molecules of Deleuze and Guattari's hypothesis, refuses to become trapped in solid, fixed configurations.

Evelyn/Eve's constant movement throughout the text produces resonances of a fugue, in both musical and psychoanalytic senses of the term. Fleeing and chasing are characteristics of all fugues. In musical fugues the theme is stated successively in all voices of the polyphonic texture, that is, it is tonally established, continuously expanded, opposed and re-established. The structure of fugues has been likened to that of formal rhetorical discourse in which a proposition is formally presented, opposing material is refuted, the initial proposition is strengthened and a forceful conclusive statement is made.[24] It has also been figured as a conversation, argument, debate, diatribe or even as a battle among various voices.[25] In psychoanalytic terms a fugue is defined as a flight from one's own identity, often involving travel to some unconsciously desired locality. *The*

Passion of New Eve is a series of chases through labyrinthine territories; it is a flight from the self but also to the self.

Eve's escape from the clutches of Mother ends in her abrupt capture and rape by Zero, the metaphorically and literally one-eyed and one-legged keeper of a harem, who believes that women are formed of 'a different soul substance to men' (87). As narrative device, the rather too frequent running-out of petrol which stops Evelyn/Eve at points along his/her journey appears conveniently coincidental and naive. Carter parodies the device as well as the arbitrariness of the groups' imprisonment of thought. Mother wishes to trap the world in mythology, Zero to plug the hole that is the 'dyke', Tristessa, so that he can stop shooting only 'sterile blanks', and the Christian Souldiers will kill to enforce their particular morality. Zero demands silence from his harem who only speak in grunts, but he can do nothing to prevent the oral flow leading out when they are outside his earshot. In a deviant way, going around the main path, they interpret the dictum of no speech to mean that whispering is permissible. While indicating how the girls subvert Zero's decree, Carter also includes their complicity in their own living conditions and their desire to hurt anyone else who might challenge these.

Zero unwittingly leads Evelyn/Eve to the object of his/her desires, Tristessa. Ageing film star and the reclusive inhabitant of a glass house, Tristessa is unmasked as a male transvestite. As Eve acknowledges of Tristessa:

> You turned yourself into an object as lucid as the objects you made from glass; and this object was, itself, an idea. You were your own portrait, tragic and self-contradictory. Tristessa had no function in this world except as an idea of himself; no ontological status, only an iconographic one.
>
> [129]

Tristessa has transformed, transmuted the sand of the desert into the glass house and the many tear-shaped objects that surround it. He/she is the icon of female suffering, 'Our Lady of the Sorrows' (122), since he/she foregrounds the social state of women in his/her elaborate masquerade of femininity. His/her glass house, the 'spinning, transparent labyrinth' (116) of the self, allows the inside to be displayed on the outside. Walter Benjamin comments on the figure of the glass house in an essay on 'Surrealism' in which he writes:

> To live in a glass house is a revolutionary virtue par excellence. It is also an intoxication, a moral exhibitionism, that we badly need. Discretion concerning one's own existence, once an aristocratic virtue, has become more and more an affair of petty-bourgeois parvenues.[26]

Benjamin, too, is aware of the revolutionary potential of excess:

> There is a residue. The collective is a body, too. And the *physis* that is being organized for it in technology can, through all its political and factual reality, only be produced in that image sphere to which profane illumination initiates us. Only when in technology body and image so interpenetrate that all revolutionary tension becomes bodily collective innervation, and all the bodily innervations of the collective become revolutionary discharge, has reality transcended itself to the extent demanded by the *Communist Manifesto.*[27]

In many ways, Tristessa's spiralling glass house is a homage to Surrealist images of the self and the revolutionary potential for freeing the repressions trapped in the unconscious. Images of the self rupture and break apart when confronted by the myriad of conflicting impressions reflected by the glass walls which the night sky has transformed into mirrors. Zero dresses Eve in an evening suit and top hat for her forced wedding with Tristessa, an act which evokes images of the gender confusion created in the similar costumes of George Sand, Greta Garbo and Marlene Dietrich. Eve describes the unsettling of gender boundaries achieved by cross-dressing to foreground the masquerade of sex and gender:

I saw him step back and I saw his reflection in the
mirror step back and the reflection of that reflection in
another mirror stepped back; an entire audience
composed of Zero applauded the transformation that
an endless sequence of reflections showed me was a
double drag. This young buck, this Baudelairean dandy
so elegant and trim in his evening clothes — it
seemed, at first glance, I had become my old self
again in the inverted world of the mirrors. But this
masquerade was more than skin deep. Under the mask
of maleness I wore another mask of femaleness but a
mask that now I never would be able to remove, no
matter how hard I tried, although I was a boy disguised as a girl and now disguised as a boy again, like
Rosalind in Elizabethan Arden...

I only mimicked what I had been; I did not become it.
[132]

Eve is married to Tristessa who wears the wedding dress
that was used on the set of *Wuthering Heights*. This device
confounds the boundaries between novel and cinema and the
intertextual representation in this immediate text, a kind of
metacinema. We hear echoes also of Catherine's cry to Nelly
Dean that 'I am Heathcliff — he's always, always in my mind —
not as a pleasure, any more than I am always a pleasure to
myself — but as my own being...'.[28]

The nature of being is most closely explored in the
rampages of Zero and his harem through the labyrinth of glass
rooms which rotate about the spiral staircase. But the flesh
mocks the lived being. When Tristessa is unveiled as a man, he
is appalled by his 'red-purple insignia of maleness' (128) and
attempts 'to swallow his cock within his thighs' (128). Eve's
dizzying confusion, which is represented in the cessation of
linear time, and which ruptures the past-tense narration with a
reflection in the present tense (124), is resolved in the realization
that 'that was why he had been the perfect man's woman! He
had made himself the shrine of his own desires, had made of
himself the only woman he could have loved!' (128–129)

Tristessa's house is littered with glass and wax statues. The gallery of wax figures is styled as a mausoleum with figures lying in glass coffins. Tristessa attempts to hide his self in one of these coffins to escape the clutches of Zero; he becomes a morbid sleeping beauty who lives only in the multiple film roles that he continues to play out. Believing Tristessa to be dead, New Eve reads the 'corpse' as a 'sign of love made flesh' (119).

Infuriated that he has been duped by his own projected hatred of dykes, Zero engages in a rampage of desecration. The girls of the harem defecate and urinate upon the glass floors and when they have dressed the bridal dolls, they delight in their travesty by pelting Tristessa 'with lipsticks, rouge pots and eye paint until his satin skirts were daubed and streaked' (134). The trappings of masquerade, of clowning, are enlisted to ridicule these challenges to gender boundaries and to punish the trans-gressors. The house itself becomes an animate force in this confusion of boundaries and surfaces when it flings body parts outwards. The girls of the harem unwittingly engage in their re-membering:

> The centrifuge of the building whirled the dismem-bered waxworks round the floor but the girls hurried to gather the limbs together and prop them willy-nilly in rows facing the make-shift altar, so we should have witnesses and a congregation. But they put the figures together haphazardly, so Ramon Navarro's head was perched on Jean Harlow's torso and had one arm from John Barrymore Junior, the other from Marilyn Monroe and legs from yet other donors — all assem-bled in haste, so they looked like picture-puzzles.
>
> [134]

We are reminded of one of the favourite parlour games of the Surrealists, who delighted in making 'exquisite corpses'.[29] Carter not only creates the corpses, but re-members them, refigures them to foreground the arbitrary allocation of gendered characteristics. Judith Butler explains well not only the allocation of gender characteristics, but also the gendered view of sex:

It is cultural assumptions regarding the relative status of men and women and the binary relation of gender itself [that] frame and focus the research into sex-determination. The task of distinguishing sex from gender becomes all the more difficult once we understand that gendered meanings frame the hypothesis and the reasoning of those biomedical inquiries that seek to establish 'sex' for us as it is prior to the cultural meanings that it acquires.[30]

The sheer difficulty of negotiating this labyrinthine basis of identity is expressed by Carter when she describes the love-making of Eve, the man who is now a woman, and Tristessa, the biological man who had always lived as a woman until his/her encounter with Eve. While they seditiously make love on top of the United States' flag, Eve remembers that:

> I beat down upon you mercilessly, with atavistic relish, but the glass woman I saw beneath me smashed under my passion and the splinters scattered and recom-posed themselves into a man who overwhelmed me.
>
> [149]

As the narrative is told retrospectively in the first person, it is a remembering of the repression of the text, an impression on a body that is both newly inscribed and atavistically chained. While the novel ends by emptying itself out into the sea, its circularity, the circulation of its language, symbols and body, is reinscribed back into the text by the retrospective narration. We are asked to participate in the mapping of new spaces which defy closure but which must remain indeterminate. Herein lies the paradox which refuses to be resolved and which glories in its complexity.

---

1   Douglas R. Hofstadter, *Godel, Escher, Bach: An Eternal Golden Braid: A Metaphorical Fugue on Minds and Machines in the Spirit of Lewis Carroll* (Harmondsworth: Penguin, 1979), the 'Waterfall' is discussed on page 11 and the möbius strip on page 30.

2   See Gilles Deleuze and Felix Guattari, *Anti-Oedipus: Capitalism and Schizophrenia* [1972] (Minneapolis: University of Minnesota Press, 1983), p. 5f. See also Deleuze and Claire Parnet, *Dialogues* (Paris: Flammarion, 1977), pp. 108–110.

3   Here I am using the term 'ideology' in the way that Althusser defines it as 'the representation of the imaginary relationship of individuals to their real conditions of existence', in Louis Althusser, *Lenin and Philosophy and Other Essays*, trans. Ben Brewster (London: New Left Books, 1971), p. 152.

4   Deleuze and Guattari, p. 5.

5   ibid., p. 4.

6   Deleuze and Parnet.

7   Julia Kristeva, 'Women's Time', in *The Kristeva Reader*, ed. Toril Moi (Oxford: Basil Blackwell, 1986), p. 205.

8   Virginia Woolf, *Three Guineas* [1938] (London: Hogarth Press, 1986), pp. 122–133.

9   Alice Jardine, *Gynesis: Configurations of Women and Modernity* (Ithaca and London: Cornell University Press, 1985), p. 216.

10   Deleuze and Guattari, p. 338.

11   Luce Irigaray, *This Sex Which Is Not One*, trans. Catherine Porter (New York: Cornell University Press, 1985), p. 141.

12   Jardine, p. 217.

13   Madeleine Cottenet-Hage, 'The Body Subversive: Corporeal Imagery in Carrington, Prassinos and Mansour', in Mary Ann Caws, Rudolf Kuenzli and Gwen Raaberg, eds, *Surrealism and Women* (Cambridge, Mass.: The MIT Press, 1991), p. 77.

14   All page references are to the edition *The Passion of New Eve* [1977] (London: Virago, 1982). This reference is to page 6.

15   Roland Barthes, *The Pleasure of the Text*, trans. Richard Miller (London: Cape, 1976), p. 36.

16   ibid., p. 36.

17   Leon Roudiez, 'Introduction' to Julia Kristeva, *Desire in Language: A Semiotic Approach to Literature and Art* (Oxford: Basil Blackwell, 1981), p. 15.

18   ibid.

19   Kristeva, pp. 86–87.

20   Judith Butler, *Gender Trouble: Feminism and the Subversion of Identity* (New York: Routledge, 1990), p. 136. Butler writes, '[t]hat the gendered body is performative suggests that it has no ontological status apart from the various acts which constitute its reality'.

21   Irigaray, p. 134.

22   The Phallic Mother is the imaginary female figure who existed with the Primal Father before the social contract. In *Desire in Language*, Kristeva describes the Phallic Mother as having 'possession of our

imaginaries because she controls the family, and the imaginary is familial' (p. 191). The Mother 'is presumed to exist at the very place where [social and biological] identity recedes' (p. 242).

23 R.G. Bury, ed., *The Symposium of Plato* (Cambridge: W. Heffer and Sons, 2nd edn 1932), p. x.

24 Don Michael Randel, *The New Harvard Dictionary of Music* (Cambridge, Mass.: Harvard University Press, 1986), p. 327.

25 ibid., p. 328.

26 Walter Benjamin, 'Surrealism: The Last Snapshot of the European Intelligentsia', in *One-Way Street and Other Writings* [1929], trans. Edmund Jephcott and Kingsley Shorter (London: New Left Books, 1979), p. 228.

27 ibid., p. 239.

28 Emily Brontë, *Wuthering Heights* (Harmondsworth: Penguin, 1965), p. 122.

29 Rudolf E. Kuenzli, 'Surrealism and Misogyny', in Caws, Kuenzli and Raaberg, p. 20.

30 Butler, p. 109.

THE AMBIVALENCE OF WOMEN'S EXPERIENCE IN ELIZABETH JOLLEY'S *MY FATHER'S MOON* AND *CABIN FEVER*

AMANDA NETTELBECK

MANY critics of Elizabeth Jolley's fiction comment on its quality of duplicity, particularly as that quality relates to Jolley's female characters. There are the mingled stoicism and vulnerability of her women; the ambivalences of their relationships with one another; their desire both for order and for flight from its restrictive codes. However, these various areas of duplicity, in which each state is shadowed by the possibility of its opposite, do not remain fixed as easily definable binaries. Rather, they become areas of shifting signification which attest to the ambiguous nature of women's social, as well as emotional, experience.

Such shifts and ambiguities emerge again in Jolley's recent novel, *Cabin Fever*, which is in fact the extension (although not in a chronological or sequential sense) of her previous novel, *My Father's Moon*.[1] The narrator, Vera Wright — the efficient and compassionate nurse, the calculating and dispassionate friend, the lonely and disappointed mother, the clinging and distant daughter of *My Father's Moon* — is enclosed in her room on the twenty-fourth floor of a hotel in a strange city. Waiting out a medical conference (which includes such titles as 'Symptoms of Panic Disorder', 'Study of Closet Relationships' and her own 'Perspectives on Moral Insanity'), Vera acknowledges that she is suffering from cabin fever. To have cabin fever is to suffocate from one's own fear of cracking the 'thin ice', of confronting 'what is hidden immediately beneath the skin' (53). Yet to have cabin fever is not only to fear gazing inwardly, but also to fear acting outwardly. In short, it is to live always within a pause. 'This cabin fever', writes Vera, 'is like the intention to speak, it is the long drawn-out pause of intention' (237).

Jolley's presentation of a problem of language for Vera, as well as for other of her women characters, makes her work ripe for discussion within the contexts of recent feminist debate. The notion that women speak through the 'blanks and gaps' of a 'prison-house of language'[2] has been central to the position of those critics who argue that language, as a most potent medium of representation, marks out a male centred and categorized world; this point is the key one to the psychoanalytic/post-humanist school of feminism, which has extended the notion of 'castration' into a metaphor for the repression of the feminine in patriarchy's organization of language and, by extension, social power. To pursue this position as a way into Jolley's work is to risk perpetuating the most self-referential model of psycho-analytic criticism. Nevertheless, the seemingly self-conscious (and even tongue-in-cheek) foregrounding in Jolley's work of the complexities and ambivalences of the social 'psyche' does offer a means of reading the recurring way in which her women characters are configured. Vera's sense of an endless existence within a space outside of empowering action — to feel that one lives always '*before* a journey' (52) rather than that the journeys of one's life can have a destination — is particularly relevant to the position of women within the patriarchy or symbolic order: the post-Oedipal, language structured social order, which is presided over by the Law of the Father.[3] To know a constant disparity between desire for lost identity with the m/other and fulfilment of that desire is the destiny of the speaking subject within the symbolic order. For the female subject, however, that recognition of division is compounded by her problematic position within the symbolic order. Kristeva argues that the female subject must face the dilemma of either becoming father-identified, which allows her identity within the male-ordered realm of the word but which represses her identification with the mother, or of remaining mother-identified, which would be to retreat from the possibility of identity within the given (that is, patriarchal) social framework.[4] Either way, in other words, she faces marginalization within that social framework. The daughter's response to the figure of the mother, then, is an ambivalent one of both desire and denial. The effect of this ambivalence is in turn problematic. On the one hand, women's lack of defined space within the symbolic implies a symbolic crippledom: one thinks of the crippled Diana Hopewell in *Miss Peabody's Inheritance*, or the lame Hester or the one-armed woman in *The Well*. On the other hand, the very spacelessness which disables women may also be empowering, for it can become the undefined space from which alternative or unsettling meaning is generated. The position of 'the in-between, the ambiguous', writes Kristeva, is the position that 'does not respect limits, places or rules'.[5] So it is that these 'crippled' women are also the writers of their own narratives: Diana Hopewell is a novelist who writes of 'strange pleasures to be had';[6] Hester becomes a storyteller whose final tale, one senses, will be one that overturns the comfortably assumed vision of communal experience. Vera Wright, too, handicapped in many ways by the relationships in her life, is the self-assigned narrator of a text-within-a-text in which there is no closure or fixity of meaning.

Thus *Cabin Fever* is a novel filled equally with images of freedom as with images of restraint. If Vera is consistently trapped within her own immobilizing panics, she also works very hard at escaping the forms of her restraint (her mother's house, the hospital, the ironically named Fairfields School and, through the writing of her narrative, the hotel room on the twenty-fourth floor). It is difficult to say, finally, whether *Cabin Fever* is predominantly a story of defeat or of triumph; the fact that it is both points back towards what Toril Moi describes as the 'difficult balancing act' that women face in being 'in a position which is at once subversive of and dependent on the law'.[7]

In the opening section of the novel, Vera's 'balancing act' is reflected in her hesitant need both to retreat into inertia (in psychoanalytic terms, to reclaim and lose oneself in the m/other) and to move forward into the given social order. Both paths involve a sacrifice, an alienation. The hotel room is restrictive — 'The heat is unbearable...The windows do not open. I'm suffocating' (52) — but it is also protective. In Lacanian terms it is aligned with the pre-structured and therefore pre-conflict state of the imaginary; in Kristevan terms it is aligned with the polymorphic, pre-gendered realm of the semiotic. 'I try to think of the design of the hotel', writes Vera, 'but...I have no sense of direction from here' (15). Both Lacan's notion of the imaginary and Kristeva's notion of the semiotic are associated with mother-identification, and indeed the hotel room has a womb-like warmth and damp; it induces a dream-state which is both seductive and threatening in its emptying of identity:

> I remember reading somewhere that in order to be able to sleep in a strange room it is necessary to clear the mind; to 'empty yourself for sleep.'
> The sound of the running water is persistent, as if it will never stop. I feel the wall above my bed. The wall is warm.
>
> [15]

And later: 'At times I find the heat overpowering. The heat induces dreams bordering on nightmare. Delirium in which harm is done...' (51)

In an effort to overcome the cabin fever, the 'pause of intention', Vera's self-set task is to write, and this taking up of the pen marks her infiltration of the male-ordered realm of the word. Since her position there is problematic, her unravelling text is itself fragmentary in structure, finding its form as a series of interweaving threads moving backwards and forwards between present and past rather than as a sequentially unfolding narrative. And this fragmented, shifting form is the source of the story's unsettling potential: in its revealing of a polymorphic life, we as readers come to understand that nothing is resolved, that each event and thought is shadowed by the unarticulated possibility of its opposite.

This tension is lived out, in one way, through the historical context of the novel. England is engaged with Germany in the Second World War, and for Vera this implies personal as well as national conflict. German is the nationality of her parents, but in particular German is the language of her mother, who struggles comically and often in vain with English. Thus German is both nurturing and shameful; it is both the language of the mother's endearments and the language of the enemy, and this dichotomy, of course, also frames Vera's relationship with her mother:

> My nightdress, which she made, is very comfortable. It wraps around me. She knitted it on a circular needle, a kind of stockingette, she said it was, very soft. My mother, handling the nightdress again, spoke to me:
> *ein weiches reines Kleid für dich zu weben,*
> *darin nicht einmal die geringste Spur*
> *Von Naht dich drückt...*
> 'Shut up,' I said, not liking her to speak to me in German in front of the woman next door. 'Shut up,' I said again, knowing it was a poem. 'Shut up,' I crushed the nightdress back into the overnight bag, 'it's only a nightgown!'
> When I stop crying I pretend that the nightdress is my mother holding me.
>
> [*MFM*, 33]

The way in which the historical context of war intersects with an ambivalent response to the figure of the mother is also apparent in Vera's account of 'My Mother's Hats'. As a child, in the pre-war years, Vera looks for her mother from a 'high up' (73) hospital window (one thinks of her ongoing cabin fever in the room on the twenty-fourth floor). The defining characteristic of the mother is the hat, soft and white, that she wears: 'She had

a white hat with a broad, soft brim...She said that when I saw
the white hat in among all the people I would know that she
would soon be there. So I waited.' (73) But Vera's mother does
not come, and here the first recollection of separation and loss
emerges. In her fear of abandonment, the child recalls an image
of her mother, dressed in hat and fox fur, leaving with her
father to attend a concert. The recalled image is one which
speaks for the proprietorial right of the father, which separates
the child and mother:

> 'Your mother has such pretty arms,' my father said.
> The glass eyes of the fox were yellow, overflowing
> with tears which did not fall.
>   The white hat was the hat I was looking for...[but]
> suddenly there was my mother beside me, laughing.
> She had a new hat. A hat of fur encircling her head
> low just above her eyes.
>
> [74]

The tension which is lived out hereafter in the relationship
between mother and daughter again has physical representation
in the 'wartime' headscarf adopted by Vera's mother: 'Even
though the actual war is over, in many ways it is still as if there
is a war. As if the war will never really come to an end.' (75)

The image of the fox — which in this scene suggests the
intrusion of the father and the child's subsequent recognition of
division — is a recurring one in *Cabin Fever*, as it is in fact
elsewhere in Jolley's fiction (in *The Well*, for instance, the father
is 'the great red fox'[8]). However, the image of the fox carries
more than just the suggestion of masculine power. By association, it carries the weight of a worldliness that shadows and
belies an imaginary innocence. In *Foxybaby*, for example, the
eyes of Miss Porch's fox fur are almost sinister in their expression
of a worldly knowledge: 'They held in their glassiness a
knowledge of things not found in a spinster's luggage'.[9] In other
words, the potential for tension or conflict is already contained
within the state of innocence (in this case, sexual innocence); so
even Gertrude's Place, which represents to Vera a space of pure

harmony, beyond the 'Pit Fall' (3) of the outside world, is touched by the presence of the fox: '"That old red fox has had a wing offer one of 'em tell mother," [Gertrude] would say about a badly maimed boiler. "Tell her as I'm sorry about the wicked fox."' (189)

So paternal law, as the reminder of a worldliness that belies an imaginary 'innocence', is at the heart of the ambivalence in this text: it structures and orders the 'way things are' but it also instigates loss and division. For Vera, the figure of the father holds the promise of both security and separation; she is drawn to her father ('wherever I was, I was seeing the same moon that he was looking at' [196]), but he is also associated with the pain of separation ('It seems to me now, when I think of it, that my father was always seeing me off either at a bus stop or at the station' [*MFM*, 25]). One of Vera's infant memories is of her father singing her to sleep. The memory is suggestive of both protection and loss, for the images he evokes in his song are both reassuring and curiously sinister:

> My father comes creaking on bent legs along the hall.
> He crawls flickering across the ceiling crouching
> double on the wardrobe. Go to sleep he says. Flicker-
> ing in fire light and candle flame. Flickering and
> prancing he moves up and down the walls, big and
> little, little and big, colliding in the corners with
> himself...I'm a pork pie that's what I am. I'm a mouse
> now, he says, I'm a mouse in the iron and steel works.
> I'm a needle and thread. I'm a cartwheel turning in the
> road, turning over and over turning...
>
> [137]

The awareness of conflict within the supposedly harmonious, pre-conflict state of innocence is powerfully marked in the figure of Vera's own reticent, anxious little daughter Helena. Even newly born, Helena carries the shadow of worldliness, of a knowledge of loss which touches the purity of that idealized first unity with her mother:

> Helena cries the whole day, the first day of her life, a
> heartbroken crying as if she knows straight away some
> secret awful thing about the world into which she has
> come...I hold my baby. She is new-born and small and
> wrinkled with grief.
>
> [95]

As the reminder of an inherited repression, Helena reflects the
sense that at some level all women are 'the owners of grief' (95).
The fact of becoming Helena's mother heightens that irresolvable
ambivalence in Vera's relationship with her own mother because,
as Vera recognizes, 'this time is the one time when the child
turns back towards the parent in that curious bond between
parent and child in which the child is always moving away'
(124). It is notable, then, that Vera sees that her baby has
'inherited' her mother's looks: 'Helena's resemblance to my
mother is striking and cancels any other resemblance' (135). And
it is equally notable that her mother tells Vera: '"She looks like
you when you were a baby"' (136). In the pre-Oedipal moment
of the new daughter's dependency, the mother and daughter are
again bound together, but the moment carries with it also the
knowledge of the future 'war': 'A curious grief seems to engulf
me. I am sorry for my mother, for her almost childlike eagerness
to show off Helena, in spite of the shame I have brought, to
someone — and for her disappointment.' (136–137)

The recurring tension within the mother/daughter relationship is played out in other ways in Vera's adult relationships with
other women. Magda Metcalf, for instance, is both a beloved
substitute mother-figure and a suffocating, manipulative rival
whose nurturing gestures are less than innocent:

> 'Isn't she just a pet,' she called out, turning me round
> and round in front of her roomful of guests. 'Isn't she
> sweet to come after work. You darling!' she kissed me.
> 'And you still wear your school coat. I love it!...Jonty,'
> she called Dr Metcalf, 'take this dear child somewhere
> and undress her. Help her out of this coat.' They were
> all laughing.
>
> [*MFM*, 111]

Yet Magda is only one of the various and often disturbing female characters who in some way parallel the ambivalent mother/daughter relationship. There are Gertrude and the bossy midwife Sister Peters, who offer warmth and maternal care but are ultimately left behind as Vera moves towards the 'Pit Fall'. Moreover the safety that they offer is not only transient but also conditional: in the demands that it sets, their love for Vera is oppressively binding, emprisoning. In her choice to slide towards the Pit Fall, Vera encounters such women as Sister Purvis and Patch: the head nurse and the headmistress, both familiar figures of Jolley's institutionalized worlds. Both are imposed 'guardians' of sorts, whose roles of authority are not so much reassuring as dangerous. The one is 'a battle axe' who, it is rumoured among the nurses, 'hasn't any sex organs' (21); the other sings 'sinister remarks in a contralto voice, which...is the prelude to trouble' (187), and her sexual invitations promise not love but conquest and control. The world of the Pit Fall, in effect, is the world of the 'censured' woman. The cost 'of censuring herself as a woman', writes Kristeva, is to be 'deprived of a successful maternal identification and [to find] in the symbolic paternal order her one superficial, belated and easily severed link with life' (*Reader*, 150).

According to this model, then, women's choice of identification is always and inescapably ambivalent. 'I yearn for the Law', says the voice of Kristeva's female subject. 'And since it is not made for me alone, I venture to desire outside the law...Nothing reassures...' (*Reader*, 175) Yet this, perhaps, is where the story of defeat intersects with the story of triumph. The women of *Cabin Fever*, and of Jolley's fiction on the whole, occupy a position that is beyond ready categorization and that is therefore evasive of the monolithic social economy which surrounds them. Jolley's fiction tends to focus on the complexities of women's relationships with each other, and in the process it draws upon some powerful stereotypes (the 'castrated' or institutionalized woman of the school or hospital; the manipulative and enveloping mother). But in the end these woman-centred relations are slippery of definition: some are homosexual and some are not; some are predatory and others are supportive; some suggest various levels and ranks of power but are usually uncertain in their terms. In effect, the fact that so many of the social and sexual relations between Jolley's women *are* uncertain, are unarticulated, makes those relations evasive of the patriarchal stereotypes they so wryly evoke. So just as the first of the companion texts ends with a question which defers any resolution — 'but is it you, Ramsden, after all these years is it?' — so too *Cabin Fever* closes with a sense of non-closure: Helena has oddly faded from the text, and the outcome of Vera's story (if there is one) is withheld. Vera is still in a state of waiting, held in the 'pause of intention', but perhaps it is in the space of this pause that the stability of the Law is most profoundly unsettled.

1   Elizabeth Jolley, *Cabin Fever* (Harmondsworth: Penguin, 1990); *My Father's Moon* (Harmondsworth: Penguin, 1989). All references are to these editions and appear in the text. Since the writing of this essay, the third of these companion novels, *The Georges' Wife*, has been published.

2   Elaine Showalter, *The New Feminist Criticism: Essays on Women, Literature and Theory* (New York: Pantheon, 1985), p. 256.

3   Jacques Lacan distinguishes between what he calls the Imaginary (the pre-Oedipal, pre-lingual state of dyadic unity with the mother and indeed the world) and the Symbolic Order. In particular, see his collection *Écrits: A Selection*, trans. Alan Sheridan (New York: W.W. Norton, 1977).

4   Lacan's distinction between the Imaginary and the Symbolic Order may be compared with and contrasted to Julia Kristeva's distinction between the semiotic (the heterogeneous, chaotic realm of symbolic disruption) and the symbolic (the ordered realm of the word). In particular, see her *Desire in Language: A Semiotic Approach to Literature and Art*, trans. T. Gora, A. Jardine and L. Roudiez (Oxford: Basil Blackwell, 1980).

5   Julia Kristeva, 'Approaching Abjection', *Oxford Literary Review*, vol. 5 (1982), p. 127.

6   Elizabeth Jolley, *Miss Peabody's Inheritance* (St Lucia: University of
        Queensland Press, 1983), p. 35.
7   Julia Kristeva, *The Kristeva Reader*, ed. Toril Moi (Oxford: Basil
        Blackwell, 1986), p. 13. All further references appear in the text.
8   Elizabeth Jolley, *The Well* (Ringwood: Viking, 1986), p. 141.
9   Elizabeth Jolley, *Foxybaby* (St Lucia: University of Queensland Press,
        1985), p. 47.

ART FOR WOMAN'S SAKE:
KATE GRENVILLE'S *LILIAN'S STORY* AS
FEMALE *BILDUNGSROMAN*

SUSAN MIDALIA

RECENT feminist theorists of the *Bildungsroman*[1] have stressed the necessity for gendering and historicizing the genre, recognizing that the very concept of *Bildung* on which it is predicated has traditionally been a male prerogative. The novel of education, formation, or vocation, as it is variously called, both requires and valorizes what is usually denied to women — autonomy, independence, self-determination. The implicit male-centredness of the genre becomes apparent when the central character is female; the female *Bildungsroman*, bound by the generic constraints of realism — an adherence to social and historical realities and a notion of typicality — has until fairly recently been obliged to depict the *obstacles* to development, the limited number and limiting nature of plots traditionally available to women. Certainly it is true that nineteenth-century examples of the genre highlight the circumscribed nature of women's social roles, confining or consigning their heroines to either marriage or death. Female *Bildung*, as novels such as *Emma* and *Jane Eyre* illustrate, is often charted through the use of the romance plot and marriage-as-resolution; whilst the refusal of romance, as in *The Mill on the Floss*, offers death as the only alternative destiny for its fictional heroine. Indeed, the paucity of choices or the denial of development in such texts has prompted some critics to see the nineteenth-century female *Bildungsroman* as almost a contradiction in terms.[2]

More recent examples of the genre, however, particularly those written in the past twenty years or so in the wake of the Women's Movement, reveal a more optimistic view of female destiny. The contemporary female *Bildungsroman* often depicts expanded social opportunities for women, notwithstanding Nancy Miller's tart observation that even now 'female *Bildung* tends to get stuck in the bedroom'.[3] In novels such as Doris Lessing's *Summer Before the Dark*, Marilyn French's *The Woman's Room*, Marge Piercy's *Fly Away Home* and Margaret Atwood's *Surfacing*, to name some of the more well-known examples, the characteristic movement is from the personal and familial to the wider public sphere, as the female protagonists question the value of their traditional roles as wives, mothers, lovers. Critics have pointed to the appropriateness of the female *Bildungsroman* as a means of exploring this contemporary search for self. Ellen Morgan, for example, claims that:

> ...the female *Bildungsroman* appears to be becoming the most salient form for literature influenced by neo-feminism. The novel of apprenticeship is admirably suited to express the emergence of women from cultural conditioning into struggle with institutional forces, their progress toward the goal of full personhood, and the effort to restructure their lives and society according to their own vision of meaning and right living.[4]

Female *Bildung* in more recent examples of the genre thus becomes a genuine possibility. The greater number, and more emancipatory nature, of the plots available to the fictional heroines reflect a more liberated and liberating social order.

None of this is to posit, of course, a crude rupture between nineteenth-century and more recent versions of the genre. The change has been evolutionary rather than revolutionary; and furthermore, neither oppression nor liberation is ever absolute. Although nineteenth-century examples often depict a frustration or denial of female development, they also often have an oppositional potential, sometimes manifested in those formal disruptions embodying the genre's inability to contain female aspiration or desire. Such disruption can be shockingly spectacular, as it is in the conclusion to *The Mill on the Floss*, with the appearance of the symbolically charged flood which destroys the heroine. In Penny Boumelha's illuminating reading of the novel, 'the damned-up energy created by the frustrated ambitions and desires, intellectual and sexual, of the woman is so powerful that it cannot be contained within the forms of mimesis — it is the repressed and thwarted potential of Maggie that conjures into being that destructive, vengeful, triumphant flood'.[5] In *Jane Eyre*, female aspiration finds expression in the heroine's polemical feminist speeches addressed to Rochester and/or the reader. Whilst these speeches have been criticized for their lack of subtlety, their political hectoring of the reader, it is surely the obviousness, the 'set-ness' of the set pieces, which is precisely the point. Jane's special pleading is a necessary disruption, both aesthetic and political, of a genre and a society unwilling to acknowledge or accommodate feminist protest. And even in a female *Bildungsroman* as formally and ideologically conservative as *Emma*, there are moments of dis-composure. The famous Box Hill scene, for example, evoking as it does a sense of the heroine's frustration and ennui in a claustrophobically decorous social order, momentarily disrupts the novel's characteristically imperturbable comic surface. The unusual emotional intensity of the scene, culminating in Emma's 'extraordinary tears', troubles the equanimity of the heroine, the social group, and the comic mode itself. In Austen, too, there is a sense, however muted and sporadic, of the force of female frustration and desire. These examples reveal that the nineteenth-century female *Bildungsroman* is not a simple and dismal replication of a repressive and restrictive patriarchal order. There is scope here, too, for opposition, subversion, resistance.

Similarly, contemporary examples should not be reduced to monolithic models of female liberation. Conclusions are often open-ended, thereby problematizing the meaning of the heroine's journey of self-discovery. In *Surfacing*, for example, the heroine's impending return to what she loathes or distrusts — the city, the man — suggests either courage, or defeatist cynicism, or both. The novel leaves her in a state of suspension, radically undecided:

> If I go with him we will have to talk, wooden houses are obsolete, we can no longer live in spurious peace by avoiding each other, the way it was before, we will have to begin. For us it's necessary, the intercession of words; and we will probably fail sooner or later, more or less painfully. That's normal, that's the way it happens now and I don't know whether it's worth it or even if I can depend on him...[6]

The conclusion to *Summer Before the Dark* is similarly inconclusive and ambiguous. The choice which signifies the middle-aged heroine's rejection of the tyrannous regime of appearances — her decision to stop dyeing her hair — may be considered either the beginning of a radical restructuring of her life or merely a token gesture. Other novels are even more equivocal about the fates of their suffering heroines: novels such as Atwood's *Bodily Harm* and Marge Piercy's *Braided Lives* have been described by Linda Howe[7] as 'narratives of survival' rather than narratives of development. Within the broadly optimistic trajectory of the contemporary female *Bildungsroman*, development, formation, the realization of aspiration remain partial and problematic.

Individual complexities notwithstanding, however, it remains true to say that the contemporary female *Bildungsroman* is more sanguine about the potential for female *Bildung* than its nineteenth-century counterpart. I want to consider in some detail the contemporary politics of optimism in the novel *Lilian's*

Story,[8] by Australian writer Kate Grenville, published in 1991. Although in mimetic terms *Lilian's Story* emphasizes the denial of female development in an oppressively patriarchal society — Sydney in the earlier part of this century — it also refers to the beginning of a more emancipated social order — the 1960s. The heroine's individual history of decline is thus placed in a wider historical context which hints at a period of enormous social change and considerable progress for women. *Lilian's Story* thus posits an ameliorative view of women's history. And in meta-fictive terms, too, the novel recognizes the possibility of constructing more personally sustaining and socially productive narratives for women. As a self-conscious female *Bildungsroman*, the novel not only charts the denial of female development through the inadequate plots of romance and education, but also employs the potentially emancipatory plot of artistic vocation and the motif of the incipient female artist figure. And whilst the story of Lilian evokes the pathos of unrealized, including artistic, potential, *Lilian's Story* — the novel — anticipates an era in which artistic vocation might indeed be a reality for women, an answer to the question of female aspiration and desire.

Lilian's Story makes explicit its gendering of genre in its list of contents: the novel's tripartite division into sections entitled 'A Girl', 'A Young Lady', 'A Woman' foregrounds the gender-specific nature of identity formation and *Bildung*. At one level, it demands to be read as an anti-*Bildungsroman*, the story of the destruction of a woman of extraordinary promise. Loosely based on the legendary Sydney eccentric of the 1950s and 1960s, Bea Miles — famous, like Lilian, for jumping into taxis and quoting Shakespeare in the city streets — Grenville's novel presents its heroine as the victim of a pervasive and invasive patriarchal ideology, as embodied in the discourses of the family, education, romance, psychiatry and the law. Her story is a history of decline. Structurally, *Lilian's Story* subverts the central assumption of linearity-as-progress which underpins male versions of the *Bildungsroman*. Indeed, the novel might more properly be read as two halves, the first of which proceeds in linear fashion to suggest the possibility of female development, the second of which relies increasingly on repetition and circularity as formal embodiments of the heroine's *lack* of development.

The novel begins by constructing Lilian as defiantly non-conformist — linguistically precocious, sexually adventurous, wonderfully appetitive. She is the 'bold girl...hungry for every-thing' (111), with 'ambitions to possess the complete works of everyone' (79) and for whom 'there was nothing that did not matter' (83). In spite of the oppressive social forces ranged against her, Lilian is initially presented as capable of choice, in charge of plotting her own life. By contrast, the second half of the novel presents her as increasingly acted upon, plotted against — as evidenced by her father's confining her to a mental asylum in the appropriately entitled section 'Up Father's Sleeve'. Lilian's increasing powerlessness and marginality, her loss of a coherent sense of self, is embodied in her repetitive street performances, reciting Shakespeare, telling stories to unsuspecting passers-by, pursuing the object of her romantic and sexual fantasies, the hapless 'Lord Kitchener'. From potential *Bildung*, then, to decline: and what separates the two halves, and provides the explanation for the transition in character, is the profoundly dis-locating experience of incestuous rape — the novel's most potent metaphor of patriarchal power. The gendering of genre is here made disturbingly explicit: the failure of female *Bildung* is attri-buted to literal and symbolic violation by the male. *Lilian's Story* is unmistakably a *female Bildungsroman* in the centrality — structurally, psychologically, politically — it accords to the father's rape of the daughter.

One of the most important consequences of the rape is the heroine's loss of a sense of coherent selfhood. The section entitled 'Too Much Skin' images her psychological trauma in terms of bodily fragmentation and dissociation: 'Things were closing down like lights going out. I looked at the skin of my hand in the daylight and it was alien to me. My sturdy feet tramped over grass and dust, carrying a large stranger to whom people spoke, mistaking her for me.' (127–128) Lilian's 'recovery' in the second half of the novel is at best partial, a testimony to her individual resilience. In her discussion of the representation of incest in *Lilian's Story*, Veronica Brady points to the heroine's inability to form intimate relationships, her retreat into a fantasy world, her 'permanent exclusion from normality'.[9] This fragmentation of the self, the psychological crippling of the woman by patriarchy, thus undermines what Penny Boumelha describes as one of the central assumptions and sources of appeal of the nineteenth-century *Bildungsroman* — 'the integrity and coherence over time of the individual'.[10] Grenville's female *Bildungsroman* makes appallingly and movingly explicit the patriarchal denial of both integrity and coherence to its fictional heroine.

Equally disturbing is the novel's presentation of the experience of rape as 'unspeakable', not just morally and socially but quite literally. The section entitled 'Telling', in which Lilian attempts to inform family and friends of what has happened, insistently registers her trauma as a loss of language, an *inability* to tell:

> I tried to begin. *Mother*, I began, and stopped. I could not start the sentence that would tell her what had happened. My mouth and my tongue were someone else's now and even the words that rose into my mind had nothing to do with me...I could not make the words come for Aunt Kitty either...all the words I had ever learnt did not seem enough, or the right ones.
>
> [126–127]

At the heart of Lilian's story is an eloquent and terrible silence. Language is here presented as painfully insufficient, inadequate, as a means of representing female experience. Lilian's temporary aphasia here, this gap in the narrative, exposes the dangerously masculinist basis of language, with its power to exclude or deny the female voice. Moreover, the heroine's inability to 'tell' — as in 'telling on' or informing — allows the authority and legitimacy of the patriarchal system to go unchallenged. Given Lilian's subsequent incarceration by her father, the political consequences of silence are ominously 'telling' indeed.

In both mimetic and structural terms, then, *Lilian's Story* can be read as an anti-*Bildungsroman*, or, in marginally less pessimistic fashion, as one of Linda Howe's 'narratives of survival'. But if the novel emphasizes the oppressiveness of social determinations, it also has a transformational impulse. At the level of both content and form, *Lilian's Story* suggests the possibility of new and better narratives for women. The novel makes brief and infrequent, but telling, references to significant social changes in the lives of women, of which Lilian as narrator is only intermittently aware. It refers, for example, to the entry of women into the work force during the Second World War; and it is part of the novel's pathos that the ageing and isolated Lilian should remain a mere witness to this historical phenomenon, and the experience of female solidarity it engenders:

> It seemed to be all women these days. I wondered where they had been all my life, these women who could drive trams and buses, and be policemen and bank-tellers. Their faces looked stern under their peaked caps, as though they wanted to make it clear that they were not enjoying this, but I heard them humming as they wound the great wheels of the buses, and laughing in uniformed groups, and I did not believe they were not having a good time. I knew they were only pretending not to care.
>
> [180]

Whilst Lilian is shown as excluded from the larger currents of history, this moment in the novel also underscores the fact that there is no tragic inevitability about her particular story. Alternative narratives for women — joy in work, independence, self-esteem — are here in the process of being constructed. Similarly, the novel's conclusion anticipates a more flexible notion of gender roles, in Lilian's brief description of the garb of the 1960s university students: 'the young girls striding in their pants, and boys with long hair and beads around their foreheads' (226). In a work pervaded by references to clothing which image the rigidity of gender stereotyping, this concluding detail suggests a more sexually and socially liberal era for both women and men.

At the level of form, too, in its appropriation of the *Bildungsroman*, the novel reveals the possibility of an emancipatory plot for women. *Lilian's Story* uses the plot of artistic vocation, and the motif of the incipient female artist figure, as a potential source of *Bildung*, and as a means of challenging patriarchal ideology. The principal figure is of course Lilian herself, although, as we shall see, the characters of Miss Gash and Aunt Kitty are also relevant. The description of Lilian's birth, with its reference to the baby's caul as 'a lucky sign', recalls the birth of Dickens's eponymous artist-hero, David Copperfield; and the allusion serves to contrast hero and heroine, his eventual success as a writer with her unrealized potential. Moreover, as a first-person narrative, *David Copperfield* assumes the 'natural' right of the male to be and to speak; by contrast, the initial use of a third-person omniscient narrator in the brief opening section of *Lilian's Story* foregrounds the heroine's lack of voice and subject position. This opening section, however, also suggests the latent power of the female as storyteller, enacting as it does Lilian's movement from silence to speech. Lilian is first described as 'the infant' — literally meaning 'without speech'; but the first word she is granted in the novel — '[f]eelingly' — suggests her capacity to challenge patriarchal values. The allusion here is to *King Lear*: 'feelingly' is the blinded Gloucester's response to Lear when asked how he finds his way; and feeling — the capacity for sympathy, compassion, imaginative identification with another — serves as a moral contrast in both Shakespeare's play and Grenville's novel to the destructive patriarchal obsession with authority, power, ownership. This contrast is pointedly made in *Lilian's Story* by juxtaposing the heroine's first word with the description of her father, Albion, having sex with his wife, as he tries yet again to 'produce a son' (4):

> *Don't move*, he told her mother, and convulsed. *Don't move*, he said again, and clapped wax paper between her legs. *Keep it in.*

[4]

Sex is here ruthlessly functional, joyless, *unfeeling,* an act whereby the patriarch reduces the woman to an instrument for the reproduction of patriarchy itself. Lilian's first word can thus be seen both as an admonishment of and as an alternative to the dehumanizing patriarchal system so starkly epitomized by the father. The opening section thus empowers the heroine as storyteller; and hereafter, the novel is narrated, 'feelingly', from the first-person — the heroine's — point of view.

Part One of the novel — 'A Girl' — establishes Lilian's status as artist figure, through a sense of her fascination with language. When, for example, Father talks of keeping '*the business afloat*', preventing it from '*going under*', Lilian imagines living on a boat with 'the sound of waves against a hull at night' (6); Father's references to his alcoholic sister as being '*constantly pickled*' make Lilian 'willing to believe that there was a barrel in Aunt Kitty's house for her to climb in after we had gone' (16). The child's comic misunderstanding of language here also reveals her inventiveness, her imaginative transformation of the sterile masculine worlds of money-making and moralizing, respectively. A similar transformational impulse underpins Lilian's later stories of heroic fantasies, with their reversal of gender stereotypes:

> At night I rescued [Rick] from burning buildings. It was a joy to feel my hair burn off in one crisp frizz. Among waves pounding the shore only I saw the pale weakening hand about to go under for the last time. When everyone else had fainted dead away I alone lanced the puncture marks on his ankle and sucked out the venom.
>
> [25]

There is of course an element of irony at the young heroine's expense, given the comically derivative nature of her fantasies and their glorification of a conventionally masculine, merely physical concept of heroism. Nevertheless, Lilian's imaginative effort here reveals an early refusal of, and desire to reconstruct, her society's stereotypically feminine narrative of helpless passivity.

Part Two of the novel — 'A Young Lady' — confirms Lilian's artistic sensibility, her status as incipient artist figure, through her rejection of the plots of conventional romance and education. She refuses both plots because they fail to appeal to her imagination. Her attitude to romance sets her apart from the era's model of decorative nullity — those 'lawn lovelies', as she calls them, who frequent the endless garden parties of her fraught young womanhood:

> I imagined those boys in their blazers drawing around me, bringing me cakes which, like Ursula, I would squash with a fork but not eat. I could imagine the way Ursula would smile at me, and wink encouragement if no-one was looking, and the way she would teach me what to say, and how to laugh daintily, and how to encourage the boy you wanted. It frightened me to think that I could also have that kind of future.
>
> [80]

The image of the uneaten cakes suggests the unseemliness of female desire or appetite; in this context, Lilian's obesity signifies a refusal to be contained by the romance plot, an insistence on taking up space, having substance, unconstrained by the sashes and corsets of stereotypical femininity. And significantly, it is Lilian's artistry here — her imagination — which proves her salvation: it is her capacity to construct a particularized scene, shaped according to an understanding of its symbolic import, which saves her from a horrifyingly conventional future.

The education plot is similarly rejected, although initially Lilian aspires to the 'wisdom' she imagines awaits her at the university. Even here, however, the ironies are apparent. Far from signifying the existence of a more progressive social order than the one available to the intellectually hungry Maggie Tulliver, Lilian's access to education in 1920s middle-class Sydney is effected by a paternalistic, if not misogynistic, gesture. The heroine is only allowed to attend the university because her obesity and non-conformity deem her, in her father's eyes, unmarriageable. The education plot is further ironized in Lilian's disillusionment with academia; her contempt for those sterile 'men in tweed' (102) signals a rejection of masculine and unimaginative forms of knowledge:

> The notes I took meant nothing: a few facts about enclosure laws, a list of the dates of battles...there did not seem to be much sense in these lists of denuded facts, dates, names. Descartes was a man with a ball of wax, I knew that much, and Philip of Spain had died an unmentionable death, but what else? Even Napoleon seemed boring.
>
> [102–103]

These 'denuded facts', like those endless 'facts, facts, facts' of Lilian's father's projected book, recall the Gradgrindian education system in Dickens's *Hard Times*, with its similar valorization of rationality and pragmatism and its denigration of the imaginative and emotional dimensions of self. The heroine's rejection, then, of the romance and education plots as delimiting, unimaginative, profoundly unsatisfying, attests to her artistic sensibility.

Finally, in Part Three — 'A Woman' — Lilian's status as artist stands as an implicit rebuke to the distorting effects of patriarchal ideology: denied a socially legitimized voice, the heroine's creative energy eventually emerges in parodic form. Her artistry manifests itself as a comic grotesque self-aestheticization, the construction of herself as a larger-than-life operatic heroine who recites Shakespeare to taxi drivers and tells stories to bemused passers-by. '*I am my own destiny*', she declaims in a travesty of Romanticism, '*and have always loved my inventions of myself*' (207). And although she tells stories which amuse and occasionally provoke her listeners, her adult artistry consists mainly of performance: it is Lilian's lot as artist to be reduced to an entertaining spectacle, the subject of *other* people's stories. It is only the reader who knows of the heroine's most important artistic endeavours — those socially subversive stories of misfits, prostitutes, the 'mad', the migrant, the homeless, and the 'ordinary men and women in the street' (226) whose lives go

unrecorded in patriarchal versions of history. Lilian speaks about
and on behalf of those traditionally silenced or spoken for in
patriarchal society — those 'poor naked wretches' of Lear's
vision of suffering humanity. She tells not only her own story but
those of the oppressed and marginalized like F.J. Stroud and
John, victimized by their failure to conform to the masculine
ideal. She tells the stories of the effaced and invisible like her
mother, whose photograph in young womanhood, taken before
her marriage, images the poignancy of lost possibilities: Lilian
describes her mother as 'standing erect and winsome, smiling,
one hand on the saddle of a stuffed donkey, a waterfall frozen
behind her, in a dress made of chips of light' (5).

Although it is clearly Lilian as artist figure who dominates
the novel, the characters of Miss Gash and Aunt Kitty also reveal
the potentially emancipatory nature and function of female art.
The painter and eccentric spinster Miss Gash, whose name
suggests the wounded nature of the female artist and the punitive
attitude of patriarchal society towards 'difference', recalls the
figure of Miss Havisham in another Dickens *Bildungsroman*,
Great Expectations. The connection is effected in Lilian's mother's
description of Miss Gash as 'a bit odd...There is some story...that
she was jilted early on, and went a little odd' (63); and in the
descriptions of her garden and house (23–24 and 61) which, with
their images of decay and the animation of the inanimate, recall
Satis House in Dickens's novel. The parallels between Miss Gash
and Miss Havisham reinforce gender stereotypes: both are
'witches', 'mad' spinsters — indeed made 'mad' by spinsterhood,
as popular mythology would have it. Grenville's allusion to
Great Expectations, however, is ironic: for unlike the embittered
and revengeful Miss Havisham, the kind and companionable
Miss Gash finds meaning in the pleasures and consolations of art.
Art for Miss Gash is a self-directed and self-delighting activity: '*I
do a picture every day*', she tells Lilian, '*then I wash them away.
It is the only thing to do.*' (64) Whereas Miss Havisham's self and
life remain defined and ultimately destroyed by the romance plot,
Miss Gash finds in art an escape from the story which has
traditionally given meaning to women's lives. As artist figure,

then, she is as affronting to patriarchal notions of woman as her physical presence — hairy armpits and pipe-smoking — would imply.

Lilian's Aunt Kitty, the blowsy, audacious merry widow, is also a subversive artist figure. Her one artistic creation recorded in the novel, a pair of embroidered slippers with green roses and purple leaves, suggests her refusal of the feminine stereotype of docile domesticity. Unlike Lilian's mother's embroidery — an emblem of the circumscribed world of genteel female accomplishments — Aunt Kitty's effort is cheekily unconventional, wittily imaginative: '*Unusual*, Mother had said, and Aunt Kitty had cried out in a soprano, *My word it is!* and laughed' (16). The reference to the slippers' green roses also points to Kitty's status and significance as artist by alluding to an early moment in Joyce's *Künstlerroman, A Portrait of the Artist as a Young Man*,[11] in which the child Stephen remembers 'the song about the wild rose blossoms on the little green place. But', he continues, 'you could not have a green rose. But perhaps somewhere in the world you could.' (16) That world, of course, is the realm of art or the imagination; and both Aunt Kitty and Joyce's artist-hero recognize and utilize its capacity to transform reality. But again the use of literary allusion is ironic; for whereas Stephen's 'mature' art is arguably an escapist and elitist refusal to engage with a squalid reality, Aunt Kitty's later artistic endeavour involves a direct confrontation with and a remaking of the real world. This is seen in her role as rescuer through story-telling: it is Kitty who secures Lilian's release from the mental asylum by threatening to use that traditional female art of gossip against the Father: '*I told him I would spread stories about his mad wife and daughter...I told him I would spread stories about him and his women and he gave in.*' (162) Kitty's stories are powerfully subversive in their potential to make public the private humiliations and degradations which lie at the heart of the patriarchal family. They are a means of exposing sentimentalized myths about the family and the moral fraudulence of paternal authority. In Lilian's case, the threat of such stories secures both physical freedom and financial independence in the form of an allowance from her father. As would-be storyteller, then, Aunt Kitty makes possible the conditions on which Lilian's continued artistry depends. The freedom — physical, psychological and financial — which Virginia Woolf described in *A Room of One's Own* as the necessary condition for the female artist is alluded to at the conclusion to the section entitled 'A Woman of Means': in confirmation of Lilian's status as artist, the novel describes her as 'having money in my hand, and a room all my own' (162).

Artistic vocation in *Lilian's Story* thus functions as a potentially emancipatory plot. And although it uses the genre of the *Bildungsroman* to document the denial of the heroine's development, Grenville's novel also anticipates an era in which the female artist might be an accepted, if not always entirely acceptable, social reality, rather than merely a literary motif. Its optimism is justified by the substantial number of recent Australian works by women about female artists, among them Marion Campbell's *Lines of Flight*, Beverley Farmer's *A Body of Water*, Sue Woolfe's *Painted Woman*, Elizabeth Jolley's *Miss Peabody's Inheritance* and Amy Witting's *I for Isobel*, and, of course, by the existence of *Lilian's Story* itself.

---

1   See, for example, Elizabeth Abel et al., eds, *The Voyage In* (New Hampshire: Hanover Press, 1984); Penny Boumelha, 'George Eliot and the Ends of Realism', in Sue Roe, ed., *Women Reading Women's Writing* (Brighton: Harvester Press, 1987); Susan Cornillon, ed., *Images of Women in Fiction* (Ohio: Bowling Green Press, 1973); Rita Felski, *Beyond Feminist Aesthetics* (Cambridge, Mass.: Harvard University Press, 1989); C. Pearson and K. Pope, *The Female Hero* (New York: R.R. Bowker and Co., 1982); and Annis Pratt et al., *Archetypal Patterns in Women's Fiction* (London: Harvester Press, 1982).

2   See Marianne Hirsch, 'Spiritual *Bildung*: The Beautiful Soul as Paradigm', in Abel et al.; and K.K. Ruthven, *Feminist Literary Studies* (Cambridge: Cambridge University Press, 1984), pp. 120–121.

3   Nancy Miller, 'The Text's Heroine: A Feminist Critic and Her Fictions', *Diacritics*, vol. 12 (1982), p. 48.

4   Ellen Morgan, 'Human Becoming: Form and Focus in the Neo-Feminist Novel', in Cornillon, p. 185.

5   Boumelha, p. 30.

6   Margaret Atwood, *Surfacing* (London: Virago, 1979), p. 192.

7   Linda Howe, 'Narratives of Survival', *Literary Review*, vol. 26 (1982), pp. 177–184.

8   Kate Grenville, *Lilian's Story* (Sydney: Allen & Unwin, 1991). This is a revised and final version of the original 1985 publication. All references are to the 1991 edition and appear in the text.

9   Veronica Brady, 'The Men Who Loved Children', in Penelope Hetherington, ed., *Incest and the Community: Australian Perspectives*, published by P. Hetherington under the auspices of the Centre for Western Australian History at The University of Western Australia, 1991.

10   Boumelha, p. 27.

11   James Joyce, *A Portrait of the Artist as a Young Man* (London: The Folio Society, 1965).

GENDER, ETHICS
AND LITERARY THEORY

ALEX SEGAL

P AUL de Man's *Allegories of Reading* offers one of the most controversial accounts of ethics in contemporary literary theory. The controversy has not concerned gender. The charge against de Man is that he severs ethical categories from 'issues of practical choice and commitment',[1] a charge based on his describing ethics as 'the structural interference of two distinct value systems', as having 'nothing to do with the will (thwarted or free) of a subject, nor *a fortiori*, with a relationship between subjects', and as 'the referential (and therefore unreliable) version of a linguistic confusion'.[2] Yet the fact that gender has not been at issue becomes surprising when de Man's cryptic claims are placed in the context from which their meaning derives.

For they must be explained partly with reference to his judgement that in the main text of Rousseau's *Julie ou la nouvelle Héloïse*, the ethical moment — 'the moment when Julie acquires a maximum of insight' — occurs when she rejects love, choosing instead 'the contractual agreement of marriage, set up as a defense against the passions and as the basis of social and political order'.[3] And this must lead us to ask if de Man is complicit with the patriarchal ideology for which Rousseau is notorious, to ask, for instance, whether the passions against which he says marriage is a defence are those of women rather, or at least more, than those of men.

The force of these questions is apparent if we recall Rousseau's view of the wife's role in marriage:

> There is a vast difference between claiming the right to command, and managing him who commands. Women's reign is a reign of gentleness, tact, and kindness; her commands are caresses, her threats are tears. She should reign in the home as a minister reigns in the state, by contriving to be ordered to do what she wants...[W]hen she despises the voice of her head, when she desires to usurp his rights and take the command upon herself, this inversion of the proper order of things leads only to misery, scandal, and dishonor.[4]

And Rousseau seems to exclude women from the social and political order altogether. Carole Pateman, a leading feminist political theorist, states his position in this way: 'Men...can use their reason to master their sexuality, and so can undertake the creation and maintenance of political society. Women have only modesty...a precarious control of sexual desire.' Pateman argues that for Rousseau, Julie's story shows the dangers posed by women's passions: 'despite all Julie's efforts to live an exemplary life as a wife and a mother, she is unable to overcome her illicit passion and takes the only course she can to preserve the haven of family life at Clarens: she goes to her "accidental" death'. For Pateman, Julie's decision to enter the contractual agreement of marriage — an agreement designed to overcome her illicit passion — seems to prefigure her death.[5]

De Man's reading of *Julie* is closely bound up with his characteristically 'textualist' pronouncements on ethics. In using the term 'ethics' to designate 'the structural interference of two distinct value systems', he treats it as cognate with the term *ethos*.

Ethos in classical rhetoric refers to the effect arising from the speaker's character, from for instance the fact that the speaker is not motivated by self-interest. It is in contrast with the term *pathos*, which in classical rhetoric refers to the emotions the speaker's words arouse in the audience. *Pathos* for de Man seems to imply an identification between speaker and hearer, writer and reader — enunciation and understanding. *La nouvelle Héloïse* — prior to Julie's decision to replace love with marriage — appears to be a conventional love story:

> Julie and Saint-Preux have been presented as stock characters in a situation of sentimental tragedy, persecuted by the social inequities of wealth and class and by the caprices of a tyrannical father. The reader's responses are solicited according to the rules of this plot, thus maintaining the homology between enunciation and understanding that characterizes monological narratives.[6]

This homology makes for the *pathos* of the novel's first part. The decision to set up marriage as a defence against the passions — a decision which de Man treats as Rousseau's as well as Julie's — manifests itself at the narrative's expense; it opposes the author's best interests — hence the shift to *ethos*. The decision 'acquires its moral dimension from the fact that it moves against the "natural" logic of the narrative and of its understanding'. In view of what has been said about the patriarchal nature of the marriage contract, the female character's real renunciation seems here to be conflated with or effaced by the male author's merely rhetorical renunciation. The gender neutrality of de Man's language would appear to be a deception: the 'renunciation', the 'sacrifice', he associates with ethics seems to demand more of women than it does of men.[7]

There would seem to be a need for a consideration of the gender politics implicit in de Man's account, and it is this task which I shall broach in the present paper. However, we should note at the outset the paradox in the notion that de Man's ethics perpetuate Rousseau's anti-feminism. The paradox becomes apparent with reference to the idea of constructions of gender. Rousseau in effect treats his construction of gender as not a construction at all. The subordination of women to men seems for him to have its basis in nature; it is in a certain sense a given rather than a cultural construct. Moreover, one might say that for Rousseau women incline more naturally than men to the nature pole of the opposition nature/culture. Moira Gatens argues that 'on Rousseau's model of social and political life it is women who are expected to provide the "natural" foundation necessary for the security and legitimacy of the conventional bond of the social contract'.[8] On the other hand, everything I have so far referred to in de Man's account of ethics suggests a rejection of the appeal to nature: 'the structural interference of two distinct value systems', 'the referential (and therefore unreliable) version of a linguistic confusion' — such phrases do not return ethics to nature. Julie is described as choosing 'the *contractual* agreement of marriage' (my italics). Clearly, we shall need to pay careful attention to de Man's treatment of the category of the natural as it appears in Rousseau's text.

First of all, however, in order to situate de Man's work, I evoke briefly the way that feminist characterizations of the patriarchal exclusion of women have had recourse to the notions of metaphor and metonymy — notions which have enjoyed a spectacular career in post-Saussurean linguistics and theory.

Amongst feminist theorists it is perhaps Luce Irigaray whose name first springs to mind here. Margaret Whitford has related Pateman's account of the social contract to Irigaray's work, arguing that it can be used to illuminate Irigaray's contentions that in modern society 'the citizen is always in fact male; that women have to become "men" in order to become citizens; that the social pact is a pact between brothers'. Interpreting Lacan's 'symbolic order [as] a symbolic contract equivalent to the social contract', Whitford argues that

> [i]n Lacan's economy, the founding sacrifice which underlies the social order is a relation of metaphor and

substitution. It is the male position in the Oedipus complex, the instinctual renunciation made by the boy, and the identification with the father.

By contrast, the girl's relation to her mother is 'metonymical, dependent on contiguity or association...[T]he two (mother and daughter) are not identified in a movement of metaphoric substitution.'[9] Irigaray, Whitford suggests, is evoking the metonymic in her controversial claims that 'woman...touches herself in and of herself without any need for mediation' and that 'if "she" says something, it is not, it is already no longer, identical with what she means. What she says is never identical with anything, moreover; rather it is contiguous [*contigu*]. *It touches* (*upon*).'[10]

Pateman argues Freud denigrates women's attachments by characterizing them in terms of contiguity and proximity. Being defined by the relationship to children, they remain particularized. For Freud, 'civilization' begins when 'the female, who did not want to be separated from her helpless young, was obliged in their interests, to remain with the stronger male'; women, he says, 'represent the interests of the family and of sexual life'. A woman's superego — the internal representative of the moral law — depends more than a man's on its emotional origins. Having less possibility of directing their attentions away from particular loved ones 'to all men alike' and towards 'a universal love of mankind',[11] women 'show less sense of justice than men'.[12]

Pateman likens Rousseau's account of 'the differing political moralities of the sexes' to Freud's 'conjectural history of the origin of social life'.[13] For Rousseau, sentiment in primitive society — based on familial relations, on kinship — is governed by contiguity and proximity, and hence cannot be universalized to all men alike. Primitive people 'had the concept of a father, a son, a brother, but not that of a man'; they were affectionate to those they knew and 'hated only those with whom they could not be acquainted'.[14] Metonymical relations are not here explicitly associated with women as opposed to men; they are, however, associated with the family, the realm women represent once civil society is established.

De Man's reading of Rousseau is attentive to his thematization of metaphor and metonymy. He argues that for Rousseau the concept *man* is metaphorical. According to Rousseau, a primitive man on encountering another is suspicious 'that, although the creature does not look like a lion or a bear, it nevertheless might act like one'; in other words, there is 'a possible discrepancy between the outer and the inner properties of entities'. This hypothetical aspect is effaced when the man expresses his fear by calling the other a 'giant', thereby positing a correspondence between the fear and the size of the external object. With experience the first man discovers the other man's height is numerically equal to his own and replaces the metaphor 'giant' by the term 'man'. But for Rousseau the term 'man' — which 'makes it possible for "men" to exist by establishing the equality within inequality, the sameness within difference of civil society' — is also a metaphor; it completes the process of domestication, the freezing of the suspense of the initial fear, that the first wild metaphor began.[15]

What goes for the term 'man' — de Man emphasizes — goes for concepts in general: 'conceptualization, conceived as an exchange or substitution of properties on the basis of resemblance, corresponds exactly to the classical definition of metaphor'. Conceptualization, which is the work of the universal, masters anxiety. And conceptual language — the foundation of civil society — seems to have a masculine bias. De Man contends that in terms of Rousseau's text, which 'associates the specificity of man with language and, within language, with the power of conceptualization', the exemplary situation described in the 'Essay' (man confronting man [as opposed to man confronting woman or man confronting thing]) is the correct linguistic paradigm.[16]

De Man also draws attention to an apparent privileging of metaphor in Rousseau's characterization of the social contract. Rousseau first defines the pact thus: 'Everyone puts his will, his property, his strength, and his person in common, under the direction of the general will, and we receive as a body each member as an inalienable part of the whole'.[17] De Man sees here 'the organic link that binds part to whole in a metaphorical synecdoche': 'The metaphorical system that unites limb to body, one to all, individual to group, seems firmly established'.[18] This unity of individual and group is apparent also in what Rousseau says about the happiness of political societies: '[men] will be united, they will be virtuous, they will be happy, and their felicity will be the well-being of the Republic; for since they receive all their being from the State, they owe everything to the State. The Republic will own all they own and will be all they are.'[19] De Man comments:

> The model for this utopia is the reconciliation of the most natural of groups, the family, with the State...It also reconciles moral virtue with economic wealth and makes property innocent by making it collective... [T]he text elaborates...[a] metaphor [of] the 'natural' political society or family.[20]

De Man's emphasis on what appears to be Rousseau's privileging of metaphor seems at the same time to be an emphasis on the patriarchal nature of his thought. We have already seen that he draws attention to Rousseau's treating the concept *man* as emblematic of concepts in general, and to the situation of man confronting man (as opposed to man confronting woman) as being for Rousseau 'the correct linguistic paradigm'. Moreover, if the model for Rousseau's utopia is 'the reconciliation of the most natural of groups, the family, with the State', then Pateman's and Whitford's claims about the patriarchal nature of Rousseau's good society seem to be confirmed. Pateman argues that for Rousseau marriage and the male headed family constitutes 'a natural base on which to form conventional ties' — the conventional ties of the society issuing from the social contract.[21] And Whitford argues that the social contract does not institute '[t]he familial — patriarchal — division of labour' but 'merely subsumes it, so that it is surreptitiously included without ever being put into question'.[22]

De Man, then, seems to be aware of the metaphorical

totalizations in Rousseau's text and of their link to patriarchy. What he proceeds to argue, however, is that the text subverts these totalizations.

De Man — unlike Pateman[23] — distinguishes between what Rousseau calls civil society and the social and political order that results from the social contract. Civil society is a particular form of society, the form under which, as one commentator on Rousseau puts it, 'men are united essentially through a form of exchange in which each regards the other as primarily a means to the satisfaction of his own need'.[24] In question is *laissez-faire* capitalism, society as governed by market forces. When de Man says that the invention of the concept man 'makes it possible for "men" to exist by establishing the equality within inequality, the sameness within difference of civil society', at stake is the quite specific social reality that Rousseau evokes in the statement that opens the second part of the *Second Discourse*: 'The first man who, having enclosed a piece of ground, bethought himself of saying "This is mine", and found people simple enough to believe him, was the real founder of civil society'.[25] After quoting this 'lapidary' statement, de Man comments: 'The passage from literal greed to the institutional law protecting the right to property runs parallel to the transition from the spontaneous to the conceptual metaphor'.[26] The advocates of civil society ascribe to it an equality — equality of opportunity, equality under the law — that is alleged to exist in spite of objective, economic inequality. De Man, following Rousseau, rejects this. For both, civil society is the target of critique; hence in tying it to metaphor, de Man is not privileging metaphor.

We can now begin to see why de Man says that the encounter between man and man is 'the correct linguistic paradigm'. The law protecting property right takes property as an object of possession 'used for the fulfillment of individual needs and desires' and as 'a structure based on similarity and on the integration of shared needs and desires'. This private point of view implies a 'principle of functional identification between the owning subject and the owned object': 'The contract is self-reflective; it is an agreement *du même au même* in which the land defines the owner and the owner defines the land'.[27] The encounter between man and man is likewise self-reflective, an agreement *du même au même*. De Man, it would seem, shares with Irigaray the view that civil society is hom(m)osexual.

If civil society is the target of critique, to connect it to metaphor is not to privilege metaphor. Moreover, de Man argues that Rousseau introduces a principle of organization entirely different from metaphorical totalization with the claim that '[t]he moral condition of a people is less the result of the absolute condition of its members than of the relationships among them'. This principle of generalization 'does *not* operate between part and whole';[28] it precludes a totalization of private and public well-being. According to de Man, Rousseau 'postulates the incompatibility between collective and individual needs and interests, the absence of any links between the two sets of forces', evokes a system in which public well-being is the source of the happiness of individuals as 'the misleading model [which] becomes pernicious when it is used as the foundation of a political society', and seeks to devise 'a model for a political order that is not natural'.[29]

All this has consequences for the status accorded to the family. Rousseau, de Man argues, rejects the idea of a utopia the model for which 'is the reconciliation of the most natural of groups, the family, with the State': 'because the family is based on natural ties, [it] is no better model for legality than imperialistic conquest or the enslavement of prisoners in time of war, and it is discussed under the same rubric as these anarchic manifestations of power'.[30] The familial — patriarchal — division of labour is no more subsumed by the social contract than is the enslavement of prisoners in war. Whitford thinks Rousseau fails to see the consequences of the fact that the 'natural family' is instituted in the stage — prior to the social contract — 'in which the strong and powerful have taken advantage of the weak to foist upon them a contract which only empowers the powerful even more'.[31] De Man disagrees.

Rousseau's critique of civil society is of a piece with his

refusal to characterize a sound political system in terms of a totalization of private and public needs. For civil society is based on the self-serving illusion that the pursuit of private self-interest makes for public well-being. Moreover, because Rousseau 'postulates the incompatibility between collective and individual needs and interests', de Man argues that the general will — which arises out of the social contract — is 'by no means a synthesis of private volitions' and that ' "the art of generalizing ideas" in order to orient them toward the general will...must then have a very different figural structure than such metaphorical processes as, for example, conceptualization, love, or even judgment'.[32] Hence such generalizing does not coincide with the male sense of community and fraternity directed at all men alike which Freud describes. On de Man's reading, such generalization or universalization seems to be characteristic of civil society; *pace* Pateman it is not oriented towards the general will.

With the new principle of generalization that 'does *not* operate between part and whole but is determined by the relationship that the different parts, as parts, establish between each other', metaphorical synecdoche is displaced by metonymy. When Rousseau considers political well-being in terms not of its derivation from private happiness but of the 'relationship of one State to another', he implies, de Man argues, that 'an entity can be called political, not because it is collective (constituted by a plurality of similar units), but precisely because it is not, because it sets up relationships with other entities on a non-constitutive basis...[T]he structure postulates the necessary existence of radical estrangement between political entities.'[33] Political units for de Man are characterized by the fact that they can be inscribed 'within diverse systems that are not necessarily compatible'.[34]

Rousseau characterizes the social contract in terms of a double commitment: 'Each individual, contracting so to speak with himself, finds that he is doubly engaged, namely toward private individuals as a member of the sovereign and toward the sovereign as a member of the State'.[35] De Man comments:

the private interests of the individual (which can be called his commitments toward himself) have nothing in common with his political, public interests and obligations. The former do precisely *not* derive from the latter as part derives from whole...The double relationship of the individual toward the State is thus based on the coexistence of two distinct rhetorical models, the first self-reflective or specular, the other estranged.[36]

The first rhetorical model we might call metaphorical; the second metonymical. In acceding to the social contract, the individual can be considered — to cite what de Man says in a closely related context — 'as the referent of two entirely divergent texts'.[37]

Such inscription within diverse systems is at stake in Julie's decision to marry. The decision involves a rejection of love, which we have seen de Man describe as a metaphorical process. He has in mind Julie's analysis of her love for Saint-Preux in terms of a system of relationships 'based on the presumption of an analogy between body and soul, between outside and inside', in terms of 'resemblances and substitutions of body and soul or self and other' — resemblances and substitutions which partake of 'the illusion of identity' that pertains to the term 'man'. This 'system of analogical exchanges ...has structured the narrative of the novel's first half', and the rejection of love 'acquires its moral dimension from the fact that it moves against the "natural" logic of the narrative and of its understanding'. Within this system of analogical exchanges, the love between Julie and Saint-Preux is treated as the locus of value, they having been presented as 'stock characters in a situation of sentimental tragedy, persecuted by the social inequities of wealth and class and by the caprices of a tyrannical father'. It is as if private happiness and social well-being are themselves in a relationship of analogical exchange. With the displacement of the metaphorical model, such love itself appears to be in solidarity with the kind of society that makes for

inequities of wealth and class. In deciding to marry, Julie no longer considers only the private interests of her love relationship with Saint-Preux, but commits herself towards a whole of which she is part, commits herself to public interests and obligations which have nothing to do with her private interests.[38]

Julie's decision itself exemplifies the kind of commitment that the social contract demands. It is the basis for the social and political order, not as a natural base for conventional ties but in the same way as is the social contract. In short it is a political decision.

It may appear that de Man is advocating loveless marriage. Love, though, is rejected in so far as it is a matter of 'resemblances and substitutions of body and soul or self and other'. And de Man's further specifications of this reciprocity must call into question platitudes about the value of love. Because Julie and Saint-Preux have thought of their relationship 'as a substitutive movement in which self and other constantly exchange their identity', she is for him 'like the omnipresence, the parousia of an element finer than air'.[39] The naivety and even the violence of such a relationship become more explicit in de Man's analysis of the *Confessions*. In question is the young Rousseau's love for his fellow servant Marion, a love which leads him to steal a ribbon from their employer in order to give it to her:

> [The ribbon] stands...for the reciprocity which...is for Rousseau the very condition of love; it stands for the substitutability of Rousseau for Marion and vice versa. Rousseau desires Marion as Marion desires Rousseau. But since, within the atmosphere of intrigue and suspicion that prevails in the household of the Comtesse de Vercellis, the phantasy of this symmetrical reciprocity is experienced as an interdict, its figure, the ribbon, has to be stolen, and the agent of this transgression has to be susceptible of being substituted: if Rousseau has to be willing to steal the ribbon, then Marion has to be willing to substitute for Rousseau in performing this act...

...to steal can be an act of love, an act performed by
Rousseau can be said to be performed by Marion.[40]

To the extent that Rousseau attempts to excuse his accusing
Marion of the theft in terms of his desire for her, his text is
characterizable in terms of *pathos*. We can begin to see here why
de Man says the shift to *ethos* and the ethical is a shift away from
pathos. And the claim that 'the agent of...transgression has to be
susceptible of being substituted' applies also to the relationship
of Julie and Saint-Preux. It is not only conceptualization but love
— another metaphorical process — which according to de Man's
account serves the interests of the subject.

To the extent that Julie's decision is political in this way,
the marriage contract that she chooses cannot be grouped with
the contracts of civil society. In the case of property, the rhetoric
of such contracts implies a 'principle of functional identification
between the owning subject and the owned object'. It confers
'the illusion of legitimacy' on private property:

> Thus it is that Marcel, in Proust's novel, understands
> the fascination of the proper names of the aristocracy
> because it is impossible to distinguish their names
> from the geographical names of their landed estate.
> There can be no more seductive form of onomastic
> identification. The fascination of the model is not so
> much that it feeds fantasies of material possession
> (though it does this too, of course) but that it satisfies
> semiological fantasies about the adequation of sign to
> meaning seductive enough to tolerate extreme forms
> of economic oppression.[41]

And it would seem that a similar account can be given of
marriage in civil society. The rhetoric associated with it creates
the illusion of natural and legitimate identification — identification between marriage partners, between each of them and the
body of the other. The equality that may seem at stake in such
identification is 'the equality within inequality...of civil society' —
an equality which, as we have seen, de Man regards as deceitful.

Just as 'the institutional, conceptual law protecting the right to property' favours the rich at the expense of the poor, so too marriage in civil society favours men at the expense of women. In civil society, marriage as well as property is inscribed in a rhetorical model that feeds fantasies of possession — in the case of marriage, fantasies of sexual rather than material possession.

De Man explicitly links material and sexual possession. Of Rousseau's attempt to excuse his accusing Marion of having stolen the ribbon on the ground that the feeling that accompanies this act is shame about himself rather than hostility towards his victim, De Man argues that the shame concerns 'a desire to possess, in all the connotations of the term'. In question is a desire to possess not only the ribbon but Marion as well. The ribbon, de Man says, '"stands for" Rousseau's desire for Marion or, what amounts to the same thing, for Marion herself'.[42] Moreover, de Man characterizes the ribbon as a trope that is inscribed in a metaphorical rhetorical system, the kind of system in which property is inscribed in civil society:

> We have at least two levels of substitution (or displacement) taking place: the ribbon substituting for a desire which is itself a desire for substitution. Both are governed by the same desire for specular symmetry which gives to the symbolic object a detectable, univocal proper meaning.[43]

Just as the double relationship of the social contract resists the desire for specular symmetry in so far as this desire informs fantasies of material possession, so too the contractual agreement of marriage — to the extent that it is recognized as contractual — resists this desire in so far as this desire informs fantasies of sexual possession.

De Man is not deluded about the marriage in which Julie in fact finds herself. Of the community of Clarens — to which Julie's and Wolmar's marriage is central — he says, 'it is difficult to decide whether it is an exemplary model for a state or an ambivalent family romance'. Julie's letter announcing her decision to marry is lucid, de Man says, in so far as it is a 'recapitulation';

but he claims that it 'bodes little good for the stability of what it proleptically announces'. This is because he sees Julie as repeating the notions she has just denounced as errors: 'there is nothing in the structure of Julie's relationship to virtue or to what she calls God that does not find its counterpart in her previous and now so rigorously demystified relationship towards Saint-Preux'. The 'virtue' that informs Julie's attempt 'to live an exemplary life as a wife and a mother' — to cite Pateman's phrase — is not an ethical category in the sense of ethics that de Man links to *ethos*. On the contrary, it seems to involve what de Man refers to as a 'relapse into metaphorical models'.[44]

This relapse, de Man argues, is not something from which Rousseau can distance himself. The difficulty in assessing Clarens bespeaks an instability in the text of *Julie*, not just in what the text describes. De Man's position *vis-à-vis* Rousseau does appear to allow for the possibility of critique. In the case of the *Confessions* and the *Fourth Rêverie*, he argues that Rousseau's attempt to excuse his denunciation of Marion fails: 'At the end of the text [of the *Fourth Rêverie*], Rousseau knows that he cannot be excused, yet the text shelters itself from accusation by the performance of its radical fictionality'. As we have seen, this excuse relies in part on Rousseau's appeal to the desire Marion arouses in him. Moreover, de Man seems to imply that the failed excuse would have been more naive had the text been 'set up in such a way as to court sympathy in the name of Marion's erotic charm' — a strategy which he points out Rousseau uses elsewhere. This strategy is tied to Rousseau's misogyny, to his fear of women for their capacity to arouse desire in men.[45]

It is true that de Man's reading of Rousseau differs radically from most feminist readings. But it finds some support in a recent essay by the feminist philosopher Lynda Lange. Against the general view, Lange argues that Rousseau has a value for feminism that goes beyond that of 'knowing the enemy': 'he understands very clearly many aspects of the structure of male dominance, which from the critical perspective of feminism function as effective criticisms of that system'. In particular he is clear about 'the links between private property, individualism, and male domination of women. The male head of family requires private property in order to have a private sphere within which to control the female.' Lange points out that one reason for the inadequate enforcement of the law that prohibits a man to attack a woman with whom he lives is the 'high value placed on the retention of a private sphere, on personal freedom in intimate relations, and on the use and disposal of private property'. We have in effect seen that for de Man Julie, in deciding to marry, is insisting on the contractual aspect of relations in the so-called private sphere, relations that civil society represents as natural. By politicizing these relations, she is calling into question the high value that civil society accords them. Lange's analysis helps us see that it is Rousseau's understanding and critique of the structure of male dominance to which de Man responds when he commends Julie's decision to marry.[46]

De Man states the motivation for his theoretical endeavour in *The Resistance to Theory*:

> What we call ideology is precisely the confusion of linguistic with natural reality, of reference with phenomenalism. It follows that more than any other mode of inquiry...the linguistics of literariness is a powerful and indispensable tool in the unmasking of ideological aberrations.[47]

Amongst these aberrations are those that are tied to the patriarchal nature of civil society. Julie's replacing the putatively natural relationship of love with the contractual agreement of marriage is an instance of the unmasking of ideology. At the beginning of this discussion, I referred to the perception that de Man severs ethics from issues of practical choice and commitment; what we have seen is that even in the case of the issue of gender — an issue which he does not thematize explicitly and to which at first sight he seems to be culpably indifferent — his account is alert to structures of dominance and oppression.

1   Christopher Norris, *Deconstruction and the Interests of Theory* (London: Pinter Publishers, 1988), p. 183.

2   Paul de Man, *Allegories of Reading: Figural Language in Rousseau, Nietzsche, Rilke and Proust* (New Haven and London: Yale University Press, 1979), p. 206.

3   ibid., p. 216.

4   Jean-Jacques Rousseau, *Emile*, trans. Barbara Foxley (London: J.M. Dent, 1911), pp. 370–371.

5   Carole Pateman, *The Sexual Contract* (Cambridge: Polity Press, 1988), p. 97.

6   De Man, p. 212.

7   ibid., pp. 216, 206.

8   Moira Gatens, *Feminism and Philosophy: Perspectives on Difference and Equality* (Bloomington and Indianapolis: Indiana University Press, 1991), p. 11.

9   Margaret Whitford, *Luce Irigaray: Philosophy in the Feminine* (London and New York: Routledge, 1991), pp. 175, 180.

10   Luce Irigaray, *This Sex Which Is Not One*, trans. Catherine Porter with Carolyn Burke (Ithaca: Cornell University Press, 1985), pp. 24, 29; quoted in Whitford, p. 180.

11   Sigmund Freud, *Civilization and Its Discontents*, trans. J. Strachey (New York: W.W. Norton, 1961), pp. 51, 54, 56.

12   Sigmund Freud, 'Some Psychological Consequences of the Anatomical Distinction between the Sexes', in *Collected Papers*, ed. J. Strachey (London: Hogarth Press, 1953), vol. 5, pp. 196–197.

13   Pateman, p. 99.

14   Jean-Jacques Rousseau, 'Essay on the Origin of Languages', in *On the Origin of Languages*, eds J.H. Moran and Alexander Gode (New York: Ungar, 1966), p. 33.

15   De Man, pp. 150–151.

16   ibid., pp. 146, 197, 153.

17   Jean-Jacques Rousseau, *Oeuvres complètes*, eds Bernard Gagnebin and Marcel Raymond (Paris: Gallimard [Bibliothèque de la Pléiade], 1961), vol. 3, p. 290. I cite the passage as it is translated by de Man in *Allegories*.

18   De Man, p. 259.

19   Rousseau, *Oeuvres complètes*, vol. 3, p. 511. I cite the passage as it is translated by de Man in *Allegories*.

20   De Man, pp. 251–252.

21   Pateman, p. 98.

22   Whitford, p. 174.

23   This claim refers to *The Sexual Contract* but not to Pateman's earlier account of Rousseau in *The Problem of Political Obligation: A Critical*

       Analysis of Liberal Theory (Chichester: John Wiley & Sons, 1979).

24   Asher Horowitz, *Rousseau, Nature and History* (Toronto: University of Toronto Press, 1987), p. 108.

25   Jean-Jacques Rousseau, *The Social Contract and Discourses*, trans. G.D.H. Cole (London: Dent, rev. edn 1973), p. 76.

26   De Man, pp. 157–158.

27   ibid., p. 262.

28   ibid., p. 253.

29   ibid., pp. 261, 260.

30   ibid., pp. 259–260.

31   Whitford, p. 177.

32   De Man, p. 261.

33   ibid., p. 254.

34   ibid., p. 253.

35   Jean-Jacques Rousseau, *On the Social Contract: With Geneva Manuscript and Political Economy*, ed. Roger D. Masters, trans. Judith R. Masters (New York: St Martin's Press, 1978), p. 164.

36   De Man, p. 265.

37   ibid., p. 264.

38   ibid., pp. 210, 216, 212.

39   ibid., pp. 212–213.

40   ibid., pp. 283–284.

41   ibid., p. 262.

42   ibid., p. 283.

43   ibid., p. 284.

44   ibid., pp. 220, 217.

45   ibid., pp. 294, 285.

46   Lynda Lange, 'Rousseau and Modern Feminism', *Feminist Interpretations and Political Theory*, eds Mary Lyndon Shanley and Carole Pateman (Cambridge: Polity Press, 1991), pp. 109, 108, 109.

47   Paul de Man, *The Resistance to Theory* (Manchester: Manchester University Press, 1986), p. 11.

TOWARDS A NEW GEOGRAPHY: BODY OF WOMEN, BODY OF THE WORLD

VERONICA BRADY

ENDER is not just a matter of politics. It can also be a matter of geography. An early engraving of the New World, by Jan van der Straet in 1600, shows America allegorized as a naked woman on a hammock surrounded by wild animals and equally wild men, feasting cannibals, looking up to great Amerigo Vespucci, the man who is to 'civilize' her.[1] As Peter Hulme remarks, the sexual dimension of the encounter is linguistically as well as visually explicit; the inscription reads '*Americus Americens retexit semel vocavit inde semper excitam*' (Amerigo changes America and summons her, at the same time awakening and arousing her).

As far as I know, we do not have a similar illustration to figure for the first European encounters with Australia. But the perceptions were similar and the reality can be traced in our literature: invasion — the metaphorical and often, for indigenous women, the literal equivalent of rape. Colonization is generally a masculine activity, an extension of warfare by another means, a form of permanent conquest. In the secondary stage of settlement, however, women are involved, and serve as auxiliaries of the invasion, makers of house and home. As for the women of the colonized, they become servants, often body-servants, objects of possession like the land itself, to be used for the invaders' own ends. Xavier Herbert's *Capricornia* is the classic account of this kind of invasion and, of course, of this connection between conquest and eroticism.

This is the reality. But the connection between the geographical and the ideological terrain is not so clear and needs to be established. Settlement involves an act of ideological as well as physical construction, a reconstruction of the metropolitan mind-set to suit the new circumstances of the frontier. Yet in many cases, this reconstruction represents an evasion rather than an accommodation to the new circumstances. Thus, Australia, perhaps one of the harshest of the new environments faced by settlers, in the long run generated one of the most domesticated of ideologies, the cult of the quarter-acre block and the 'glorious home'. But even in the early days, notions of home and family tended to crowd out the brutal realities of settlement. Letters and diaries, usually written by women, celebrated 'homes', mostly only bark huts which their men had built for them in the wilderness, but which often figured as if they were fine English houses, if not homes.

Partly, no doubt, these accounts represented for the writer an act of reassurance; having left Home, they need to still feel at home. Charlotte Bussell, for instance, wrote from the Swan River Colony in 1840 to describe her house: 'so thoroughly comfortable and so English-like that all strangers who visit us expressed the greatest admiration of it'. But she insists so much on its excellence that one suspects the opposite:

> At the end is one very large window which overlooks our pretty river in the direction of Cockatoo Valley, opposite this to the other end is the most comfortable fireplace I ever beheld. You can never see the like in England, Emily. The fire is upon the hearth which burns ever so brightly with its beautiful blocks of wood mixed with blackboy which is exactly like Kennel coal and send out such a cheerful blaze that it is worth taking a trip to Australia to see.[2]

The myth of the home which pioneer women constructed, evident here, might be seen as an extension of Wemmick's house and garden in *Great Expectations*; like Wemmick, Charlotte Bussell was constructing for herself a retreat from unpleasant reality.

Certainly many colonial settlers of Bussell's genteel kind were in search of Arcadia, of some lost innocent and prosperous world in which the 'good old days' and 'good old values' continued to flourish. In Henry Kingsley's *The Recollections of Geoffry Hamlyn*, for instance, the homestead which Colonel Buckley manages to build for himself reflects this dream. Having set out into the wilderness like Abraham with his flocks,[3] Kingsley's settlers have found their Promised Land, in an imagined return to rural England as they imagined it was before the Industrial Revolution had arrived to threaten the prosperity, peace and social position of the landed gentry.

The description of the homestead, Garoopna Station, in chapter XXVII, significantly entitled 'The Golden Vineyard', is idyllic. But it is an idyll, in which class distinctions are comfortably in place — comfortably, that is, for the gentry. When young Sam Buckley arrives on a visit, a groom arrives on cue to take his horse, for instance, and the Buckleys and their friends seem to spend more time in genteel leisure pursuits than in work. Even more importantly, perhaps, is a beautiful young woman, Alice, whom he meets here and who becomes in due course his wife and is the centre of the scene. Home and family are the goal of this kind of colonization, as the following passage from the *Perth Gazette*, March 1859, suggests:

> We now think that a man who is happy in his home, at his own fireside, with the partner of his life smiling gently upon him and his little children looking like smiling content...is to all intents and purposes a 'Serene Highness'.[4]

The conquest of Empire is also a conquest on another front. Geoffry Hamlyn's imperial dream of 'walking irresistibly on to the conquest of an empire greater than Haroun Al Raschid's[5] is also grounded in domestic reality. Woman is 'orientalized', so to speak, as the other to be conquered, possessed and enjoyed. So significantly, Sam Buckley's first glimpse of Alice echoes the engraving already mentioned of Amerigo Vespucci's encounter with the young and beautiful America:

> Under the arch between the sunlight and the shade, bareheaded, dressed in white, stood a girl, so amazingly beautiful that Sam wondered for a few minutes whether he was asleep or awake. Her hat, which she had just taken off, hung on her left arm, and with her delicate white hand she arranged a vagrant tendril of the passion flower, which in its luxuriant growth had broken bounds and fallen from its place above.[6]

Like America, she is beautiful and innocent. But, like America, she is also shadowed by savagery from which she must be rescued by her man. Alice's attendant is an Aboriginal woman, 'a hideous, old savage, black as Tophet, grinning; showing the sharp gap-teeth in her apish jaws, her lean legs shaking with old age and rheumatism'[7] — the epitome of evil as Alice is of good, both being defined in physical terms, terms of the Manichean allegory of colonization in which white is to black as good is to evil.[8] So, here, Alice is not only goodness but civilization personified. Possessing her, Sam will possess that civilization and establish it in the wilderness, tame it and render it decorously fruitful. To do so, however, it is implied that he will need to eliminate or at least civilize the Aborigine, one of the lesser breeds 'outside the law'.

Towards the end of the nineteenth century, writers like Lawson and Furphy attacked this model of colonization. Furphy, for instance, characterized Kingsley's heroes as 'slender-witted, virgin souled and overgrown schoolboys',[9] pointing to the element of fantasy and emotional immaturity involved in their Arcadian dream. More extensively, the whole of *Such Is Life*, 'temper, democratic; bias, offensively Australian', as Furphy described it, is an attack on the politically reactionary and Anglophile temper of novels like his. Like most of the other writers of the nationalist school of the 1890s, Furphy attempted to come to terms with the actual experience of pioneering instead of idealizing it, and wrote from the point of view of ordinary settlers, not the privileged and successful.

Significantly, however, this attempt had little to say about women. The few women who appear in *Such Is Life* are peripheral figures, objects of anxiety rather than of sustained attention. The most interesting of them, Mollie, jilted by her fiancé when she is disfigured in an accident, survives by disguising herself as a man, working as a boundary rider on one of the stations visited by Tom Collins, the novel's narrator. Cross-dressing, it seems, was often a woman's only defence on the frontier. At the other end of the scale, the freest of the women in the book, significantly called 'Jim' by her family, terrifies Tom by this freedom. He only manages to control his terror by turning her into a figure of romance and fancying himself as the man she demurely adores.

For all that, there is in Furphy's work a poignant sense of woman's vulnerability. Far from seeing her as the embodiment of the land, confirming the link between women and nature, he sees her as its victim. Mary O'Halloran, daughter of Tom's old friend Rory, idealized in Tom's first description of her as 'a child of the wilderness, a dryad among her kindred trees',[10] is killed by that wilderness. Going off in search of her father who has been away from home longer than usual, she gets lost in the bush and dies of exhaustion and exposure.

But as Furphy also suggests, women are vulnerable economically as well as physically. Nineteenth-century Australia was a 'man's country' and colonial society was essentially patriarchal. There was little or no paid work for women: their place was in the home. Unmarried women were more or less placeless. Mrs Beaudesart, the mock-heroine of *Such Is Life*, a widow intent upon marrying Tom, is a figure of desperation, however ironically this desperation may be presented. Without a husband, she is dependent upon the charity of friends like the wife of the station owner who offers her a position as housekeeper at

Runnymede Station. In his description of her life after the death of the husband who squandered all her money, leaving her penniless, Furphy is clearly, if ironically, aware of the humiliations of the genteel poverty she must endure trapped in social obligations she no longer has the means to fulfil:

> For the next two years, the poor gentle woman hung round the scene of her former glories, wearing garments that were out of fashion, and otherwise drinking to its very dregs the cup of bitterness which a heartless society holds to the lips of its deposed queens.[11]

His picture of Ida, daughter of a poor squatter, is even more poignant. Ugly as well as poor, she is condemned to a life of drudgery as a kitchen servant at Runnymede, mocked for her unattractiveness by men as well as women and yet fortunate to have a job.

Henry Lawson's famous story 'The Drover's Wife' offers an even more powerful picture, linking the woman's plight more explicitly to the environment. Here, also, the land is anything but feminine. It is rather an emptiness, an annihilating force in which the woman, left alone, must struggle to exist, battling with flood, drought and bushfire and looking after the children while her husband is away. Significantly, the only help she gets is from a blackfellow who cheats her when she asks him to stack wood. The 'civilization' she represents is therefore fragile indeed. Poor settlers, she and her husband have failed to put their mark on the land and struggle to survive. Not for them the dream-like abundance with which Kingsley rewards his settlers; only the negation of everything the woman knows and hopes for, the civility represented for her in the *Young Ladies Journal* she reads and the solitary promenade she takes through the bush on Sundays, dressed in her best:

> Bush all round — bush with no horizon, for the country is flat. No ranges in the distance. The bush consists of stunted, rotten 'native apple trees'. No undergrowth. Nothing to relieve the eye, save the

darker green of a few 'she-oaks' which are sighing
above the narrow, almost waterless creek. Nineteen
miles to the nearest sign of civilisation — a shanty on
the main road.[12]

The Manichean allegory of colonization turns against the
colonizer here. The snake, the epitome of evil which threatens
her and her children, represents the savagery which the Imperial
dream believed existed to be conquered and transformed. But in
the bush, it is an ever-present danger. True, the woman and her
dog finally kill the snake. But the battle is a desperate one. It is
also in a sense unending as its description suggests as the dog
shakes 'the snake as tho' he felt the original curse of Toil in
common with mankind'.[13] This curse, of course, is one of the
consequences of the Fall, condemning women to 'bring forth
children in pain' and men to 'toil all the days of their lives' — a
curse of which women like this drover's wife must have been
grimly aware, battling as they were for sheer physical and
psychic survival.

Lawson makes explicit here what is implicit elsewhere in
his work: that Australia is not the paradise of imperial myth but its
opposite, a place under a curse, in which people in general were
condemned to incessant and often unsuccessful battle with nature
and the elements and women in particular were subject to sexual
oppression and continual childbearing, often with little or no help,
far from civilization. The stories of Lawson's contemporary,
Barbara Baynton, give a powerful impression of the state of near
hallucination, a sense of vulnerability and terror, which this
struggle induced, at least in some women, matching the terrors of
Marcus Clarke's description of the convict system in *For the Term
of His Natural Life* and suggesting that women suffered perhaps
from a deeper imprisonment of a psychic and social kind.

This is very different, then, from Kingsley's dream of a
'new heaven and a new earth' and of woman as the embodiment
of the land rendered benign and fruitful. But I would argue that
it was probably closer to the actual experience of most settlers,
especially of women. At the end of the nineteenth century,

when Lawson, Furphy and Baynton were writing, Australian society was still essentially patriarchal. Perhaps it still is today — certainly most contemporary writing by women suggests that it is.

Helen Garner's *The Children's Bach* (1990), for instance, is about a woman's struggle against the oppressive, if well-meant, power of her husband. It opens with a tableau of patriarchal power, the more powerful perhaps for its ironic tone, a picture of the Victorian poet Tennyson:

> To the modern eye it is a shocking picture: they are all, with the exception of the great man himself, bundled up in such enormous, incapacitating garments. Eye lines: Tennyson looks into the middle distance. His wife, holding his arm and standing very close to his side, gazes up into his face. One boy holds his father's hand and looks up at him. The other boy holds his mother's and looks into the camera with a weak rueful expression. Behind them, out of focus, twinkles the windy foliage of a great garden.[14]

Consciously or unconsciously, this echoes a similar tableau towards the end of *The Recollections of Geoffry Hamlyn* in which Sam Buckley, now full of years and prosperity, returns to England to resume the position of country gentleman which his father, Major Buckley, had been unable to sustain:

> The wife and son are both leaning over the father's shoulder, and the three faces are together. Sam is about forty. There is not a wrinkle in that honest forehead, and the eyes beam on you as kindly and as pleasantly as they ever did...Alice, whose face is pressed against his, is now a calm young matron...if it were possible, more beautiful than ever, only she has grown from a Hebe into a Juno. The boy, the son and heir, is much such a stripling as his father at the same age, but handsomer and while we look, another face comes peering over his shoulder; the laughing face of a lovely girl, with bright sunny hair, and soft blue eyes; the face of Maud Buckley, Sam's daughter.[15]

Patriarchal power is a constant as the phrase 'the boy, the son and heir' implies. It weighs differently perhaps today but it still weighs not only on bodies but on minds which are still, many of them, wrapped metaphysically in the incapacitating garments of ideology, what Hélène Cixous calls the 'masculine realm' of property.[16] By and large, women remain powerless in Australian society. In a moving passage in *West Block*, a novel set in Canberra, about women and political power, Sarah Dowse, for instance, imagines the generations of women waiting for some share of power:

> How long they would wait. The women in the factories. The lonely ones, who spoke in foreign tongues. The children who stood in the morning cold before locked school gates. The pensioners, hounded. The women who went mad in those suburbs; dingy or maniacally clean. The women with bruises, inside and out, that none, least themselves, dared to see. They ran for their lives, or stayed, for the same reason. Daring to be human; abused for that.[17]

Increasingly, many women are no longer willing to wait, and are challenging the patriarchy. But there is also a growing sense of the complexities involved in this challenge, that what may be needed, first and foremost, is a redefinition of 'power'. In *The Children's Bach*, for instance, Athena goes back to her marriage after a brief affair with a young musician. This return is, however, not seen as a defeat: Athena has learned the art of polyphony, mastered the music of existence which up till now she has only played mechanically and now, therefore, she is able to operate at different levels, secure in the ground bass of her own identity.

At first this resolution to the problem we have been describing may seem sentimental, working off in words feelings the situation does not really support. If one accepts, however, the argument that the power of the patriarchy is essentially ideological, a matter of imaginative cooption into imperial power, then it is best challenged on these ideological terms. Imperial ideology is essentially 'masculine' in Cixous's sense, preoccupied with power, possessions and mindless pleasure, the inertial and indifferent passions of consumer society, and these terms have been traditionally accepted by women in our own society as well as by men. What some contemporary women writers are suggesting, in contrast, however — Helen Garner, Beverley Farmer, Marion Campbell and Joan Dugdale, for instance — is the need to imagine and then live by a different kind of economy, characterized by Cixous as 'feminine', a realm of giving and receiving, of generosity and freedom of movement.

So Marion Campbell's *Lines of Flight*, for instance, is about a young woman who lives along 'lines of flight', according to some potential for movement which comes to her from outside the frame of a society which is organized in terms of property, propriety and appropriation. Her centre of gravity lies within herself, is not transferred outwards onto objects to be possessed, but is bound up with some mystery of love, whatever that may mean (it is ambiguous in the novel). Similarly, in *A Body of Water*, Beverley Farmer quotes from Paul Valéry's notebooks:

> I cannot *believe* either in the *sub* or the *ob-jective*; that
> is, I feel that nothing, not even oneself, could be of
> interest except in crossing some strange threshold —
> itself an illusion, and moreover uncrossable.[18]

Elsewhere she writes of Virginia Woolf's idea that 'we are sealed vessels afloat on what it is convenient to call reality' but also notes, as Woolf does too, that 'at some moments, the sealing matter cracks'[19] — something which the stoic woman like Lawson's Drover's Wife would not allow, but which Baynton and, in his own way, Furphy do.

Writers like Garner, Farmer and Campbell are concerned with some 'transvaluation of value'. But this concern also represents a political move. This is clear in Joan Dugdale's *Struggle of Memory*, an attempt to subvert the myth of history in the name of another history, the story not of the 'winners' — the story of progress which underpins present Australian society — but of the losers — poor people like the timber workers whom the novel's protagonist, Miriam, gets to know as a child at her father's mill, and Aborigines and migrants like the German she marries who is later destroyed by the patriotic frenzy of the First World War, and most women.

The subversive intent of the novel is made explicit in its title which also serves as its epigram: Milan Kundera's proposition that 'the struggle of [people] against power is the struggle of memory against forgetting'. It is also apparent in one of the key scenes in the novel, during the First World War. Miriam has just read a letter from the front describing the truce on Christmas Day 1917 and her imagination conjures up an image of the fragile community this truce creates:

> No man's land: a place where men could cease from war, sharing their smokes and songs around a glowing brazier in that horrendous dark. The image had flared, transforming the wilderness for Miriam into a place of celebration.[20]

But the truce is also, she realizes, 'no woman's land', the place in which the victims of power may begin to hope for something more, for release from 'the boundaries of ownership, the paths of certainty, all surveyed and mapped for a single high perspective',[21] which are controlled by the imperial and patriarchal gaze. So Miriam is drawn into the past, into her childhood intuition of some 'land...where belonging transcended ownership and a knowledge more fluid than certainty led some feet among the trees'.[22]

This brings us to a crucial, but probably contentious, point in my argument: the link between the situation of women and that of Aboriginal Australians. To establish this link, we need to return to the initial point, the relations between geography, ideology and power. By definition, geography as a strategy of space has to do with the conflicts of power which traverse and organize it.[23] This is especially the case, as we suggested earlier, with settlement. For colonizers, place then becomes an aspect of strategy, first of all of a military and political and then of an economic kind[24] — as J.M. Coetzee remarks, the type of the settler is the man with a gun.[25] The land figures as an object to be conquered, penetrated and made fertile and in this sense settlement is analogous to rape. But the result is that it becomes a place of death, its interior a place 'where the dead men lie'. To its Aboriginal inhabitants, in contrast, however, it is the source of life, material, an aspect of memory, of all that is abiding, sustaining and worshipful. It is not a mere contrast of self and world, as in colonial ideology; one's own body and the body of the earth are aspects of the one dynamic reality. As the Aboriginal leader Bill Neidjie puts it:

> Listen carefully this, you can hear me.
> I'm telling you because earth just like mother
> and father or brother of you.
> That tree same thing
> Your body, my body I suppose,
> I'm sure as you...anyone,
> Tree working when you sleeping and dream.[26]

Another recent novel, Heather Grace's *Heart of Light*, explores the ways in which two white women begin to be aware of and come to share this Aboriginal sense of reality. More significantly, in discovering this sense they come to discover themselves and to break free from patriarchal oppression. At the beginning, driving across a long stretch of desert country to take up a job as cook on a Kimberley cattle station, the words of a song, 'Water of love deep in the ground, but there ain't no water here to be found', play through one of the character's, Julie's, mind.[27] In the context, she realizes, the maps on which the settlers relied are no longer useful instruments of power since they do not really tell about this country. The more she gets to know the country, however, the more she realizes her affinities with it. Lying on a hot stone at the pump waterhole, for instance, she imagines 'she can hear the tree roots pushing at the rock beneath her',[28] and it becomes for her and her friend, Kass, the station school teacher, a 'spirit country' as they discover their affinity with it and with generations of Aboriginal people who have been here before them. So when they drive out from the station, they choose to sleep at places where there are signs of past Aboriginal presence: 'it seems somehow propitious to sleep where others before them have also chosen to spend time'.[29]

The type of the male explorer and settler, the man with the gun, is a figure of loneliness:

> Destroyer of the wilderness...[moving] through the land cutting a devouring path from horizon to horizon. There is nothing from which [his] eye turns, [he is] all that [he sees]. Such loneliness...what is that that is not [himself]? [He is] a transparent sac with a black core full of images and a gun.[30]

This is the self of the settler, described earlier. But for women today, *Heart of Light* implies, it is different. The novel is about the discovery of a different mode of being, 'feminine' rather than 'masculine', a knowing which to rationalistic Western thought is a 'not knowing', and in this way it breaks through the impasse represented by Lawson, Furphy, and even Baynton. Julie and Kass are aware of new possibility, brought up short by a strange rock which looms before them:

> In the sunlight its hard white surface contrasts with the charred rock, and Julie imagines it glowing at night, a full white moon in the dark. There is nothing to explain its presence. Stranger than all the paintings they have seen, the shells and stones and skeletons, this rock embodies her fear and she realises, staring at it, that what she is afraid of is not-knowing, and this stone, no less than the great Pyramid of Egypt and the soaring cathedrals of Europe, represents human hope and fear and trust.[31]

The patriarchal ideology of conquest saw this country as empty, 'terra nullius', devoid of interest, with no history, no monuments or stories. Its history therefore 'began' with our arrival in 1788. That history, as we have been arguing, has also tended to write out the experience and achievements of women, achievements which have usually been different in kind, more inward than those celebrated by the patriarchal culture of power and possession. But Heather Grace glimpses here the symbol of the moon, the symbol par excellence of women, fluid, bound to the natural cycle and yet free, clean and yet not clean, dynamic, not static. She is only one of many women writers for whom this country and its Aboriginal inhabitants are becoming part of an exploration of new possibilities within the self. A new geography, a new sense of self and world which entails a new affinity with Aboriginal people and their culture, may thus be beginning to emerge.

---

1   Peter Hulme, *Colonial Encounter: Europe and the Native Caribbean 1492–1797* (London: Methuen, 1986). This engraving is the book's frontispiece.

2   Marion Aveling, ed., *Westralian Voices: Documents in West Australian Social History* (Nedlands: University of Western Australia Press, 1979), p. 280.

3   J.D.S. Mellick, ed., *Portable Australian Authors: Henry Kingsley* (St Lucia: University of Queensland Press, 1982), p. 137.

4   Aveling, p. 278.

5   Mellick, p. 233.

6   ibid., p. 224.

7   ibid., p. 226.

8   Abdul Jan Mohamed, 'The Economy of Manichean Allegory: The Function of Racial Difference in Colonialist Literature', in Henry Louis Gates, ed., *'Race', Writing and Difference* (Chicago: University of Chicago Press, 1986), pp. 78–106.

9   John Barnes, ed., *Portable Australian Authors: Joseph Furphy* (St Lucia: University of Queensland Press, 1981), p. 164.

10   ibid., p. 73.

11   ibid., pp. 109–110.

12   Leon Cartrell, ed., *Portable Australian Authors: The 1890s; Stories, Verses, Essays* (St Lucia: University of Queensland Press, 1977), p. 234.

13   ibid., p. 241.

14   Helen Garner, *The Children's Bach* (Melbourne: Penguin, 1990), p. 1.

15   Mellick, pp. 422–423.

16   Toril Moi, *Sexual/Textual Politics* (London: Macmillan, 1985,) pp. 110–111.

17   Sarah Dowse, *West Block* (Melbourne: Penguin, 1983), p. 285.

18   Beverley Farmer, *A Body of Water* (St Lucia: University of Queensland Press, 1990), p. 209.

19   ibid., p. 79.

20   Joan Dugdale, *Struggle of Memory* (St Lucia: University of Queensland Press, 1991), p. 270.

21   ibid.

22   ibid., p. 271.

23   Michel Foucault, 'Questions of Geography', in Colin Gordon, ed., *Power/Knowledge; Selected Interviews and Other Writings 1972–7* (Brighton: Harvester Press, 1980), p. 63.

24   ibid., p. 68.

25   J.M. Coetzee, *Dusklands* (Harmondsworth, Middlesex: Penguin, 1983), p. 79. Paul Carter, *The Road To Botany Bay* (London: Faber, 1988), makes a similar point, more moderately.

26   Bill Neidjie, *Story About Felling* (Broome: Magabala Books, 1989), p. 3.

27   Heather Grace, *Heart of Light* (Fremantle: Fremantle Arts Centre Press, 1992), p. 17.

28   ibid., p. 31.

29   ibid., p. 54.

30   Coetzee, p. 79.

31   Grace, pp. 137–138.

NOTES ON CONTRIBUTORS

PHILIPPA BECKERLING teaches part-time in the English Department of The University of Western Australia, and is at present completing a PhD on medieval romance. She has an MA in the area of Anglo-Saxon poetry.

PENNY BOUMELHA is the Jury Professor of English Language and Literature at The University of Adelaide. Her publications include *Thomas Hardy and Women (1982)*, *Charlotte Brontë (1990)*, and articles on nineteenth-century fiction, realism, and literary manuscripts. She is the editor of *Jude the Obscure: New Casebook* (1994), and is currently editing Brontë's *Shirley* and Hardy's *The Return of the Native* for Penguin Classics.

VERONICA BRADY is Associate Professor of English at The University of Western Australia. She gained her first degree from The University of Melbourne and her MA and PhD from The University of Toronto. She is the author of four books, the most recent being *Caught in the Draught*, a collection of essays on Australian literature and culture, and has published widely in journals in Australia, the United States, France, Spain, Italy and India.

ANN CHANCE is a postgraduate student at The University of Western Australia, currently working towards a PhD in the field of early modern English literature and social history.

D.W. COLLIN's edition of Elizabeth Gaskell's *North and South* was published by Penguin. She has published articles on Gaskell's novels in *BJRL* and gave the annual Gaskell Lecture in England in 1993. She is a Senior Lecturer in the Department of English at The University of Western Australia.

CHRISTINE COUCHE is completing her PhD in Shakespeare and the representation of women, and has research interests in the areas of feminist theory, Renaissance sexual politics, and the Australian novel. She was awarded a British Council Scholarship Bursary to further her PhD studies, which she took up at Oxford University in mid-1992.

TIM DOLIN completed his PhD at The University of Western Australia, and now works in the Department of English at The University of Newcastle, New South Wales. He has published articles on Elizabeth Gaskell, Charlotte Brontë and Charles Dickens, and is presently writing a book on Dickens and Victorian art, as well as preparing a new edition of Hardy's *The Hand of Ethelberta* for the new Penguin Classics series.

LUCY DOUGAN is a postgraduate in the Department of English at The University of Western Australia. Her doctorate involves a study of representations of women and metamorphosis in Victorian literature and art. She has published poems and an article in the *Fremantle Arts Review* and book reviews in *Westerly.*

HILARY FRASER is Associate Professor of English at The University of Western Australia. Her publications are mainly in the area of nineteenth-century literature and culture, and include *The Victorians and Renaissance Italy* (Oxford: Blackwell, 1992) and *Beauty and Belief: Aesthetics and Religion in Victorian Literature* (Cambridge: Cambridge University Press, 1986). She is currently preparing a critical study of nineteenth-century English prose for the Longman's Literature in English series.

ANDREW LYNCH is a Senior Lecturer in English at The University of Western Australia, where he teaches medieval and modern literature. His publications include essays on Chaucer, Malory and gender in medieval romance.

CARMEL MACDONALD-GRAHAME is a graduate of The University of Western Australia. She is a peripatetic teacher of literature(s), currently working part-time in the Department of English and Comparative Literatures at Murdoch University and engaged there in PhD research. In addition to her critical interests, she has published short fiction in Australia and Canada. Her primary area of interest is now located at the juncture of feminist and post-colonial criticisms.

SUSAN MIDALIA has taught for many years at The University of Western Australia and more recently at Edith Cowan University. She is currently a full-time PhD student at The University of Western

Australia, writing on the topic of female identity and the politics of form in contemporary women's fiction.

AMANDA NETTELBECK taught at The University of Western Australia for two years and is now a Lecturer in English at Flinders University. She is editor of *Provisional Maps: New Critical Essays on David Malouf,* and is currently working on a collection of Australian women's ficto-criticism.

IAN SAUNDERS teaches in the areas of literary theory and cultural studies. His *Open Texts, Partial Maps: A Literary Theory Handbook* was published in 1993.

ALEX SEGAL is a Lecturer in English at Charles Sturt University. Prior to that he was a Research Fellow in the Department of English at The University of Western Australia.

JANE SOUTHWELL lives in Perth, Western Australia, with her husband and four children, dog and goldfish. While her real talent is as juggler, her present daytime job is teaching English and Literature. At present, she is completing a doctorate in the sexual politics of Angela Carter's novels. She has published on women's health and the politics of the women's movement.

BOB WHITE is Professor of English at The University of Western Australia. He has published on Shakespeare, Keats, and Australian topics, the best known book being *Innocent Victims: Injustice in Shakespeare's Tragedies* (London: Athlone Press, 2nd edn 1986). *The Merry Wives of Windsor* (Harvester New Critical Introductions to Shakespeare, Hemel Hempstead: Harvester, 1991), and *Macbeth* (Horizon Studies in Literature, Sydney and Oxford: Sydney University Press, 1994) are both written from a feminist point of view. He is revising for publication *Natural Law in English Renaissance Literature* (Cambridge University Press).